INTERIOR DESIGN CHOICE

THIRD ANNUAL EDITION

A publication of
Indecs Publishing Inc.

President and Publisher: David Jaeger
Treasurer: Vladimir Losner
Marketing Director: Kelly Rude

Book Design & Production:
Jaeger Graphics
Cover, Title Pages, Upfront Section Design:
Taylor & Browning Design Associates
Cover illustration:
Wendy Wortsman
Typesetting:
XY Typesetting Services

Printed in Japan by Dai Nippon

ISBN 0-9692019-2-3
ISSN 0829-5298

Published annually by
Indecs Publishing Inc.
23 Brentcliffe Road,
Suite 317
Toronto, Ontario,
Canada M4G 4B7
(416) 421-5227

Distributed in Canada by:
Firefly Books Ltd.
3520 Pharmacy Avenue, Unit 1 C
Scarborough, Ontario M1W 2T8
(416) 499-8412

All other countries:
Rockport Publishers Inc.
5 Smith Street
Rockport, Massachussets 01966
USA
(617) 546-9590

The third annual edition of
Interior Design Choice once again records
excellence and achievement in an industry
which has been demonstrating tremendous
growth and no less capacity for unceasing
qualitative development throughout
the '80s. In the context of a continuous
upsurge in interest in design, growth and
quality have been its constant hallmarks.
It is only natural to see in the
achievements of the interior design
industry the true source of the growing
success of Interior Design Choice.
The quality of presentations in this
edition, as in its predecessors, is proof
that today's interior design responds to
the needs and aspirations of an
increasingly knowledgeable, demanding
end user.
Supporting this showcase of talent and
competence, we are uncompromisingly
pledged to quality, to the highest
production values.
Interior Design Choice remains committed
to fulfilling its role as vehicle of reference
and front of contact between the best of
creative talent and an increasingly
enlightened environment.

La troisième édition annuelle de Choix
se veut, une fois de plus, un reflet de
l'excellence et des performances d'une
industrie dont la croissance dans les
années 80 a été remarquable et la capacité
de développement qualitatif non moins
exceptionnelle. Dans le contexte d'un
intérêt puissant et continu de la part du
public, qualité et croissance sont bien ce
que le design d'intérieurs a aujourd'hui
de plus caractéristique.
Il n'est que naturel de voir dans les
réalisations du design d'intérieurs la
source profonde du succès croissant
de Choix.
La qualité des présentations dans cette
édition, comme dans les précédentes, prouve
que le design d'intérieurs satisfait de nos
jours les besoins et les souhaits d'une
clientèle toujours plus avisée et exigeante.
En créant le cadre pour cette vitrine de
talents et de compétences, nous avons
souscrit sans concession aucune à la
cause de la qualité, du plus haut niveau
de la production.
Choix reste engagé comme avant à
remplir sa mission d'ouvrage de référence
et de moyen de rencontre entre l'élite des
talents créateurs et un environnement
toujours plus éclairé.

David Jaeger
Publisher/Éditeur

Design credit for the lounge at
Toronto's Terminal One (appearing on
page 86 of Interior Design Choice 1986 as
part of the Tribute feature) is due to
David Bodrug, under the direction of
Stan White, architect-in-charge, for the
Department of Transport, 1960-61.

INDEX

RESOURCES

INTERIOR CONTRACTORS

CONSULTANTS

EXHIBIT / DISPLAY

INTERIOR LANDSCPING

ART / ANTIQUES

DESIGN AWARDS

RENDERERS PHOTOGRAPHERS

DESIGN SCHOOLS

QUICK CHOICE DIRECTORY

ALPHABETICAL INDEX

A

B

C

Design credit for the lounge at
Toronto's Terminal One (appearing on
page 86 of Interior Design Choice 1986 as
part of the Tribute feature) is due to
David Bodrug, under the direction of
Stan White, architect-in-charge, for the
Department of Transport, 1960-61.

SPACE

YABU PUSHELBERG

Les Cours Mont-Royal Montreal
Contruction in Progress

elevation, twisting forms in ways

which reinforce the overall design

theme, integrating them to produce a

very strong statement. The result is

the realization of a place with power

that is consistent in every detail.

The key to Yabu Pushelberg's success

and reputation is found in their

Stephen K Toronto

problem-solving orientation. Each

project is defined as requiring a

particular solution. Collectively with

the client, Yabu Pushelberg defines

an overriding principle which

becomes the basic element for the

design. Once this very specific

concept is defined, it is applied and is

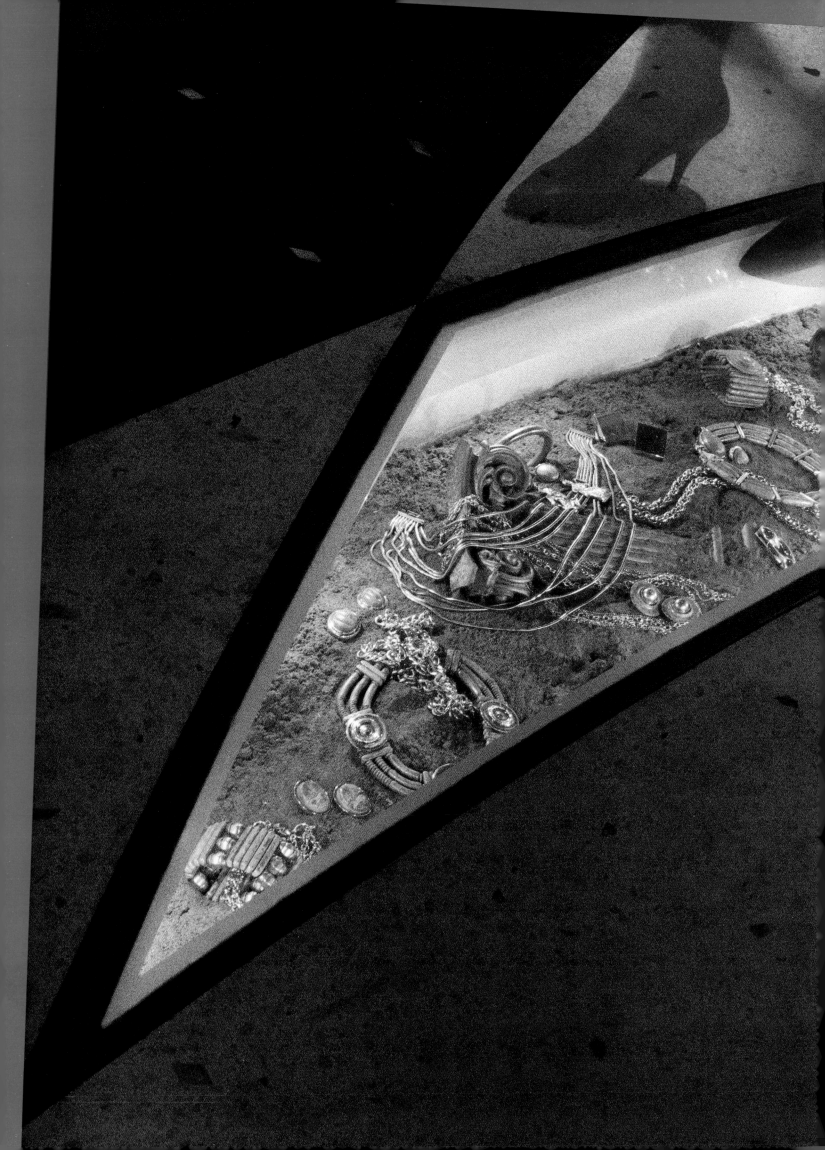

Yabu Pushelberg's approach to design

is unique. Out of space, a sense of

place and identity is established

which is particular to the needs of

each client. The firm's capacity to

combine creativity and reality is the

trademark of their work.

Yabu Pushelberg's attitude to design

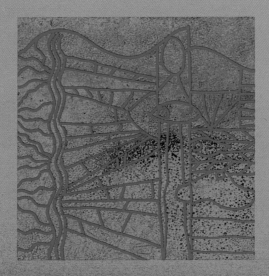

is the difference. Yabu Pushelberg

creates a very specific and personal

theme for each client. The results

attest to this difference. Yabu

Pushelberg's designs are dynamic,

expressive and very personal. They

combine elements such as

shifts in scale of space and

responsible for the consistent and

unified nature found in every one of

the firm's diverse projects.

Yabu Pushelberg's conceptual

problem-solving strategy explains

why their designs are appropriate to

the requirements of each individual

project and client. Working with each

Yü Fashion Accessories Toronto

client, Yabu Pushelberg is able to

clearly assess the client's needs. By

developing a client-based marketing

strategy, the Yabu Pushelberg design

team creates an image that is both

suitable and seductive to the client's

needs and desires. The firm's

commitment to a flexible, client-

oriented strategy produces results.

By addressing the actual needs and

problems of both the space and the

market, the result is a space which

produces a strong individual image.

By employing strong visual meta-

phors, a sense of identity is created

for both the user and the client.

The Irish Shop for Men Toronto

Yabu Pushelberg's refreshing

approach to solving design problems

does not rest at the level of image.

Yabu Pushelberg extends the concept

throughout the design process,

resulting in a unified space, detailed

and finished. From concept to

completion, from abstract through to

material and spatial realization, the

concern is to create visual images

which last. Yabu Pushelberg's vision

is their ability to create personal and

evocative architecture while meeting

the very real needs of the project.

This total design approach benefits

everyone — the client and the user.

Scènts Toronto
Yushi Toronto

11

Yabu Pushelberg's difference is their

strength. By employing a sensitive

client and market-based problem-

solving approach, they resolve

diverse design problems in an

appropriate and exciting manner.

Their flexibility is their style,

bringing with them a dynamic and

Yushi Toronto

Rasa Design San Antonio Texas
New Orleans Louisiana

fresh approach to a field ridden

with imposed, preconceived

solutions. Their style is not

decoration, it is an affirmative act

of creation.

Yabu Pushelberg has established its

reputation on taking a concept and

transforming it into a space, playful

yet interesting, not jarring or

overwhelming. They are at once fun

and sensitive, appropriate and

meaningful. Their ability to solve

very real problems and to create a

workable vision is their magic.

The Milli Showroom New York

Yü Fashion Accessories Toronto

Club Monaco Toronto

Les Cours Mont-Royal
I.C.S.C. Exhibit Canada

Cravings Toronto

Yushi Toronto

Yabu Pushelberg 359 King Street East Toronto, Canada M5A 1L1 (416) 362-1414.

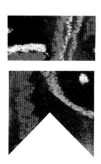

D E S I G N

C O R P O R A T E

AID 2000 Inc.
101 Freshway Drive
Unit 66D
Concord, Ontario
L9K 1R9
(416) 661-6433

V. Flander
B.A. Architecture, Interior Design,
Furniture Design

B. Papernick
Design Consultant

AID 2000
Professional interior design/custom
production and installation for home
and office. All custom work is
personally executed and supervised by
our own experienced staff. From
design concept through to complete
installation, AID 2000 will even custom
build a new home or office for you,
or renovate an existing one.

INTERIOR DESIGN CHOICE 3 © AID 2000 Inc.

agnelli • orsini inc.
2 phoebe street
toronto, ontario M5T 1A7
416 593 0633

Our design work is as individual as these chairs –
custom created for a perfect fit.

INTERIOR DESIGN CHOICE 3 © Agnelli • Orsini Inc.

Mary Kathryn Angus, B.I.D., L.I.D.   Jerilyn R. Wright, B.I.D., L.I.D.   Westcoast Petroleum   Trans Canada Resources

ANGUS WRIGHT

INTERIOR · DESIGN · CONSULTANTS · LTD.

The success of Angus Wright Interior Design Consultants Ltd. has been our ability to listen to our clients and to develop unique reflections of their personalities. We do this through our experience in creating functional and efficient design concepts that blend the realities of cost control with tight schedules.

306 Mount Royal Village, 1550 - 8th Street S.W., Calgary, Alberta T2R 1K1 (403) 229-2717

INTERIOR DESIGN CHOICE 3 © Angus Wright Interior Design Consultants Ltd.

**Benitz & Benitz
Designs Canada Ltd.**
355 Berkeley Street
Toronto, Ontario M5A 2X6
Studio: 360 Dundas Street East
Toronto, Ontario
(416) 926-1632
Ottawa
(613) 564-0208

David Jefferies Benitz
Principal, ARIDO, A.S.I.D.
Margaret Jean Benitz, B.A.
Principal; Art Consultant

Full and bilingual design service
accross Canada for 25 years.

Evaluation of space requirements for
maximum efficiency and realistic
move-in budgets.

Professional art consulting services.

INTERIOR DESIGN CHOICE 3 © Benitz & Benitz Designs Canada Ltd.

INGER BARTLETT

Reception Area

Elevator Lobby

cMaster Meighen, Toronto Reception Area. As we move into the future, the need to express individual identities in the corporate environment increases. In a traditional business setting, Inger Bartlett and Associates was able to achieve a progressive visual statement of confidence and style based on strong planning skills.

Through careful attention to overall planning and individual requirements, the Toronto offices of McMaster Meighen are highly functional and efficient. This design reflects our commitment to listen to our clients and respond with a high degree of professionalism.

Inger Bartlett and Associates Limited, 2A Gibson Avenue, Toronto, Canada M5R 1T5 (416) 926-8247
Interior Planning and Design

INTERIOR DESIGN CHOICE 3 © Inger Bartlett and Associates

INTERIOR PLANNING AND DESIGN

houghtful and careful attention to detail allows us to achieve a cohesive corporate image on every project. Architectural themes developed on a large scale are integrated into individual elements, such as custom designed furniture, to present consistent and innovative solutions.

But more than that, we recognize that the design process is a partnership. Successful design cannot exist in isolation. Inger Bartlett and Associates believes that incisive communication with clients makes the difference. Through innovative methodology, client objectives are met with creativity and imagination.

Floor Detail

Edge Detail

Boardroom Table

nger Bartlett and Associates provides the full range of design functions; from initial planning of the design concept through working drawings to construction and installation of the client. Our objectives are to complete the project with integrity, on budget and within the planned time schedule. We are able to achieve these goals through personal attention from senior people within our project teams.

Inger
Bartlett
and Associates

Partial Client List: *McMaster Meighen, Magnasonic Canada Inc., The Royal Bank of Canada*
Photographer: *Ian Samson*

INTERIOR DESIGN CHOICE 3 © Inger Bartlett and Associates

Now that we've got your attention, we'd like to make a few points.

Yes, we do consider design to be a blast. One never gets really good at anything unless one is totally enthralled by it. And has some fun in the process. We're very serious about that.

Citiworks Design Inc.
296 Richmond Street West, Suite 300
Toronto, Canada M5V 1X2 (416) 531-5749

No, we don't build buildings. Or cities for that matter. We design interiors. And we've gained a reputation for being very good at it.

Finally, we'd like you to remember our name.
Citiworks.

Linda

Cindy

Renée

Charlotte

Peter

Stacey

Maria

Jane

Jeannie

Sandra

Joyce

Ed

Christien

Lynnore

Design Planning Associates takes pride in presenting its exceptional people. As professional consultants, we strive to interpret each client's individual project objectives through the integration of our collective experience, professionalism and personality. Every client is the beneficiary of our people - oriented approach to design.

Design Planning Associates

322 King Street West
Toronto, Canada
M5V 1J2
(416) 977-2355

Design Planning Associates is an independent professional consultancy specializing in the programming of corporate interior environments.

Principals Edward Hoffert and Joyce O'Keefe manage a group of talented, self-motivated personalities who represent this company's most important and vital resource.
The focus at Design Planning Associates is on a more personal approach to the serious subject of providing facilities that work for people.

Each client's objectives and project limitations are thoughtfully and creatively translated into a pleasant, productive business environment through our need to achieve design excellence.

INTERIOR DESIGN CHOICE 3 © Design Planning Associates

Nesbitt Consulting
Toronto

Adirect
Toronto

**cecconi
eppstadt
simone**
designers/planners

663 Queen Street East
Toronto, Canada
M4M 1G4
416 462-1445

Renaissance Plaza
Toronto

Robert Mann
Toronto

INTERIOR DESIGN CHOICE 3 © Cecconi/Eppstadt/Simone

D.Chenier Associates Limited

236 Avenue Road
Suite 202
Toronto, Ontario
M5R 2J4
(416) 964-1545

At D. Chenier Associates we design solutions, individual environments which meld pure art with the skilled, functional engineering of space.

Behind each one is a story of client rapport and trust, tireless teamwork, innovative flexibility and effortless, concept-to-completion management and planning that ensures D. Chenier Associates a primacy amongst Canada's preferred design resources.

1. Mr. L. Kerzner
   Private Study

2. Mr. L. Kerzner
   Bath area

3. Sack Charney Goldblatt & Mitchell,
   Barristers, Solicitors – Reception area

4. Private corporate meeting room

5. Clothes Encounters, Toronto

Our clients are among the most successful corporations and professional firms in Alberta. These businesses are directed by exacting individuals who have developed clearly formulated corporate programs focussed on thoughtful, managed growth. These individuals understand that office design must reflect and enhance their corporate identity. They also realize that an effective office design is a lasting corporate resource which must be professionally created and knowledgeably maintained. We provide the human and technical resources to achieve these objectives.

The Cohos Evamy Partnership believes that office design is nothing less than a process of asset development which requires total control in its planning, specification, realization and use. Our firm has drawn together a group of dedicated and experienced design professionals who command all of the most modern computer-assisted design technology necessary to achieve such control.

We work with each of our clients to successfully translate their business vision into concrete expression. Our firm's ability to sensitively accomplish this expression in space planning, material, furniture and equipment selection is the essence of our creative strength.

Through computer modelling we permit flexible visualization of design alternatives and through computer-assisted drafting we are able to rapidly create complete and accurate plans and specifications.

Once our designs are in place we ensure that our clients retain knowledgeable, on-going control of their office space and inventory. The records and documentation which we develop provide our clients a detailed understanding of their resources and permit their flexible allocation. Our clients' experience shows that this facility management capability results in a significant reduction of costs.

MEMBER OF THE ALBERTA ASSOCIATION OF ARCHITECTS.

THE COHOS EVAMY
PARTNERSHIP

BAIN
EZINGA
GABRIELE
GOODWIN
POFFENROTH
SINGLETON

Corporations

ARCHITECTS
ENGINEERS
INTERIOR DESIGNERS
PROGRAMMERS
FACILITY MANAGERS

200 · 902 · 11 AVE. S.W., CALGARY, ALBERTA, T2R 0E7 · (403) 245-5501

INTERIOR DESIGN CHOICE 3 © The Cohos Evamy Partnership

Professional Interior Designers

90 Albert Street

Winnipeg, Manitoba R3B 1G2

(204) 942-2129

From the inside-out Designworks Inc. is on the leading edge of contemporary design, creating functional spaces for the client with distinctive taste.

Angles Hair Design
Winnipeg

Manitoba Premier's Award
for Design Excellence

300 North Queen Street
Suite 204
Etobicoke, Ontario
M9C 5K4
(416) 626-6767

Practical, productive, yet highly attractive work environments that stand the test of time and the rigors of competing in business. That's how companies such as **Westinghouse Canada, Monsanto Canada, VG National Trust, Firestone Canada, Canadian General Life, The Woodbridge Group**, and a number of other companies large and small, have come to view the work of Fielding and Associates.

Here is a team of specifiers, space planners and designers with a long and successful track record. Their experience is wide and varied. And it has primarily required taking projects right from the initial feasibility study to final construction. Fielding and Associates: matching the practical demands of comfort and work flow efficiency with the timelessness of sophisticated design.

1. Lobby Concept
   Multi tenant building

2. Secretarial Area

3. Executive Secretary

4. Lobby Concept

5. General Office

6. Lobby

7. Reception Working Area

INTERIOR DESIGN CHOICE 3 © Fielding and Associates

EATON'S CONTRACT INTERIORS

HALIFAX   MONTREAL   TORONTO   WINNIPEG   REGINA

INTERIOR DESIGN CHOICE 3 © Eaton's Contract Interiors

L'Industrielle-Vie
Montréal offices

L'Industrielle-Vie
Montréal offices

Bell Canada Enterprises
Montréal Head-office

GSM Design
Interiors, Visual Communications
and Exhibitions Inc.
317, place d'Youville
Montréal, Québec
H2Y 2B5
(514) 288-4233

A multidisciplinary firm offering
comprehensive design services in the
field of interior design and visual
communications.

INTERIOR DESIGN CHOICE 3 © GSM Design

David Bodrug and Ian Dubienski know that design sense makes good sense

GROUP 5

Group 5 Design Associates Ltd.
Corporate Interior Designers
1305 West Georgia Street
Vancouver, B.C. V6E 3K6
(604) 681-8155

For over 20 years, Group 5 Design Associates Ltd. has been designing award winning corporate interiors for some of the toughest customers in Canada.

Companies like Citibank, Merrill Lynch, Alcan and the Jim Pattison Group have looked to Group 5 for sensible solutions to complex design problems. They have

found that the interiors we create have improved their outlook and productivity, as well as their image.

If you prefer to deal with people with a reputation for clear understanding of the functional needs of your workplace as well as creative excellence, delivered on time and on budget, give us a call. It only makes sense.

Photo: Group 5 principals Ian Dubienski and David Bodrug in the new Vancouver headquarters of the Jim Pattison Group

GTDA

GIO TAN DESIGN ASSOCIATES INC.

Space planning
Interior architecture
Project Management

169 Carlton Street
Toronto, Ontario M5A 2K3
(416) 926-1937

Consumers' Gas
Head Office, Toronto

HOLMBERG AULD INC

260 Richmond Street East, Toronto, Canada M5A 1P4 (416) 364 2950

Ottawa Airport A T B Expansion

Design and Planning Consultants
FORREST/BODRUG PARTNERS INC.

439 University Avenue, Suite 1401
Toronto, Ontario M5G 1Y8
(416) 598-2965

H. Gordon Forrest A.S.I.D., ARIDO

TORONTO
(416) 598-2965

OTTAWA
(613) 236-9473

CALGARY
(403) 266-6612

MONTREAL
(514) 875-8507

ARIDO Award Winners 1984 & 1985.

Forrest/Bodrug Partners Inc. have a commitment to design excellence based on satisfying functional requirements on a qualitative basis: to deliver projects on time, on budget. We are in the forefront in the application of new office technology.

F B P are first in the programming of corporate office facility requirements – in planning for a new building, a move to new premises or the retrofit of existing space.

1. Centre Concourse
Ottawa Airport

2. Council Room
The Canada Council, Ottawa

3. Elevator Lobby
Ault Food Limited, Toronto

4. Staircase Detail
Ault Food Limited, Toronto

**Jeffrey/Bullock
Design Consultants Inc.**
55 University Avenue
Suite 300
Toronto, Canada
M5J 2H7
(416) 868-1616

Partners:
**Allan Jeffrey
Doug Bullock**

In an ever changing world…
Jeffrey/Bullock delivers the constant
denominator: **Service.**

We pride ourselves in our ability
to complete projects on **Schedule**
and within **Budget**.

Our clients are our best reference,
among them: Barclays Bank, Dai-Ichi
Kangyo, Bank of Tokyo, The Royal
Bank, Bankers Trust, Burgess Graham,
Ontario Hydro, The Guarantee Co.,
Towers, Perrin, Forster & Crosby

Project:
**H.J. Heinz
Company of Canada Ltd.**
1. Elevator Lobby
2. Reception
3. Lobby Floor Detail
4. Reception Desk Detail

Services:
**Space Planning
Interior Design
Project Management**

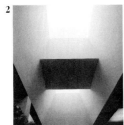

Attention to architectural detail reflects an attitude towards interior design. That attitude or expression, we believe, is one that encompasses an awareness to all elements of interior space; thorough, not just cosmetic, application of design concept; and image creation personifying the culture/personality of the client. We welcome the opportunity to discuss your needs.

1, 2 William Neilson Ltd.
    Georgetown, Ontario

3, 4, 5 William Neilson Ltd.
    Toronto, Ontario

INTEFAC

Facilities Design Group
A Division of Intefac Inc.
5420 Timberlea Blvd.
Mississauga, Ontario
L4W 2T7
(416) 624-6700

INTERIOR DESIGN CHOICE 3 © Intefac Inc. Facilities Design Group

Donald Ketcheson Limited

Thirteen Clarence Square, Toronto, Ontario M5V 1H1 **(416) 593-0744**

Since its inception twenty-five years ago, Donald Ketcheson Limited has dedicated itself to excellence both in design standards and in service to its clients.

The firm specializes in corporate office design. Its commitment to strongly held design principles has resulted in interiors which project a feeling of quality. Finishes and fabrics are skillfully integrated with the functional requirements of the client.

Donald Ketcheson Limited prides itself in developing carefully detailed spaces that reflect the architectural integrity of the buildings that contain them.

Mole·White & Associates Ltd.

260 King Street East
4th Floor
Toronto, Ontario
M5V 1H9
(416) 867-1414

Design is a symbiosis requiring the thoughtful consideration of the client together with the creative and organizational skills of the designer. When these are fully integrated with enthusiasm, a successful imaginative solution is the result.

Client:
Eye Care Centre
Toronto, Ontario

INTERIOR DESIGN CHOICE 3 © Mole · White & Associates Ltd.

Marshall Cummings+Associates

D E S I G N E R S · P L A N N E R S

43 Davies Avenue
Toronto, Ontario
M4M 2A9
(416) 461 · 3563

404 Park Avenue South
Suite 1208
New York, N.Y. 10016
(212) 889 · 0830

221 10th Avenue SW
Studio 1
Calgary, Alberta T2R 0A4
(403) 233 · 8423

INTERIOR DESIGN CHOICE 3 © Marshall Cummings + Associates

Marshall Cummings + Associates is a finely tuned team of individual talents dedicated to servicing our clients to the last detail.

From the rigors of space analysis, planning, design and construction, through the complexities of ongoing facility management, our people provide the assembly of knowledge, experience, creativity, thoroughness and professionalism that are Marshall Cummings hallmarks.

Individually, we're great; collectively, we're even better. Join us as we launch into our second decade.

Photography: Ted Yarwood

McWatt Anderson
Design Consultants Inc.

67 Mowat Avenue
Suite 339
Toronto Canada
M6K 3E3
Telephone (416) 530-4800

Roger McWatt
BAA, ARIDO, IDS

Helen Anderson
BA, BAA, ARIDO, IDC

INTERIOR DESIGN CHOICE 3 © McWatt Anderson Design Consultants Inc.

1986
ARIDO AWARD
for
DESIGN EXCELLENCE

Molson Breweries of Canada Limited
1. Boardroom
2. General Office Area
3. Reception Area
4. Executive Office
5. Detail General Office

**Creative
Interior
Architecture**

Corporate
Commercial
Residential
Special Projects

Byers Casgrain
Avocats
Lawyers

Belcourt
Promoteur immobilier
Developer

McLeod Young Weir
Courtiers en valeurs
Stock Brokers

**Moureaux
Hauspy**
Design Inc.

2140, rue St-Mathieu
Montréal (Québec)
H3H 2J4
(514) 935-4321

Moureaux Hauspy Design Inc.

Haworth
Salle de montre
Showroom

Zellers
Bureau chef
Head Office

Rodine Investments
Investisseurs financiers
Financial Investors

**Moureaux
Hauspy**
Design Inc.

2140, rue St-Mathieu
Montréal (Québec)
H3H 2J4
(514) 935-4321

INTERIOR DESIGN CHOICE 3 © Moureaux Hauspy Design Inc.

Ove

S P A C E
M A N A G E M E N T

G E S T I O N
D E   L ' E S P A C E

CLAUDE BÉRUBÉ SDEQ, I.D.C.
Associé

BRENDA BJARNASON ARIDO, I.D.C.
Associate

Our Computer assisted survey analysis program was developed to help our designers and clients to rapidly establish the spatial, organizational and personal needs in facilities planning. This computerized program, combined with Ove Design's experience in planning millions of square feet, enables our interior design team to create solutions that provide increased productivity, efficiency and ultimately, a more profitable enterprise.

L'informatique nous permet d'analyser l'information recueillie sur place et subséquemment d'automatiser le rythme des changements. Ce programme informatisé de planification d'espace et une expérience d'aménagement de millions de pieds carrés, permettent à nos designers d'accroître la productivité et par conséquent les profits de votre entreprise.

OVE DESIGN INTERIORS INC.
29 Commercial Road
Toronto, Ontario
M4G 1Z3
(416) 423-6228

OVE DESIGN INTÉRIEURS INC.
356, rue Le Moyne
Vieux-Montréal, Québec
H2Y 1Y3
(514) 844-8421

FEASIBILITY STUDIES	ÉTUDE DE FAISABILITÉ
INFORMATION RETRIEVAL	CUEILLETTE DE L'INFORMATION
COMPUTERIZED DESIGN PROGRAMS	PROGRAMME INFORMATISÉ DE DESIGN
SPACE PLANNING	PLANIFICATION DE L'ESPACE
INTERIOR DESIGN	DESIGN D'INTÉRIEUR
PROJECT MANAGEMENT	GESTION DE PROJET
SIGNAGE	SIGNALISATION
VISUAL ART CONSULTATION	CONSEILLER EN ART VISUEL

PULSANN

111 Queen Street East
Suite 340
Toronto, Ontario
M5C 1S2
(416) 865-1196

Ann Marsolais

The successful completion of an office environment which reflects your unique corporate image and function requires the right combination of many people and many things. These in turn must be orchestrated by highly skilled experienced professionals.

We are professionals.

PRESTON    The Corporate Interiors
Resource Group

1947 – 1987
40 years of service to North America's business community.

500 University Avenue   310 Somerset Street West
10th Floor   3rd Floor
Toronto, Ontario   Ottawa, Ontario
M5G 1V7   K2P 0J9
(416) 598-3540   **(613) 232-7175**

The Preston Interior Resource Group was selected by Royal Trust to plan, design, supply and service their more than 250,000 square feet of corporate office space in Toronto.

The challenge which the Preston team met was to provide Royal Trust with the most flexible and productive office space, able to encompass the rapidly-changing and growth-oriented requirements of this dynamic company.

Royal Trust
Royal Trust Tower
Toronto Dominion Centre
1. Typical floor reception
2. Elevator lobby
3. Cafeteria
4. Typical floor reception

INTERIOR DESIGN CHOICE 3 © Preston

PRESTON

1947 – 1987
40 years of service to
North America's business community.

Toronto, Ontario

Ottawa, Ontario

As one of Canada's most successful space planning, office design and furniture supply firms, Preston is dedicated to providing a complete range of services for your office environment.

OUR AIM is to provide a plan that is functional and aesthetically conducive to a sustained, productive work effort in a way that reflects a corporation's goals and personality. This is our single, vital task.

OUR PRODUCT is productivity achieved through the application of proven design, analytical processes, a keen sensitivity to the corporate aesthetic and an applied knowledge in work-stations solutions.

OUR SERVICE incorporates project management. After 40 years in the business, these are not empty promises.

Royal Trust
Royal Trust Tower
Toronto Dominion Centre
1. Meeting room
2. Typical floor - closed offices
3. Detail – shelf support
4. Detail – elevator lobby

RBL

Rice Brydone Limited

635 Queen Street East Toronto Ontario M4M 1G4

(416) 466-4446

PRE-LEASE CONSULTATION ACCOMODATION STUDY INTERIOR DESIGN PROJECT MANAGEMENT RESTORATION RENOVATION

COMPUTERIZED: PROGRAMMING, PLANNING, DRAFTING, FACILITY SUPPORT, FURNITURE PROGRAMMES ART CONSULTING GRAPHICS

INTERIOR DESIGN 3 © Rice Brydone Limited, Toronto

RBL

Rice Brydone Limited

706 – 7th Avenue S.W. Suite 600 Calgary Alberta T2P 0Z1

(403) 233-8865

PRE-LEASE CONSULTATION ACCOMODATION STUDY INTERIOR DESIGN PROJECT MANAGEMENT RESTORATION RENOVATION

Photo: Shin Sugino

INTERIOR DESIGN 3 © Rice Brydone Limited, Calgary

COMPUTERIZED: PROGRAMMING, PLANNING, DRAFTING, FACILITY SUPPORT, FURNITURE PROGRAMMES ART CONSULTING GRAPHICS

design consultants

**design consultants
business furniture
& furnishings**

33 Wyecroft Road
Oakville, Ontario
L6K 2H2
(416) 842-5183

Larry E. Sikorski
ARIDO, I.D.C., A.S.I.D.

A team of professional business interior consultants dedicated to providing a quality concious design service.
As systems furniture specialists, their expertise with office interiors allows **SIL & ASSOCIATES** to select the best available solutions to both functional and aesthetic requirements.
As a result of many successful years of professional experience, **SIL** possesses a creative, yet functional attitude towards commercial interior design.

SERVICES

– **Feasibility Reports**
– **Space Planning**
– **Interior Design**
– **Specifying**
– **Architectural Working Drawings**
– **Budgets**
– **Tendering**
– **Project Management**
– **Complete installations of
furniture & furnishings.**

Paul A Stocks Limited
Professional Interior Design
Commercial Space Planning
Systems Specialists
Project Management
35 Coldwater Road, Don Mills, Ontario   M3B 1Y8   (416) 449-9733

1. Shell corporate offices
Reception – Toronto

2. & 3. Stelco Credit Union
Branch Bank – Hamilton

INTERIOR DESIGN CHOICE 3 © Paul A Stocks Limited

 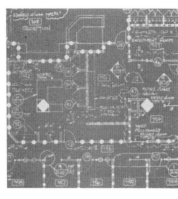  

today's

AND

317 Adelaide Street South
London, Ontario
N5Z 3L3
(519) 681-8585

The process is complex,
but the result is simple...
we create business interiors
that work for our clients.

Today's Business Interiors   **(416) 292-5155**
393 Nugget Avenue, Scarborough, Ontario, Canada   M1S 4G3

**total
environmental
planning
limited**

265 Hood Road
Markham, Ontario
L3R 4N3
(416) 474-0510

Ludwig O. Schindler
ARIDO, I.S.P., I.D.C.
Design Director

When we founded Total Environmental Planning Limited we conceived an operating philosophy to develop, design, space plan and perform related management services to bring total professional objectivity and independence to each client's unique situation.

INTERIOR DESIGN CHOICE 3 © Total Environmental Planning Limited

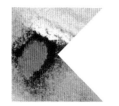

I N T E R I O R

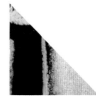

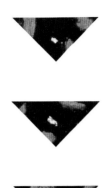

D E S I G N

R E T A I L

Joseph Bigio Interior Design Inc.
204-600 Eglinton Avenue West
Toronto, Ontario
M5N 1C1
(416) 481-5423

Joseph Bigio, ARIDO, I.D.C.

1. Revlon International, Toronto
2. Cosmelux Inc., Toronto
3. Bryan's Cookies, Toronto

Stephen Campbell Design Ltd.
Store Planners
2nd floor, 224 – 11th Avenue SW
Calgary, Alberta
T2R 0C3
(403) 262-7416

Innovative Solutions

Project Locations:
Victoria • Vancouver • Calgary
Edmonton • Lethbridge • Banff
Lake Louise • Innisfail • Sexsmith
Lacolme • Saskatoon • Swift Current
Winnipeg • Toronto • Ottawa
Halifax • Santa Barbara

1. Facemakers • Saskatoon
2. Dinnerware Studio • MRV • Calgary
3. & 4. Bloomers • MRV • Calgary

Getting attention is important. Especially if you're in retail. Our retail design has been getting a lot of attention recently.
And while that's all very nice for us, it's all very critical for you.
Of course you don't have to be in retail to want people to notice you.

Citiworks Design Inc.

296 Richmond Street West, Suite 300
Toronto, Canada M5V 1X2 (416) 531-5749

Everyone has customers. Our corporate clients are pleased as punch to be noticed. If you'll pay us a little attention we'll pay you a lot. So will others. Remember our name. **Citiworks.**

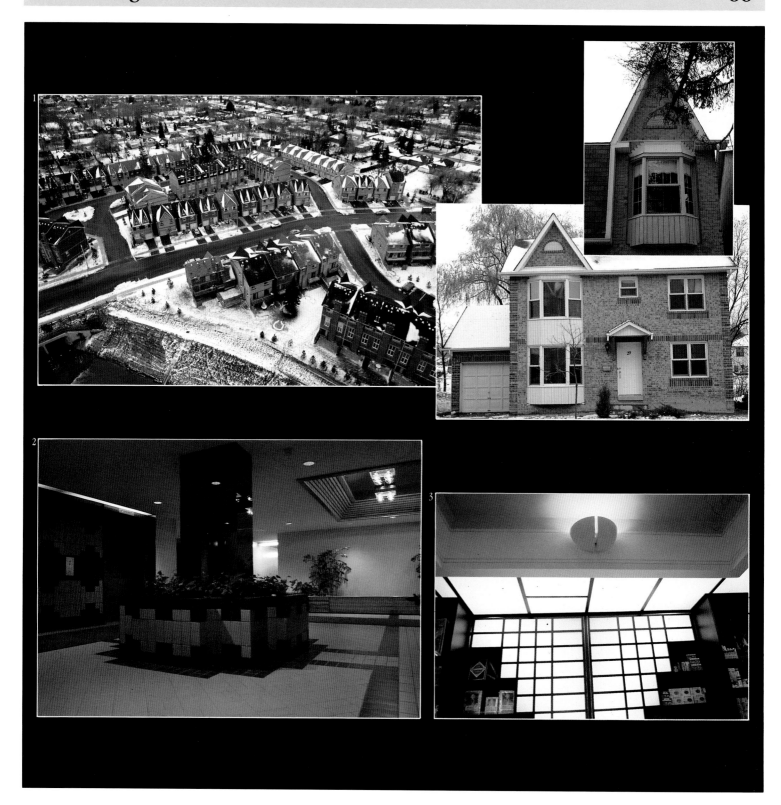

ID

Inter-Design
Architectural &
Industrial Design
Consultants
30 Ridley Gardens
Toronto, Ontario
M6R 2T8
(416) 532-9435

1. Wilcroft Mews, Scarborough, Ontario
104 Townhouse–condominium
development at Kennedy & Sheppard
for Lebovic Enterprises.
One of the ten finalists nominated for
an urban planning design award in
1986 by the City of Scarborough

2. Peel Non-profit Housing Corporation
Mississauga, Ontario
Lobby

3. The Gourmet Touch
Sheraton Centre, Ontario

INTERIOR DESIGN CHOICE 3 © Inter-Design

isometricdesigngroupinc.

24 Beisel Court
Brampton, Ontario
L6Z 1P4
(416) 846-8675

The Designer
We are neither cold, nor inhuman.
We are flights of fantasy and romance,
crystal ice palaces rising out of nothing,
floating in a calm, dream-like world
far from reality and its chaos. We are
what we are – the designer.
We see a project as the creation of a
space where shopping is meant to be
an escape from the mundane. The bare
bones of retail are spun into an ongoing
journey where sight and senses fuse in
visions and illusions sought, from this
place to another.

My belief is that good creative and
functional design, limited only by the
imagination, will be revered as long as
humans have the capacity to appreciate
design. Let us take your dream and
transpose it to reality where others
can then dream.

Morrie Serber, ARIDO

Thank You: Jonathan Smith
Alena Drozd

1. Jolene
   Yorkdale Shopping Centre, Toronto

2. & 3. Raphael Jewellers
   The Promenade, Toronto

4. Riordan's
   Fairview Park Mall,
   Kitchener, Ontario

5. & 6. Fenzi
   Yorkdale Shopping Centre, Toronto

INTERIOR DESIGN CHOICE 3 © Isometric Design Group Inc.

chris kyranis +associates ltd.

5233 Dundas St. W. Islington (Toronto) Ont. M9B-1A6 239-0549

1. Pennington's
St. Laurent Shopping Center
Ottawa, Ontario

2. Silverberg's Toys
Yorkdale Shopping Center
Toronto, Ontario

3. Liz Porter
Rideau Center
Ottawa, Ontario

4. Young Canada
Yorkdale Shopping Center
Toronto, Ontario

M.D.I.
Design
Consultants Inc.

At M.D.I. DESIGN CONSULTANTS INC.,
we think our work speaks for itself.

72 Fraser Avenue
Suite 216
Toronto, Ontario
M6K 3E1

(416) 533-4642

(416) 535-0746

Our business is Retail Store Design, our projects are international.

1. Charlie's Burger & Ice Cream Parlour
   Charlie's Plaza
   Bradford, Ontario
2. Rubin's Jewelers
   Bayside Marketplace
   Miami, Florida

3. Maxi Boutique
   Toronto, Ontario
4. The Squire Restaurant
   Antioch, Illinois

5. Mammina's Ristorante
   Toronto, Ontario
6. Chocolateur
   Masonville Place
   London, Ontario

7. Lustig Jewelers
   Hawthorn Center
   Vernon Hills, Illinois
8. Adam's Garden Restaurant
   Toronto, Ontario

Our strength is
the success of our work.

Sam Marouhos & Associates
Interior Designers, Planners
17 St. Joseph Street, Suite 402
Toronto, Ontario M4Y 1J8
(416) 923-4074
Facsimile (416) 960-3382

Our services:
Visual merchandising
Feasibility studies
Planning and design
Colour rendering
Architecture
Engineering
Project co-ordination

INTERIOR DESIGN CHOICE 3 © Sam Marouhos & Associates

MICHAUD
DESIGN CONSULTANTS

24 Kew Beach Avenue
Toronto, Ontario
M4L 1B7
(416) 690-6422

INTERIOR DESIGN CHOICE 3 © Michaud Design Consultants

Photo: Fraser Day

⬡OMNIPLAN

Omniplan Design Group Limited
92 Church St. South
Suite 108
Pickering (Toronto), Ontario
L1V 2S6
(416) 427-2902

Chester Niziol, ARIDO, A.C.I.D.
President, Design Director

Omniplan is a retail planning and design firm. What distinguishes Omniplan from other design firms is that all of our design solutions are based on the principle of "Strategic Creativity"... that is, the integration of marketing, design and research disciplines to generate Business Design Solutions.

We believe that creativity is essential to all parts of the problem solving process: in defining the problem, in developing a strategy for solutions,

and finally in creating the actual design solutions. While we operate on the leading edge of creativity, the orientation of our professionals is towards marketplace performance, the ultimate test of any Business Design Solution.

1. Reception area
Omniplan Design Group Limited
Pickering, Ontario

2. Computer Innovations retail facility
Standard Life Building
Toronto, Ontario

INTERIOR DESIGN CHOICE 3 © Omniplan Design Group Limited

Photo: Frank Prazak

lynn raitt interiors

190 St. George Street
Suite 801
Toronto, Ontario
M5R 2N4
(416) 923-1244

Lynn Raitt
ARIDO

Commercial and residential interiors.

Cemi Shoe Boutique
77 Bloor Street West, Toronto

INTERIOR DESIGN CHOICE 3 © Lynn Raitt Interiors

Leonard Ostroff Design Associates Ltd.

A. Gold & Sons	Men's Storefront	Anthony Saks	Storefront	Old River	Storefront
A. Gold & Sons	Men's Furnishings	Anthony Saks	Interior	Old River	Interior
A. Gold & Sons	Ladies' Storefront	Dalmys	Storefront	Pegabo	Storefront
Antels	Storefront	Dalmys	Interior	Pegabo	Interior

LEONARD OSTROFF DESIGN ASSOCIATES LTD.

1200 DE LOUVAIN ST. WEST
MONTREAL, H4N 1G5, CANADA
TEL.(514) 382-0571

Interior Design/Retail

Interior Design Choice 3

Shirley K.	Storefront	A. Gasco	Storefront	Jacob	Storefront
Addition-Elle	Storefront	Suzy Shier	Storefront	Jacob	Interior
Au Coton	Storefront	L.A. Express	Storefront	Mia	Storefront
M.G.A.	Storefront	Aldo Shoes	Storefront	Mia	Interior

LEONARD OSTROFF DESIGN ASSOCIATES LTD.

1200 DE LOUVAIN ST. WEST
MONTREAL, H4N 1G5, CANADA
TEL. (514) 382-0571

INTERIOR DESIGN CHOICE 3 © Leonard Ostroff Design Associates Ltd.

9 West, Toronto   Calderone, Toronto   Lipton's, Toronto

SHIRO/ROBERTS +ASSOCIATES

15 Gervais Drive
Suite 703
Don Mills, Ontario
M3C 1Y8
(416) 449-1529

INTERIOR DESIGN CHOICE 3 © Shiro/Roberts + Associates

Heritage House, Toronto   Harry Rosen, Toronto   Harry Rosen Women, Toronto

SHIRO/ROBERTS +ASSOCIATES

15 Gervais Drive
Suite 703
Don Mills, Ontario
M3C 1Y8
(416) 449-1529

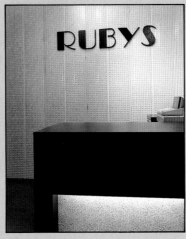

G.L.SMITH
PLANNING & DESIGN INC

IIII FINCH AVE WEST, SUITE 351, DOWNSVIEW, ONT.
M3J 2E5 TEL (416) 736-1290

1. Diva
   New concept, Canada

2. Joseph's
   Mississauga, Ontario

3. Rubys
   New concept, Canada

Photo: Ellen Taub

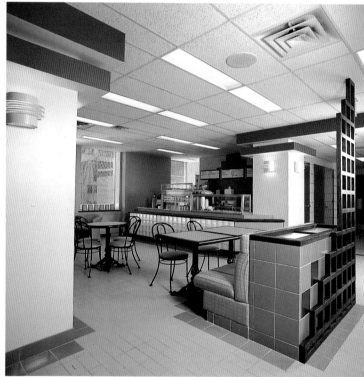

**total
environmental
planning
limited**

265 Hood Road
Markham, Ontario
L3R 4N3
(416) 474-0510

Ludwig O. Schindler
ARIDO, I.S.P., I.D.C.
Design Director

We believe we must be free to
assemble and utilize those components
which will most appropriately
represent solutions to the client's
functional and aesthetic design needs.

INTERIOR DESIGN CHOICE 3 © Total Environmental Planning Limited

Peter C. Cotton Inc. specializes in development, retail and restaurants and has designed projects from coast to coast.

Clients include:

Development
Champlain Mall, Moncton
Brunswick Square, Saint John, N.B.
Portage Place Mall, Peterborough
Saint John City Market, N.B.
Scotia Square, Halifax

Retail & Corporate

McTavish & Robinson, Ottawa
Factory Carpet – New Image Stores
Municipal Savings and Loan,
   Peterborough

Restaurants

The Fish House Expansion, Toronto
The Hayloft, Toronto, Ottawa
Clipper Cay, Halifax
Rosa's Cantina, Halifax

1.-3. The Barking Fish
   Ottawa

4. Moviolas

5. ...It Stores

Interior Designers
56 The Esplanade
Suite 408
Toronto, Ontario
M5E 1A7
(416) 863-6743

I N T E R I O R

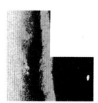

H O S P I T A L I T Y

D E S I G N

Robert J. Chaban & Associates is a highly motivated hospitality design group that understands and responds to the requirements of the industry.

PARTIAL LIST OF OUR CLIENTS

Ramada Inns

Hilton International Saint John

The Valhalla Companies

CP Hotels/The Algonquin Hotel

Hilton International Quebec

Loew's Westbury Hotel

Howard Johnson's Motor Hotels

Our company has the depth of knowledge and experience to provide the total design involvement for your projects. Whether the program is a new development or the renovation of an existing property, our success is based on our ability to create the exciting design statements while working closely within the functional, timing and budget restraints established.

Our commitment is to excellence.

ROBERT J. CHABAN & ASSOCIATES

Suite 200,
268 Lakeshore Road East
Port Credit, Ontario L5G 1H1
(416) 274-1510

Skyline Hotels

Winston's Restaurant

Commonwealth Holiday Inns

Citadel Inn

Bonaventure Hilton International

21 McGill Women's Club

CP Hotels/Royal York Hotel

Sheraton Centre Hotel

INTERIOR DESIGN 3 © Robert J. Chaban & Associates

EATON'S CONTRACT INTERIORS

HALIFAX MONTREAL TORONTO WINNIPEG REGINA SASKATOON CALGARY EDMONTON VANCOUVER VICTORIA

Interior Design/Hospitality

Pickle Barrel
Toronto

Duncan Street Grill
Toronto

GIANNA
DESIGN
ASSOCIATES
commercial interiors

593 Yonge Street
Suite 200
Toronto, Ontario
M4Y 1Z4
(416) 967-1761

Photo: Mindy Doerr

Ingrid Herczegh Inc.
54 Austin Terrace
Toronto, Ontario
M5R 1Y6
(416) 533-7034

Ingrid Herczegh
ARIDO, I.D.C.

Commercial and Residential Design
Specializing in Hospitality

Partial list of completed projects:

The Daily Planet
Eglinton and Yonge, Toronto

The Daily Planet
in The Promenade, Toronto

Hazelton Lanes
Toronto

Fenton's
Fenton's Fine Food
Toronto

Albany Club
Library Bar and Dining Rooms
Toronto

Rue Franklin Café
Buffalo, N.Y.

Eaton Hall Hotel
Jamaica

INTERIOR DESIGN CHOICE 3 © Ingrid Herczegh Inc.

INTERIOR DESIGN CHOICE 3 © Albert Hui Design Associates

ALBERT HUI DESIGN ASSOCIATES
742 Queen Street West, Toronto, Ontario M6J 1E9 (416) 869-0894

Total design SERVICES.

Davids' Deli

Mrs. Vanelli's

Tea Masters Cafe

innovation

Sweet Sue Pastries

Beaver Canoe

Davids' Deli

**Martin Hirschberg
Design Associates Ltd.**
334 Queen Street East
Toronto, Ontario
M5A 1S8
(416) 868-1210

INTERIOR DESIGN CHOICE 3 © Martin Hirschberg Design Associates Ltd.

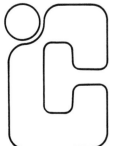

Idea Consultants Inc.
250 The Esplanade
Suite 102
Berkley Castle
Toronto, Ontario
M5A 1J2
(416) 860-1679

Thomas Wayne, President
Raul Corres, Vice-President

Idea Consultants Inc. is "The Total Concept Development Company" that provides a complete service of Design, Project Management and Operational Consulting. The results are facilities of international standards and recognition.

Idea's corporate philosophy is based on the premise that it is not how much money you spend but how you spend it. The substance of the ideas measures the success of the results.

Partial Client List:
Commonwealth Holiday Inns
Ramada Inns
Howard Johnson's (Canada)
Triland International (Dallas)
Nepentha Internacional S.A. (Mexico)
Inducon Development Corporation
The Palm Restaurants Ltd.
Queens Hotel Group
Marathon Realty

Robert M. Ledingham INC.

2327 Yew Street
Vancouver, British Columbia
V6G 3H1
(604) 734-1281

Expo '86 – Vancouver, B.C.
Canada Pavillion
Commissioner General's Suite
1. Reception Area
2. Commissioner General's office
3. Lounge
4. Dining Room
5. Hallway

Patricia McClintock Associés Inc.
Designers-conseil/Design Consultants

1167 St. Marc Street
Montreal, Quebec
Canada H3H 2E4
(514) 932-1860

- Hotel/Restaurant Design
- Corporate Interiors
- Retail Planning & Design
- Image Development

A sophisticated team of professionals providing complete design services for the hospitality industry and corporate interiors; in retail planning and design, building renovations and image development.

With a classical and structured approach to design, we transform space into functional areas; with flair and by close consultation we create innovative and personalized design solutions translating our international client's expectations into visual form.

C.N. Hotels
Projects – 1985

1   Main Lobby
    Hotel Beausejour
    Moncton, N.B.

2 & 3 Junior Suites
    Hotel Queen Elizabeth
    Montreal, Quebec

Pat and Mario's Restaurant, Mississauga, Ontario

DEL McMILLAN DESIGN

Glendale Avenue at
Queen Elizabeth Way, Box 566
Niagara-on-the-Lake, Ontario L0S 1J0
(416) 688-1165
A division of N.O.T.L.
Design Group Ltd.

Elegant, cost-effective designs for the
food and hospitality, corporate,
institutional and residential markets.

We provide comprehensive and
integrated client services in
• Interior and exterior design
• Food service design
• Contract supply
• Project management
• Graphic design
• Advertising and marketing
From concept through construction

Our Clients
Pat & Mario's Restaurants, Inc.
Pat & Mario's Restaurants, Florida
Casey's Restaurants
Asti's Ristorante
Porter's Steakhouse
The Prince of Wales Hotel
Venture Inn Hotels
Wildwood of America, Inc.
Laredo Junction Restaurants
McCabe's Restaurants
Prudhomme's Landing Hotel
P.J. Mellon's
Controlled Foods International

INTERIOR DESIGN CHOICE 3 © Del McMillan Design

Photo: Shin Sugino

INTERIOR DESIGN CHOICE 3 © Rice Brydone Limited

RBL

Rice Brydone Limited

635 Queen Street East Toronto Ontario M4M 1G4

(416) 466-4446

RESTAURANTS LOBBY BARS LOUNGES PUBLIC AREAS BALLROOMS MEETING ROOMS GUESTROOMS

The Hair Cutting Place
Toronto

Rainbows
Miami

Le Connaisseur
Toronto

Mark III Productions
Miami

Rafaell Cabrera International

914 Yonge Street
Suite 1701
Toronto, Ontario
M4W 3C8
(416) 964-6947
(416) 964-8678

246 West End Avenue
Suite 2B
New York, New York
10023
(212) 787-3851

Rafaell Cabrera
Dennis Abbé

INTERIOR DESIGN CHOICE 3 © Rafaell Cabrera International

The Last Detail

Wood Wilkings Limited
Interior Architects
Head Office
65 Front Street East
Toronto, Canada M5E 1B5
(416) 865-9980
Telex: 065-24703
Facsimile (416) 865-1073
Branch Offices: Los Angeles, Sydney

Hotel and Resort Design
Bally's Park Place, Atlantic City
Hyatt Regency Hotel, Toronto
Sheraton Landmark, Vancouver
Hyatt Regency, San Francisco
Registry Resort, Naples, Florida
Sonesta International Hotels, Boston

**Purchasing and
Project Management Division**
Sheraton Villa, Vancouver
Registry Resort, Naples, Florida
Sheraton Landmark, Vancouver

''Special Project Design'' Division
Chrysalis Restaurants
Mövenpick Restaurants
Lime Rickeys Restaurants
4-D Diner
Max's Diner, San Francisco
Second City
Plymouth Rock Restaurants

INTERIOR DESIGN CHOICE 3 © Wood Wilkings Limited

tdi assoc.
design inc.

363, rue Le Moyne
Suite 201
Montréal, Québec
H2Y 1Y3 Canada
(514) 288-8303

- Space Planning
- Interior Architectural Design
- Contract Documentation
- Construction Drawings &
  Specifications
- Scope of Work
- Construction Supervision
- Graphics & Signage

商業インテリアデザイングループ
業種範囲
- ●市場調査
- ●マスタープラン
- ●スペースプランニング
- ●コントラクトドキメンテーション
- ●詳細図、仕上表
- ●仕様書
- ●現場管理
- ●グラフィックデザイン

1, 2, 3, 5
Katsura Restaurant
Photo: Takashi Seida
4
Ogilvy Department Store
6, 7
Château Champlain
8
Sushi Bar
9, 10
Executron
Photo: Takashi Seida

INTERIOR

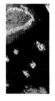

D   E   S   I   G   N

M   O   D   E   L   S   U   I   T   E   S

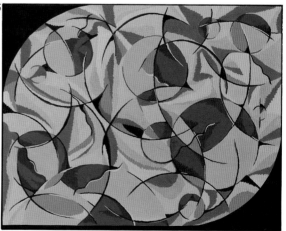

ALEX CHAPMAN DESIGN LTD.

Alex Chapman Design Ltd.
49 Spadina Avenue
Suite 507
Toronto, Ontario
M5V 2J1
(416) 597-1576

1. The Bromley, New York
2. Residence, Montreal
3. Symphony House, New York
4. 55 Prince Arthur, Toronto

5. Polo Club II, Lobby Carpet Design, Toronto
6. Greenwich Court, Sales Office, New York
7. Queen's Quay Residences, Toronto
8. You'll love it.

**Cheryl L. Duncan
& Associates**
80 Front Street East
Suite 301
Toronto, Canada
M5E 1T4
(416) 967-6090

Photo: Ralph Brodie

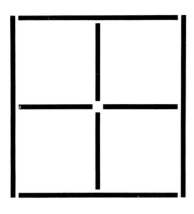

Tanner Hill Associates Inc.
25 Overlea Blvd., Suite 205, Unit 2
Toronto, Ontario M4H 1B1
(416) 429-1600
Paul Maggiacomo, President
Beverley Maggiacomo
Elli Kester
Nicolas Marton
Peter Maggiacomo
Helen Horner
Barbara Clewley-Gagnon
Lisa Robinsky
Stephen Wagg
ARIDO, I.D.C. and A.S.I.D. Members

Tanner Hill Associates Incorporated was formed in 1975 by Paul Maggiacomo. His firm is a multi-faceted interior design company encompassing design expertise in high-rise condominiums, model suites, and interior specifications. The company is responsible for many condominium projects throughout Canada and the United States, e.g. Houston, Denver, Florida and Toronto.

1. & 2. 70 Rosehill – Costain Limited

3. 130 Carlton – Tridel Corporation

Partial list of clients:
Tridel Corporation
Camrost Group of Companies
Costain Limited
Cadillac Fairview Corporation Ltd.
Ronto Corporation
Shipp Corporation Limited
The Daniels Group

INTERIOR DESIGN CHOICE 3 © Tanner Hill Associates Incorporated

Condominium Model Suites

THE PROMENADE
New York, New York

Norma King Design Inc.
114A Sackville Street
Toronto, Canada
M5A 3E7
(416) 862-9180

INTERIOR DESIGN CHOICE 3 © Norma King Design Inc.

Condominium Model Suites

THE PENTHOUSE
309 East 49th Street
New York, New York

GREENWICH COURT
New York, New York

52 Park Avenue
New York, New York

THE SYMPHONY HOUSE
New York, New York

INTERIOR

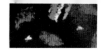

DESIGN

RESIDENTIAL

Start at the top...see
and touch our spectacular
collection of interior
furnishings, many levels
above the ordinary in more
ways than one.
Excellence endures...
 the Interior Design Studio,
 Barbara Angela

Residential and Corporate Design

Barbara Angela Interiors
145 Trafalgar Road
Oakville, Ontario L6J 3G7
(416) 842-2103

bydesignonly

By Design Only/David Burnell
3015 Queen Street East
Suite D-11
Scarborough, Ontario
M1N 1A5
(416) 699-0352

I have been creating and designing residential environments for the past ten years. My success comes from the realizations that one's dwelling place must be a complimentary extension of the personalities that live and evolve within. It must express for some a feeling of warmth in a calming sanctuary; a pleasant, welcoming environment to entertain in; and for some, a gallery of your most precious possessions and collections.

Mobilier Philippe Dagenais
1600, Sherbrooke ouest
Montréal, Québec
H3H 1C9
(514) 931-7294

Mobilier Philippe Dagenais
116, rue Principale
Grandby, Québec
J2G 2V2
(514) 372-8366

A challenge well met.
Result: "Trajectoire", signed
Philippe Dagenais.
Furniture collection in five themes,
destined to five types of different
personalities. Pure lines that join
harmoniously together living, dining
and bed rooms.

Talent, determination and relentless
work place this designer on an equal
step with the bests of Europe.
"Trajectoire" is entirely Canadian made.
A story to follow.
Philippe Dagenais was gratified with the
Canada Award of Excellence in Design
for 1983. He was also laureate of two
Habitas '85 trophies. One for Design,
and the other as Retail Store of the year.

Un défi relevé avec succès.
Résultat: "Trajectoire", signée
Philippe Dagenais.
Collection de meubles en cinq thèmes,
traduits par des noms de vents, et qui
s'adresse à cinq personnalités bien
distinctes.
Des lignes pures, racées qui défient les
modes, et relient salon, salle à manger
et chambre à coucher.

Le talent, la détermination et le travail
acharné place ce designer sur un pied
d'égalité avec les meilleurs d'Europe.
"Trajectoire" est une fabrication
entièrement canadienne. Une histoire à
suivre.
Récipiendaire du prix Excellence '83 en
Design, et de deux trophés Habitas '85,
en tant que Designer et Magasin au
Détail de l'année.

Helena Interiors
103 Ava Road
Toronto, Canada
M6C 1V9
(416) 787-7595

Helena-Lynn Neinstein ARIDO

Michael Lerch Interiors Inc.
1448 Sherbrooke Street West
Montreal, Quebec
H3G 1K4
(514) 287-0851

H. Michael Lerch
Design Consultant

BURT MANION INTERIOR DESIGN LIMITED • RESIDENTIAL AND COMMERCIAL
283 MacPherson Avenue, Toronto, Ontario (416) 923-6611 • 191 Escarpment Crescent, Cranberry Village, Collingwood, Ontario (705) 445-7226

Associate Designers: **Burt M. Manion** A.O.C.A., ARIDO, A.S.I.D., I.D.C
                       Paul Sinnott, B.I.D., ARIDO

Morel Interiors Ltd.

Renaissance Court
162 Cumberland Street
Toronto M5R 3N5
961-3385

R E S I D E N T I A L

R E N O V A T I O N S

- Planning
- Design
- Construction
- Project Management
- Kitchens & Baths
- Custom Cabinetry
- Custom Furniture

A team of professionnals capable of handling all phases of your renovating and decorating needs, from planning through conception to final execution.

No shortfalls.
No compromises.

Award winning kitchen
International
Kitchen & Bath Expo 1986

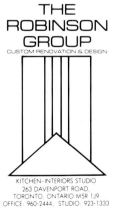

THE ROBINSON GROUP
CUSTOM RENOVATION & DESIGN

KITCHEN-INTERIORS STUDIO
263 DAVENPORT ROAD,
TORONTO, ONTARIO M5R 1J9
OFFICE: 960-2444 STUDIO: 923-1333

INTERIOR DESIGN CHOICE 3 © The Robinson Group

DEALERS

DESIGNERS

EATON'S CONTRACT INTERIORS

HALIFAX MONTREAL TORONTO WINNIPEG REGINA SASKATOON CALGARY EDMONTON VANCOUVER VICTORIA

**DIANE NICHOLLS, ANDREA RACKETT & HEATHER LAMORIE
CREATE BUSINESS INTERIOR DESIGNS
AS REFRESHING AS THE GREAT OUTDOORS.**

Their undeniable talent and youthful enthusiasm have combined to produce some rather outstanding examples of contemporary interior designs for business.

830 BROCK ROAD SOUTH, PICKERING, ONTARIO   416•683•6222   TORONTO 416•282•6161

Intefac Showroom
Mississauga, Ontario.

Intefac's horizon of services spans the corporate office market, the health care environment, and the industrial market place, with a facilities design group and an installation team to complete the offering.
Our showroom illustrates vanguard product in the fields mentioned.

Intefac Inc.
5420 Timberlea Blvd.
Mississauga, Ontario
L4W 2T7
(416) 624-6700

INTERIOR DESIGN CHOICE 3 © Intefac Inc.

POI Business Interiors
120 Valleywood Drive
Markham, Ontario
L3R 6A7
(416) 479-1123

2 Robert Speck Parkway
Mississauga, Ontario
L4Z 1H8
(416) 272-1530

Office environments for busy,
industrious people to perform to the
utmost of their capabilities — where
every inch of space is utilized to
produce a perfect melding of function
and aesthetics, precisely tailored to the
customer's needs, image and budget.

INTERIOR DESIGN CHOICE 3 © POI Business Interiors

This has been the achievement — and the commitment — of everyone at POI since our very beginning in 1953. From establishing initial criteria and design concepts to implementation and ongoing service, our teams of professionals interpret every client requirement, and translate them into bold, dynamic statements of form and function.

Through our wide selection of fine office furnishings and years of experience, we maintain our position of leadership. We will continue to make available the highest possible calibre of expertise, and to introduce new products and innovations as market demands over the years.

POI Services:
- Consultation
- Feasibility studies
- Concept development
- Space planning
- Facilities management
- Leasehold improvements
- Project management
- Furnishings selection
- Delivery/installation
- Warranty fulfillment

INTERIOR DESIGN CHOICE © POI Business Interiors

Preston supplies office furnishings. We believe that it is too important to leave the quality of materials and construction to chance. Preston is a preferred distributor of a selected group of North America's most prestigious builders of fine office furniture.

Our account managers have been professionally trained to represent this product and to ensure that its application best suits the client's requirements. We are committed to a long and lasting relationship with each client.

Whether you are designing an entirely new office environment, or simply refurbishing the one you have, you are bound to ask: Why buy through Preston? In fact, there are some very good reasons. Our buying power and relationships which we enjoy with our suppliers mean that we can assure availability of products, specifications, prices, and delivery times to a degree the average individual cannot.

Secondly, and perhaps more importantly, is what you get when you buy your furniture through Preston: Service. Rather than having truckloads of crates arriving at your office a few at a time, Preston will dispatch trucks from our own fleet. Our crew of expert installers will set it all up and make sure that it works. After you have had a chance to settle in and assess your new office, Preston will conduct detailed follow-up interviews and inspections. If there is a problem, it will be corrected. We guarantee it!

We trust that the quality of our work will be evident in everything you see. The quality of the people who do it, however, is our reponsibility and Preston is committed to the very best.

Robert J. Bridel
President

PRESTON   The Corporate Interiors
Resource Group

1947 – 1987
40 years of service to North America's business community.

500 University Avenue	310 Somerset Street West
10th Floor	3rd Floor
Toronto, Ontario	Ottawa, Ontario
M5G 1V7	K2P 0J9
(416) 598-3540	**(613) 232-7175**

INTERIOR DESIGN CHOICE 3 ©Preston

Photo: Joanne Gilmour

Form and function with the future in mind.

1220 Ellesmere Road
Scarborough, Ontario
M1P 2X5
(416) 292-0090
Telex: 06-986683 E.O.R.-TOR

INTERIOR DESIGN CHOICE 3 © Salix Systems Limited

One smart, sure source for anything to do with interiors.

No matter what kind of business you're in, Simpsons Commercial Interiors & Design is a single dependable source for anything you need in interiors. We do it all. We do it well. We do it affordably.

Interior Design

Our accredited design professionals know how to help you get the most out of the money you put into your space. They can work out every detail of things like traffic flow, lighting, color co-ordination, materials, and furnishings. They present you with meticulous plans and estimates that make sense.

Interior Construction

Here we act as your general contractor overseeing the tradesmen who construct and install such things as lighting, partitions and finishes. We make sure it's done right, right on time and inside the budget.

Floor Coverings

We can help you find your way through the maze of hundreds of kinds, styles and colors of floor covering to find the one that's just right for your needs and budget. Custom carpeting, resilient tile, carpet tile... whatever! We've got the ones that are easy to care for, look great and wear well.

Business Interiors

When your employees and customers feel better, work better and interact better in your office, then chances are your business will get better. We can make it happen with well-planned office environments that make a good impression, improve productivity and reflect your professional attitudes.

Food Service Interiors

From kitchen equipment to cafeteria or restaurant furniture, we have the technical know-how and experience to help make food service operations both more appealing and more efficient.

Hospitality Interiors

We know the ins and outs of hotel and motel interiors very well. Our designers and consultants have helped to create welcoming surroundings for travelers — and profitable environments for owners — right across the country.

Health Care Interiors

Simpsons Commercial Interiors & Design has the capability to completely plan and furnish hospitals, senior citizen facilities, nursing homes and other health care facilities.

Across The Nation

Corporations and banks with nationwide operations rely on us for such things as the storage, distribution, assembly and installation of standardized furniture.

49 Gervais Drive
Don Mills, Ontario
M3C 1Y9
(416) 449-0110

Cataraqui Town Centre
945 Gardiners Road
Kingston, Ontario
K7M 7H4
(613) 389-5750

275 Slater Street
Ottawa, Ontario
K1P 5H9
(613) 237-3996

Colborne Centre
400 York Street
Suite 200
London, Ontario
N6B 3N2
(519) 679-4811

96 Larch Street
Sudbury, Ontario
P3E 1C1
(705) 673-4181

7 Edison (B.P. 1133)
Place Bonaventure
Montréal, Québec
H5A 1G4
(514) 866-9991

240 Leonard Street North
Regina, Saskatchewan
S4N 5V7
(306) 775-1955

Bay 2
3040 Miners Avenue North
Saskatoon, Saskatchewan
S7K 5V1
(306) 933-4311

Simpsons Commercial Interiors & Design

A Division of Simpsons Limited

Where design gets down to business.

Today's Business Products Ltd.

HEAD OFFICE

393 Nugget Avenue
Scarborough, Ontario
M1S 4G3
(416) 292-5155

1785 Matheson Boulevard
Mississauga, Ontario
L4W 1V2
(416) 625-3335

30 Manitou Drive
Kitchener, Ontario
N2C 1L3
(519) 893-2510

317 Adelaide Street South
London, Ontario
N5Z 3L3
(519) 681-8585

790 Industrial Avenue
Ottawa, Ontario
K1G 4H3
(613) 738-7611

TODAY'S QUEBEC INC.

1895, 46ᵉ Avenue
Lachine, Quebec
H8T 2N9
(514) 636-4606

Ontario's fastest growing dealership
because **we offer more.**

INTERIOR DESIGN CHOICE 3 © Today's Business Products Ltd.

855 Harrington Court
Burlington, Ontario
L7N 3P3

Burlington
(416) 639-7474
Toronto
(416) 827-6445

"Ours is a dedication to surpass,
rather than, to simply meet our
client's expectations."

Designs West's commitment to
quality in interior design is expressed
throughout the corporate, hospitality
and health care sectors of the
industry.

Dental Clinic
Dr. Robert Weber
Oakville, Ontario

Combined with the imaginative input of
the client, a functional and innovative
environment, incorporating a creative
use of colour, materials and architectural
elements was successfully developed.

INTERIOR DESIGN CHOICE 3 © The Ultimate Source Group Inc/Designs West

Product Design

Toronto 927-0353

Toronto 927-0353

Designwerke

Designwerke, the dynamic partnership of Jack Smith and Stephen Boake, specialize in product design solutions that are not only innovative but also technically resolved. The scope of our work extends from furniture, consumer products to electronic equipment. In 1986 we received an Award from the Philips Concours Design Competition for the Tricycle Lamp which is now in production.

366 King Street East Toronto Ontario M5A 1K9 Telephone 362 6000

D E S I G N E R S

M A K E R S

WITH THE SUPPORT OF:

LOOMIS & TOLES CO. LTD.

INDECS PUBLISHING INC.

Photo: Peter Hogan

Photo: Saltmarche

▶
Leaning Light 1986
Black dyed swiss pear, pigments on maple
68" × 7" × 4"

●
Silkscreen yardage 1986 (Detail)
Pigments on canvas

■
Menzefricke Sideboard 1986
Australian lacewood, African bubinga,
East Indian rosewood
60" × 20" × 36"

The Design Cooperative
135 Tecumseth Street
Toronto, Ontario
M6J 2H2
(416) 947-1684

Studio open by appointment

▶
The right object announces itself by its ability to communicate a presence that goes beyond marks on the sketch book page. The rhythm of positive and negative space, its stance, its silhouette and the overall surface are the components that I enjoy creatively.

The overlay of these intentions lends a richness and duration of curiosity over time.

Joel Robson

●
The process of silkscreening enables choices of exact repetition of images but also the freedom of random printing, breaking of the patterned surface. The marks vary, strong colour contrast, layering, texture and dimension are a concern. The prints are usually small in length and have a multitude of uses.

Gitte Hansen

■
Recently my designs have incorporated line and form in a technical method through the use of segmented or articulated joinery. Since joinery is a basic element in woodworking I've chosen to emphasize its effect visually while still retaining its structural purpose. Thus the process of joining the vertical and horizontal planes provides the setting for an event.

Robert Diemert

Photo: Peter Hogan

● End Table 1986
Curly maple, amaranth
16" × 16" × 24"

■ Rug 1986
Wool, Linen, Cotton
52" × 78"

◄ An Early Spring Table
Hard maple with epoxy inlay
15" × 15" × 30"

● *I am a craftsman because I am impatient. This is a bit of a contradiction when discussing such a long and sometimes tedious process as woodworking. However, this process and scale of production allows me to be intensely involved in that magical and bittersweet experience of the transmutation of idea into form. This involvement gives me control over the production of my work and lets me see results in a relatively short time.*

John Ireland.

■ *I am a weaver of rugs and tapestries. My work is concerned with the layering of marks and rays of color on different planes, of transposing one field on top of another and the interaction each individual plane has with one another. I work on a commission basis as well as producing pieces for exhibition.*

Barbara Walker

◄ *My search is not for perfection, but rather for what I imagine as "appropriateness", an appropriateness of scale, of form, of materials, of function both aesthetic and actual.*

I wish to achieve a sense of animation in the objects which I create; a vestigial personification of the beast. The viewer is to be engaged as a participator in my pieces, a relationship between the user and the used; humour is definitely an element in this dialogue.

Peter Fleming

The Design Cooperative is a group of individuals with a shared commitment to the expressive possibilities of craftsmanship and design, innovative design and technical competence in furniture, fabric, and interior furnishings.

From conception to completion each piece is designed and made by a single member of the cooperative.
Unique pieces are available for purchase and commissions are invited.

INTERIOR DESIGN CHOICE 3 © The Design Cooperative

Virtu

Forum & Function
Directions in Canadian Design
749 Queen Street West, 2nd Floor
Toronto, Ontario M6J 1G1
(416) 364-7251

'VIRTU', noun, 1. objects and articles of beauty and quality; 2. a taste for such objects; 3. such objects collectively. VIRTU is the only annual national competition/exhibition for residential furniture design in Canada.
VIRTU is organized by Forum & Function Directions in Canadian Design, a non-profit organization.
VIRTU has the mandate of developing

and encouraging new design within the residential context and providing a critical forum for the evaluation of the quality and integrity of these works.
Forum & Function is currently compiling archives of contemporary work from across Canada and is functioning as a source for curators, design professionals, manufacturers and consumers.
To receive competition briefs or to purchase VIRTU exhibition catalogues or items from VIRTU collections contact Forum & Function.

Selected works from the VIRTU 2 collection:
1. "Mach IV", Michael Hosaluk, Saskatoon
2. "Strala", Scot Laughton/ Tom Deacon, Toronto
3. "Mailbox", Brigitte Shim/ Howard Sutcliffe, Toronto
4. "Desk", Brian Gladwell, Regina
5. "This Is Not A Zoo", John Tong, Montreal
6. "Nera", David Dumbrell, Vancouver

Stephen Harris
Peter Pierobon
35 Booth Avenue
Toronto, Ontario
M4M 2M3
(416) 466-5892

Gordon Peteran
248 Dupont Street
Toronto, Ontario
M5R 1V7
(416) 925-5342

1. **Stephen Harris**
Entrance Door
Teak and wenge, bronze door knob
and rosette – 85'' high

2. **Peter Pierobon**
''Madonna'' Clock
Ebonized mahogany and gold leaf
73'' × 28'' × 10''

3. **Gordon Peteran**
Secretary
Pine, birdseye maple, ebony
72'' × 25'' × 16''

R E S O U R C E S

R E S O U R C E S

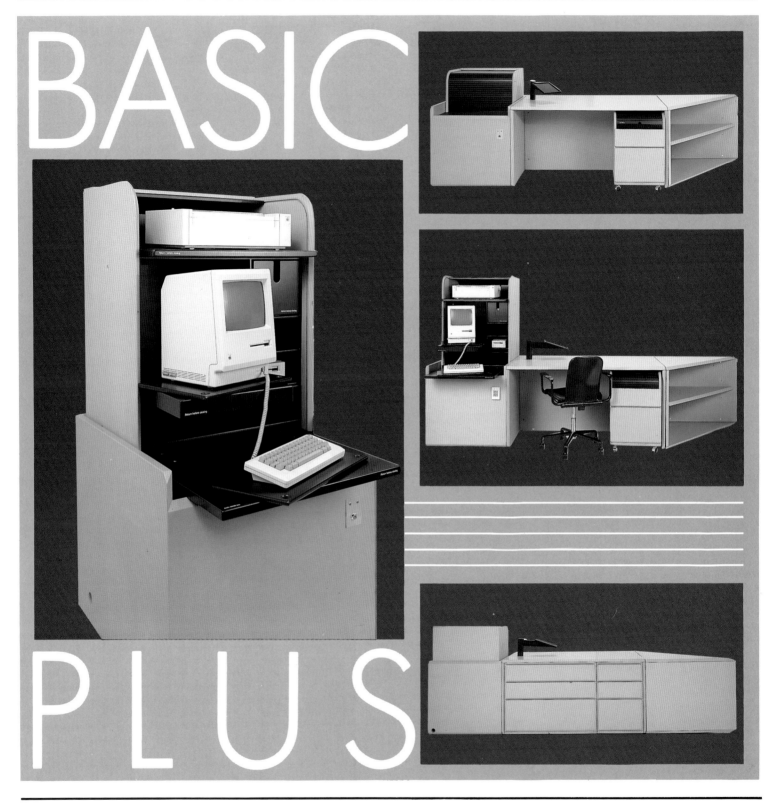

BASIC

PLUS

AID 2000 Inc.
101 Freshway Drive
Unit 66D
Concord, Ontario
L9K 1R9
(416) 661-6433

V. Flander
B.A. Architecture, Interior Design,
Furniture Design

B. Papernick
Design Consultant

A modular system for general office use, rich in functional detail, incorporating today's business machinery in a clean uncluttered environment. All pieces are amply scaled using a minimum amount of floor space, ideal for installation where a combination of panelled and free standing components are integrated into an esthetically pleasing environment.

BASIC PLUS was designed by V. Flander, winner of many international competitions in Europe for furniture and industrial design. Mr. Flander brings this experience and expertise to the North American furniture market.

BASIC PLUS was designed for several reasons:
1. To alleviate space management problems by restricting key board, screen, disk drive and software to 22.7 cubic feet of recessed space

with a surface area of just 7.1 square feet.
2. To facilitate the simultaneous access of the computer by two users, offering full rotation of keyboard and screen to left and right.
3. To keep the system dust free and protected
4. To improve the esthetic quality of office systems, that because of their size, shape and varied colours, clutter up the visual landscape of office interiors.

Abstracta Systems Inc.

abstracta

Abstracta Systems Inc.
30 Malley Road
Scarborough, Ontario
M1L 2E3
(416) 751-2717

Showroom
411 Richmond Street East
Toronto, Ontario
M5A 3S5
(416) 363-0657

Abstracta has been variously described as a unique catalyst to creative design, as imaginative, generating new forms of design thought, and abstract concepts.

Whatever the description, the imperative is that Abstracta Systems for retail displays, exhibition booths, P.O.P. racks, just to mention a few, will be a challenge and joy to your design creativity.

INTERIOR DESIGN CHOICE 3 © Abstracta Systems Inc.

Alexander's Fine Furniture
717 Kipling Avenue
Etobicoke, Ontario
M8Z 5G4
(416) 252-9347

Being interior designers ourselves we understand the nature of the business and the problems that can occur; consequently Alexander's has now become a significant resource for other design firms as well as for our own clients offering hand made traditional reproductions and custom designed transitional and contemporary case goods, tables and upholstery.

We also pride ourselves in being able to offer genuine restored 18th and 19th century furniture and accessories of superb quality from our ''in stock'' antiques inventory.

Good interior design, we feel, is born out of the knowledge and installation of fine crafted furniture that withstands the test of time.

Alexander's

ALLSTEEL

Allsteel Canada Ltd.
3500 Cote Vertu
St. Laurent, Quebec
H4R 1R1
(514) 334-0150

H. Astley,
V.P. Sales & Marketing

Bühk 100 Seating

Allsteel established several rigid criteria in preparing to design a chair that would symbolize its continued dedication to ergonomics and quality workmanship: Comfort, Function, Aesthetics & Quality. The Bühk 100 Seating not only meets all these criteria, it surpasses them.

The end result, Bühk 100 Seating is an ergonomically sound and aesthetically pleasing line, built to Allsteel's high standards of quality, yet affordable for most applications. Furthermore Bühk 100 Seating is versatile. It is designed for people of different sizes, shapes and occupations.

1. Allsteel's Bühk 100 Seating Models

2. Bühk 100 Seating Professional Chair

3. Bühk 100 Seating Operational chair

arconas

Arconas Corporation
580 Orwell Street
Mississauga, Ontario
L5A 3V7
(416) 272-0727

Arconas Corporation
150 East 58th St.
New York, N.Y.
10155
(212) 753-4960

Hotels, Offices, Lounges, Reception Areas, Dining Rooms and Embassies in Canada, U.S.A. and various parts of the world are home to Arconas seating. As our name means 'Innovative Leader', Arconas uses innovative designers and techniques from Europe, Canada and the U.S. to provide for the hospitality, commercial and institutional market. Our steel frames molded into high resiliency urethane provide the durability, comfort and fire retardency that allows us to warrant our product for 5 years (subject to conditions).

1. Flora
   Designer – Conrad Marini

2. Aurora
   Designer – Andre Vandenbueck

3. Gemello
   Designer – Conrad Marini

4. Our construction
   Designer – Arconas Staff

INTERIOR DESIGN CHOICE 3 © Arconas Corporation

REVIVAL

was designed for **BILTRITE** by Thomas Lamb.

BILTRITE'S innovative modular executive office furniture with co-ordinated seating. Work surfaces and casegoods stack and link together to easily facilitate personalized arrangements to suit the most particular executive.

1 Shown: typical lateral work wall arrangement with a round run off desk conference work surface supported by a single column leg. Finish: French walnut faces with solid wenge wood edges.

2 Shown: conventional two pedestal desk with optional recessed modesty panel. Also a five case modular credenza with two outside 1/4 round bar units. Finish: French walnut faces with solid wenge wood edges.

10251, boul. Ray Lawson
Ville d'Anjou, Quebec, Canada
H1J 1L7
Telephone (514) 352-7770
Telex 05-828560

BILTRITE

BILTRITE NIGHTINGALE INC.

INTERIOR DESIGN CHOICE 3 © Biltrite Nightingale Inc.

BONAVENTURE

894 Bloomfield
Montreal, Quebec
H2V 3S6
(514) 270-7311

146 Dupont Street
Toronto, Ontario
M5R 1V2
(416) 961-5900

BRUNSWICK
MANUFACTURING
COMPANY LTD.

21 Research Road
Toronto, Ontario
M4G 2G7
(416) 421-5858

Every detail speaks volumes
about the craftsmanship you thought
belonged to another era.
For excellence in office furnishings
Brunswick, since 1957

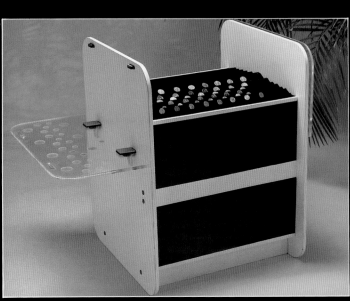

A combination of design knowledge, woodworking quality and experience, applied to:
- custom furniture design and manufacturing
- store fixtures

1. P.D.Q. Laundries of Canada
   Toronto
   Design: Citiworks Design Inc.
2. Residential bar – Arborite and brass
3. Coin Display – Prototype

Cardell Design Inc.
85 Bowes Road
Units 18 & 19
Concord, Ontario
L4K 1H3
(416) 738-1035

CENTRAC

INDUSTRIES

LIMITED

2650 St. Clair Avenue West, Toronto, Canada M6N 1M2

(416) 763-4551   **(416) 763-3893**

Founded over 30 years ago, **Centrac** has grown to become North America's foremost manufacturer of premium quality Hotel and Restaurant furniture. Our completely integrated production facilities combine sophisticated equipment with the personal craftsmanship of highly skilled tradespeople.

Centrac manufactures a diverse line of casegoods, soft goods, seating, tables, bars, millwork, and other related products.

If a client's individual requirements cannot be met from one of our standard product lines, our flexible production methods permit modification or custom building of furniture to meet designer specifications.

The finest woods, finishes, and fabrics, as well as meticulous attention to detail, make **Centrac** the obvious choice for beautiful Hotel and Restaurant interiors.

Featured: *Ascot Collection* by **Centrac.**

INTERIOR DESIGN CHOICE 3 © Centrac Industries Limited

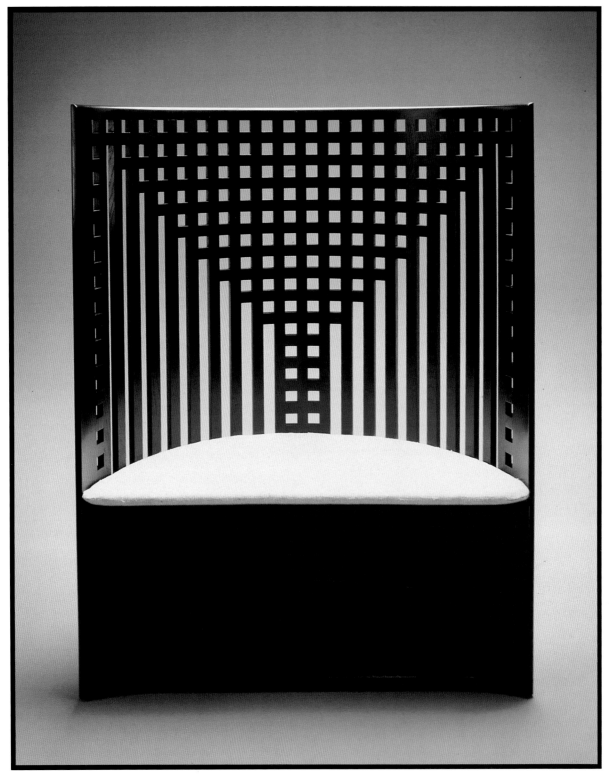

Cassina

WILLOW 1 (1904)
by Charles R. Mackintosh
Curved lattice back chair, ebonized
ashwood frame. Seat cushion
upholstered in a special fabric either
green or beige.

THE GREAT MASTERS OF CONTEMPORARY DESIGN

LE
CHÂTEAU
D'AUJOURD'HUI

INTERNATIONAL
PRESTIGIOUS
FURNITURE

Cassina 🅐

VERANDA (1983)
by Vico Magistretti
Armchair and two seat sofa with frame made of folding steel units. Fabric or leather upholstery.

CASSINA, SAPORITI, B & B ITALIA, INTERLÜBKE, POLTRONA FRAU, FIAM, ACERBIS INTERNATIONAL, CASTILIA, MOLTENI, MONTIS, PASTOE

LE CHÂTEAU D'AUJOURD'HUI
Head Office

1828, Le Corbusier Blvd
Laval, Quebec   H7S 2K1
(514) 382-4710   Telex: 055-61580

Complexe Desjardins
Montreal, Quebec   H5B 1B8
(514) 288-4191

Residential and Office (contract)
Delivery all over North America

INTERIOR DESIGN CHOICE 3 © Le Château d'aujourd'hui

We are a wholesale resource to the trade. Our collection of classic chairs and tables leaves our workshops in a limitless variety of finishes.

Custom finishes vary from traditional stains and paints to the more contemporary lacquer treatments. Upholstery is tailored to meet your individual needs.

Our continually changing selection of important accessories varies from the primitive to the sophisticated.

Codd and Company
Office and showroom: 344 Dupont Street, Toronto, Ontario M5R 1V9 **(416) 923-0066** Showroom: 85, rue St-Paul ouest, Montréal, Quebec H2Y 3V4

Contract furniture built to specifications.

Conspec–Viacraft products and services available through leading architects, designers, dealers and specifiers.

C O N S P E C

Contract Furniture Built to Specification

146 Laird Drive
Suite 203
Toronto, Ontario
M4G 3V7
(416) 429-5206

Semi-Tech Microelectronics
Markham, Ontario
Board Room

INTERIOR DESIGN CHOICE 3 © Conspec–Viacraft

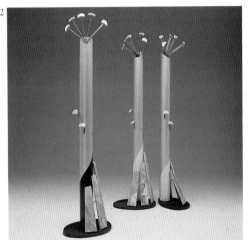

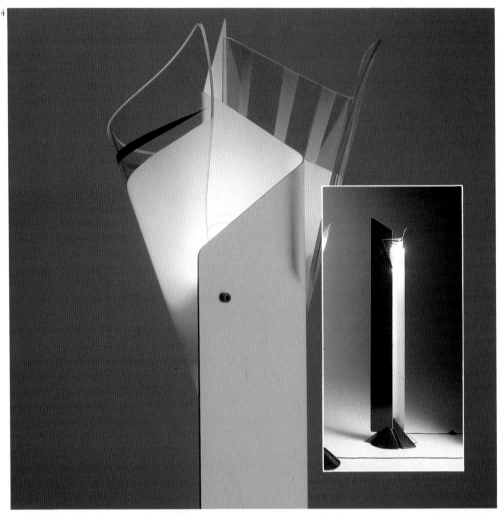

CONTEMPORA
DESIGNS INTERNATIONAL INC.

**Contempora Designs
International Inc.**
887 Yonge Street
Toronto, Ontario, Canada
M4W 2H2
(416) 964-9295
(416) 964-9327
Telex: 06-218939

Part of the **Ycami Collection,**
represented exclusively in Canada by
Contempora Designs International Inc.

1. Ruber Table
   Design: Tito Agnoli

   Regia Chair
   Design: Antonello Mosca

2. Palomar Coat Tree
   Design: Paolo Deganello

3. Primula Chairs
   Design: Tito Agnoli

4. Duala Lamp
   Design: Paolo Deganello

5. Gentiana Chairs
   Design: Tito Agnoli

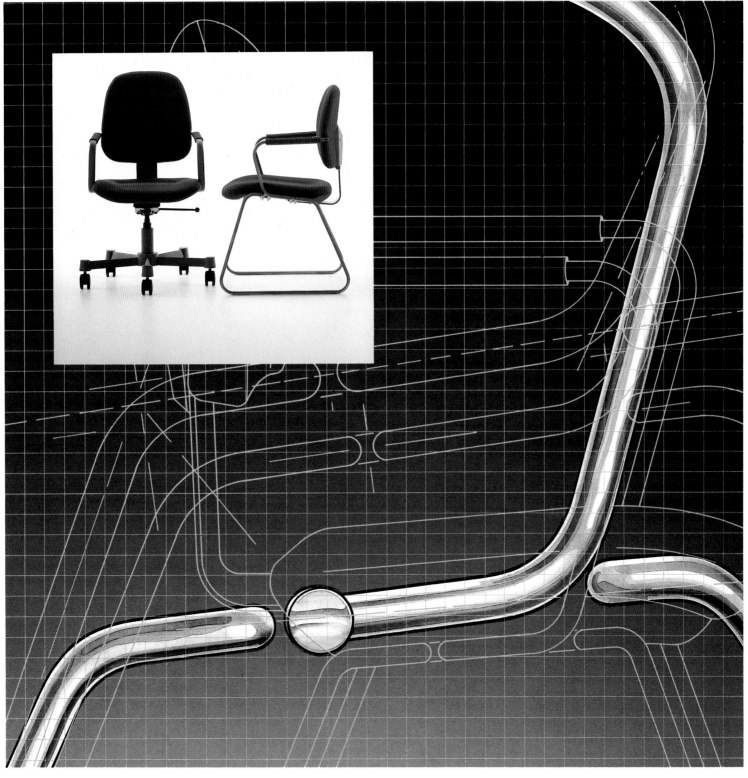

Curtis Products Ltd.
495 Ball Street
Cobourg, Ontario, Canada
K9A 4P9
(416) 372-2184

Telex 06-981277

NETWORK
THE
CHAIR
FROM
CURTIS

INTERIOR DESIGN CHOICE 5 ©Curtis Products Ltd.

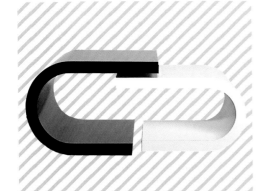

Dacota
INC.

175 Toryork Drive
Unit 35
Weston, Ontario
Canada M9L 1X9
(416) 747-6282

Aimé Maman, a painter, an artist, and a craftsman was first taught to build by his father in France. Aimé tells of his work "...Good design is not simply a matter of playing with structural concepts until you think they'll work... Good furniture achieves the nearly impossible: fresh, exciting expression of the familiar... Pleasing appearance, functionality and simple practicality combined with cost-effectiveness."

With his designer wife, Yana – that's Yana's strikingly beautiful desk and shelf unit at bottom right – they are Dacota's principal design team: "we want to show how important shape, form and colour are to the quality of office life and one's sense of well being."

There are gentle touches of Art Deco, cubist futurism in the shapes; simple, practical taste in colour combinations, and modular design freedom to create timeless environments that inspire and serve for years to come. Fully integrated work stations, ingenious retractable computer tables, non-tipping cabinets... Sturdy high fashion furniture.

INTERIOR DESIGN CHOICE 3 © Dacota Inc.

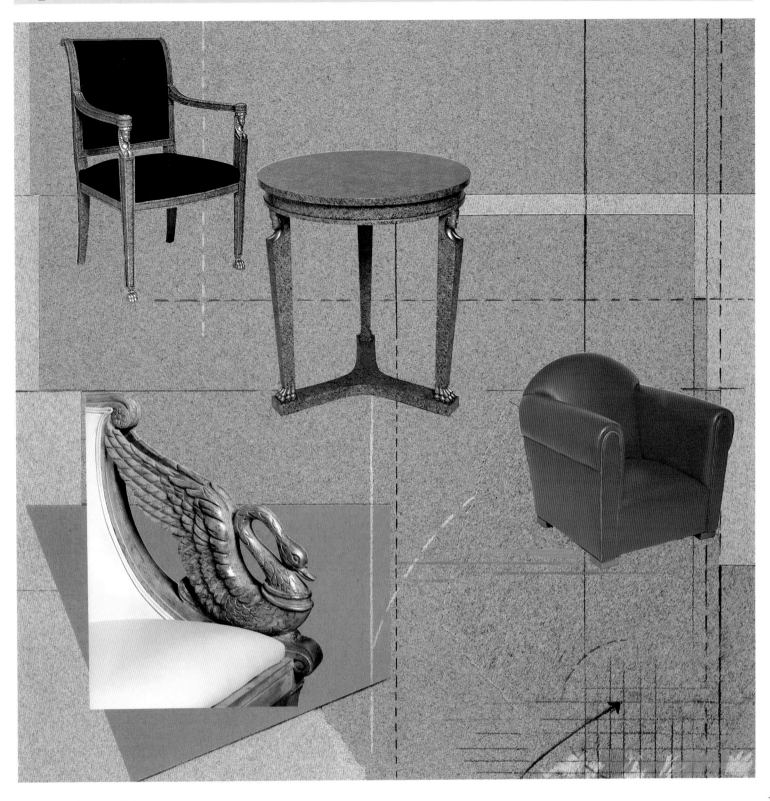

Epoca Interiors Co. Ltd.
Antique & Fine Furniture,
Props & Artifacts
Sales and Rental
(416) 530-4140

28 Atlantic Avenue
Toronto, Ontario, Canada
M6K 1X8

 Where a replica becomes an original

Fraser Contract Furniture Inc.
5525, Côte de Liesse
Montréal, Canada H4P 1A1
(514) 748-7306
Telex 05-826832

Design by
Adamson Industrial Design Inc.

Fraser Contract has been servicing the contract market for the past quarter-century...and our Montreal-based parent, Fraser Bros. Ltd., has serviced the Canadian, U.S. and international residential, office and contract furniture markets for more than a hundred years.

We know and understand the needs of today's management office environment, be it in the boardroom, the executive office, or the reception area. Each Fraser Contract piece combines proven technology and traditional craftsmanship in a rich blend of classic design, superb construction, fine detailing, exceptional fabrics and finishes.

Fraser Contract sets the highest standards for our furniture, and backs each piece with quality service and a five-year guarantee. More than a business commitment, it's a personal and family commitment, with our name on the line. Fraser.

FraserContract

INTERIOR DESIGN CHOICE 3 © Fraser Contract Furniture Inc.

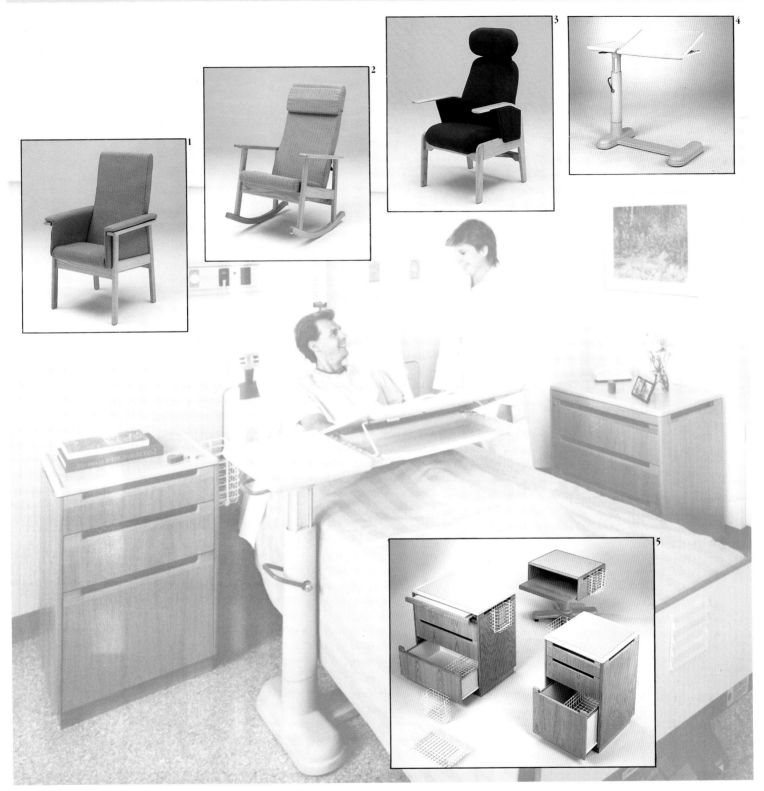

GLOBAL**care**

Canada
325 Limestone Crescent
Downsview, Ontario, Canada
M3J 2R1

Telephone: (416) 736-8700
Telex: 06-22448

United States
17 West Stow Road
Marlton, New Jersey, U.S.A.
08053

Telephone: (609) 596-4570

GLOBALcare presents a complete family of high performance health care furniture systems.
The products are carefully designed to meet the full range of home and institutional user needs.
The furniture systems offer safe, adaptable, efficient solutions; and create a comfortable, non-clinical environment.
These cost-effective, attractive systems address the criteria of administrators, architects and designers.

1. Flemming 7530 Armchair
2. Flemming 7511 Rocking Chair
3. Muller Armchair with swing-up armrest and fold-away headrest
4. Muller Overbed Table
5. Muller Case Goods System: Bedside Cabinet, Dresser, T.V. Table and accessory baskets

Background: Baycrest Hospital Patient Room

The Flemming System.
Registered Designs of Flemming Hvidt
The Muller Furniture System:
Registered Designs of Keith Muller Ltd.

Guildhall Cabinet Shops Limited
11 Jutland Road
Toronto, Ontario, Canada
M8Z 2G6
(416) 255-3425

Guildhall has been manufacturing the highest quality traditional reproduction furniture and custom contemporary furniture for the most prestigious corporate and residential environments for the past 35 years. The furniture is manufactured at 11 Jutland Road, Toronto, from a collection of hundreds of English, French and Oriental designs meticulously developed over the years. The pieces illustrated are typical examples drawn from this extensive

collection, which includes boardroom tables, desks, cabinets, lamp, coffee and console tables, chairs and sofas. The furniture has a completely hand applied French Polish finish developed by **Guildhall** over the years to give a durable and resistant finish which enhances the woods and imparts the timeless beauty and patina of fine antique furniture. This makes **Guildhall** the perfect choice for new furniture which is required to blend compatibly with existing antiques.

1. DESK
Mahogany with crotch mahogany

2. CLUB CHAIR
Mahogany

3. MINIATURE CHEST
Mahogany with burl walnut

4. ARMCHAIR
Mahogany

Guildhall Cabinet Shops Limited
11 Jutland Road
Toronto, Ontario, Canada
M8Z 2G6
(416) 255-3425

Lorna H. Rennet
President
R.F. Rennet
Secretary-Treasurer

All of the furniture is manufactured to the specific requirements of the client with an extensive selection of woods, detailing and hardware. Where necessary, designs are carefully adapted to suit the specific needs of each discerning client. Hardware is imported directly from England, France and China, and the woods are carefully selected for each piece.

The combination of fine craftsmanship. the highest quality materials, and meticulous attention to detail creates furniture which is both beautiful and functional in today's world.
Personal service, which includes a full range of wood samples and photographs for presentation purposes, is extended to the furniture specifier.

1. ORIENTAL CABINET
Mahogany with crotch walnut

2. BOOKCASE
Mahogany with crotch mahogany

3. SOFA

4. ORIENTAL CONSOLE TABLE
Ebony polish with crotch mahogany

HarterMartinStoll D6

"Chairs are more than just objects for sitting on.

They are also an expression of social, functional,

and aesthetic relationships." Martin Stoll

Guelph, Ontario 519.824.2850

HARTER®

intarc

Intarc Limited
3300 Yonge Street
Toronto, Ontario
M4N 2L6
(416) 482-1804
Closed Mondays

FLEDERMAUS beech bentwood chair
by Josef Hoffman – recreated by
Franz Wittmann.

VILLA GALLIA designed by Josef Hoffman,
recreated by Franz Wittmann.

Elegant, timeless design in exquisite
furniture from Intarc.

Design: Antonio Citterio

INTERIOR DESIGN CHOICE 3 © Intarc Limited

Meeting the needs and challenges of the workplace has been a Haworth tradition for more than 35 years. A tradition rich in service dedication and product innovation. Achieving the perfect balance between aesthetics and ultimate efficiency. Form meeting function.

Our exciting showrooms in Toronto and Montreal are showcases for office systems design ingenuity. Office systems with structural integrity that can easily be specified, installed and reconfigured. Ergonomically designed. Office systems created to customize the work environment for any purpose.

INTERIOR DESIGN CHOICE 3 © Haworth Office Systems, Ltd.

We invite you to visit our showrooms. Talk to our dedicated team of sales, technical and design consultants and experience first hand what our commitment to design excellence in Canada is all about.

Versatility. Innovation. Dedication.

33 Yonge Street, Suite 270
Toronto, Ontario M5E 1G4
(416) 363-0702

2000 McGill College Ave., Suite 500
Montreal, Quebec H3A 3H3
(514) 842-2622

EXCELLENCE IN OFFICE FURNISHINGS

Jeffrey-Craig Limited

Unlimited variations in form, function and color, a flexible approach to design and manufacturing, with the highest standards of quality, cost competitiveness and customer service – Jeffrey-Craig's tradition of excellence for over 15 years.

For a closer look at our capabilities and our extensive selection of materials and colors, call for our new brochure and catalog. And for an innovative and practical solution to your furniture requirements, talk to us first.

Jeffrey-Craig. Canada's premiere custom laminate furniture people.

Jeffrey-Craig Ltd.
763 Warden Avenue
Scarborough Ontario M1L 4B7
(416) 757-4153

INTERIOR DESIGN CHOICE 3 © Jeffrey-Craig Limited

contract seating

946 Warden Avenue
Toronto, Ontario
Canada M1L 4C9
(416) 759-5665

Keilhauer's name stands for excellence in seating. Nothing more. Because we don't want you to know us for anything less.

Keilhauer decided years ago that seating would be our only business. We design and build chairs and soft seating that specialize in looking good and making people comfortable throughout the office. From the reception area right through to the chief executive's suite. For five years guaranteed.

From left to right:
Fan chair
Anshin chair

KRUG

KRUG FURNITURE INC.

P.O. Box 9035
421 Manitou Drive
Kitchener, Ontario
Canada N2G 4J3
(519) 893-1100

Showroom
550 Queen Street East
Toronto, Ontario
Canada M5A 1V2
(416) 366-7246

The DRUM TABLE SERIES offers many selections. Tables are available both round and square in 18'', 24'' and 30'' modules. Heights available are 16'', 21'' and 29''.
Selections include either Walnut or Oak in a wide variety of finishes. Chrome and Brass inlays are optional extras.

INTERIOR DESIGN CHOICE 3 © Krug Furniture Inc.

Loomis & Toles Co. Ltd.
Furniture Showroom
214 Adelaide Street West
Toronto, Ontario
M5H 1W7
(416) 977-8877

Flax Seating – The chairs that came to work; and Flax chairs do work, in any office environment.
By combining the highest standards of German engineering and precision with our specifications for the optimum chair, you are assured a high degree of quality and excellence in Flax seating. Flax chairs are designed and constructed to respond to a variety of human functions, shapes and movements. In some chairs you just sit; in a Flax chair you perform. They are ideal for all types of people, in any working environment, whether for artists, architects, CRT operations, secretaries, managers, executives or home users. For all day seating comfort and reduced fatigue, Flax chairs will help improve work productivity and provide proper back support and circulation.

Horizon Workstation – Customized furniture system styled to meet the present and future needs of the design professional.
The Horizon Workstation is a sleek, modular studio set up that puts all the tools of the trade at finger tip touch: An adjustable electric drawing table surrounded by abundant filing storage and flat space. A built-in writing desk, bookshelf and free standing storage taboret. A swiveling monitor arm for instant computer access. And ample room for everything else.
Horizon Workstations provide maximum flexibility for creating a space efficient layout. Each complete workstation is specially designed for either a side-to-side or back-to-back orientation with another complete unit.

Louis
Interiors
Inc.

2539 Yonge Street
Toronto, Ontario, Canada
M4P 2H9
(416) 488-8844

Founded in 1961, Louis Interiors Inc. has since built a firm reputation in the manufacturing of top-end-quality furniture.

The Company and its products emerged from a simple idea: **To build furniture to consistently exceptional standards of quality workmanship.**

It is this idea that has been the force behind all of the furniture pieces that leave the shop floor of Louis Interiors Inc.

Louis Interiors Inc. products consist of:
• Upholstered Boardroom Chairs
• Reception Area Seating
• Executive Office Sofas, Chairs

• Restaurant Banquettes

• Hotel Tub Chairs, Sofas, Desk Chairs

• Residential Chairs, Sofas, Setees, Headboards, Valences, Upholstered Walls

INTERIOR DESIGN CHOICE 3 © Louis Interiors Inc.

Svend Nielsen Ltd.

Custom Contract Furniture

280 Signet Drive
Weston, Ontario, Canada
M9L 1V2
(416) 749-0131

With more than 30 years experience in the custom contract furniture industry, working with designers and architects, we have proven that we are able to manufacture a product of the highest quality relevant to the budget involved.

Supported by first rate facilities, we combine fine craftsmanship with the best of materials to produce a truly distinctive product.

Product range:
- Contemporary and traditional executive furniture: desks, credenzas, consoles, wall units.
- Boardroom tables, coffee and end tables.
- General office and computer furniture.
- Furniture for banks, libraries and private residences
- Custom seating for lounge and reception areas, etc.

1. Walter Maves and Associates Ltd. Toronto – Reception desk
Design: Britacan Business Interiors Ltd.

2. 3. 4. McMaster Meighen, Toronto
Design: Inger Bartlett and Associates

INTERIOR DESIGN CHOICE 3 © Svend Nielsen Ltd.

Nienkamper

386 West Broadway New York N.Y. Phone 212-431-3202
300 King Street E. Toronto Canada M5A 1K4 Phone 416-362-3434
306 Place d'Youville Montréal Canada H2Y 2B6 Phone 514-842-8939
Corporate Office 415 Finchdene Square Scarborough Canada M1X 1B7 Phone 416-298-5700

designed by Richard Schultz

PRISMATIQUE
DESIGNS LTD.

265 Davenport Road
Toronto, Ontario
M5R 1J9
(416) 961-7333

Montreal: (514) 845-1106
Ottawa: (613) 722-5343
Winnipeg: (204) 956-2098
Calgary: (403) 290-0900
Vancouver: (604) 684-7792

INTERIOR DESIGN CHOICE 3 © Prismatique Designs Ltd.

reff

System 6: a fully integrated office system, combining panel hung components and free standing casegood products. Shown above in ''Driftwood Grey'', System 6 is available in a variety of wood and laminate finishes.

Reff Incorporated
1000 Arrow Road
Weston (Toronto), Ontario
Canada M9M 2Y7
(416) 741-5453
Telex: 065-27300

Showrooms:
Atlanta, Boston
Calgary, Chicago
Dallas, Houston
Los Angeles, New York
Philadelphia, Toronto

INTERIOR DESIGN CHOICE 3 © Reff Incorporated

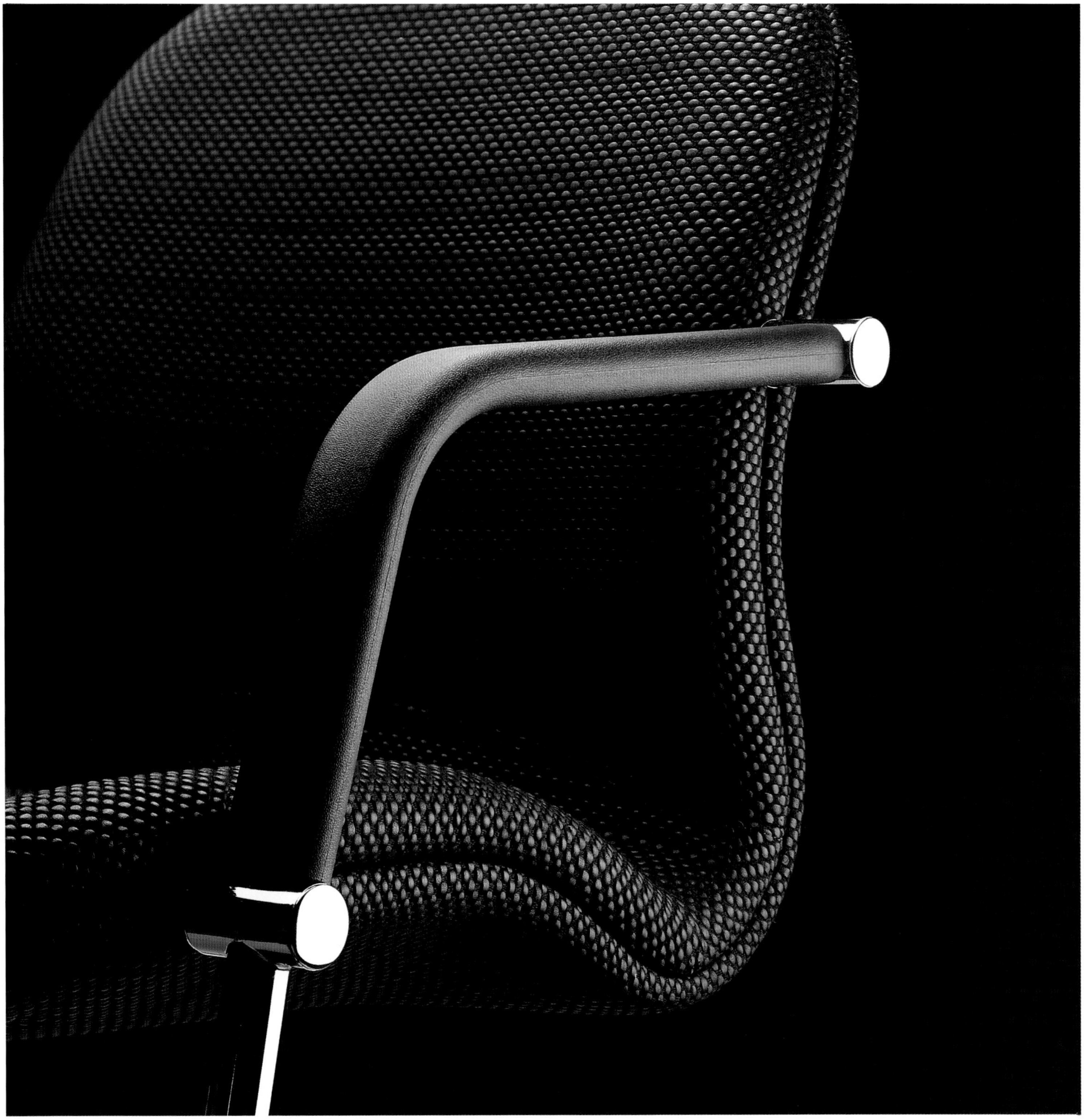

reff

Seating: available in a complete line of
Executive, Task and Lounge Seating.
Beautifully detailed, Reff seating is
designed to provide exceptional value,
quality and comfort.

Reff Incorporated
1000 Arrow Road
Weston (Toronto), Ontario
Canada M9M 2Y7
(416) 741-5453
Telex: 065-27300

Showrooms:
Atlanta, Boston
Calgary, Chicago
Dallas, Houston
Los Angeles, New York
Philadelphia, Toronto

INTERIOR DESIGN CHOICE 3 © Reff Incorporated

Shelagh's of Canada
Furniture & Design

Designers Walk
354 Davenport Road
Toronto, Ontario M5R 1K6
(416) 924-7331

A collection of:

• French, English, Irish and Austrian antique country pine

• French Provincial hand carved pickled pine reproductions

• Unique accessories from Spain, India and the Orient

1. Coffee Table
2. Breakfast Table
3. Armoire as T.V. cabinet or mirrored bar

INTERIOR DESIGN CHOICE 3 © Shelagh's of Canada

1000 boulevard St-Martin ouest
Laval, Québec, Canada
H7S 1M7
(514) 663-3030
Telex: 05-24469
Fax: (514) 663-9022

STANDARD DESK, already famous for its quality wood system and office furniture, now offers its most popular lines in a whole new range of colors.

From mahogany to walnut to black, white, pink or grey stained oak, by way of all the shades of natural oak, a whole new palette is ready for use by the most demanding designers and architects.

INTERIOR DESIGN CHOICE 3 © Standard Desk Business Furniture

Snyder Furniture Limited
87 Colville Road
Toronto, Ontario
M6M 2Y6
(416) 247-6285
Telex 06-969659

Jordan Boffo
President
Alfred Boffo
Vice President
John Dyk
National Marketing Manager

Snyder Furniture, founded in 1940, has established an enviable reputation in the quality furniture field. The ability to combine traditional craftsmanship with contemporary styling and to reproduce the enduring classics, has made Snyder Furniture the choice of todays designer.

With installations from coast to coast in Canada, USA, Europe and the Middle East, Snyder's versatility means travelling business people may work at their desk, attend a board meeting, lunch at their favourite restaurant, relax at the airline's V.I.P. lounge and stay at a fine hotel all furnished by Snyder.

When a designer's requirement cannot be met from our regular lines, we will make custom furniture according to specifications, be it boardroom, office, institution or residence.

Leathers or fabrics, fine wood finishes or lacquers, all are applied with skill and care by the Snyder professionals. We are pleased to count among our clientele governments, airlines, major hotels, restaurants and many corporations. A specific list of installations can be supplied on request.

Halifax • Moncton • Montreal • Ottawa
Winnipeg • Calgary • Vancouver
New York • Washington • Buffalo
Minneapolis/St. Paul • Dallas • Houston
Costa Mesa, California

INTERIOR DESIGN CHOICE 3 © Snyder Furniture Limited

Painted wood, cotton and styrofoam set: The Studio Store   Photo: Gill Alkin

THE STUDIO STORE

Innovative solutions for
difficult design problems.

Custom furniture,
paint treatments,
constructions, and
special effects for
commercial, residential,
retail, and exhibit.
Interior / exterior.

T H E   S T U D I O   S T O R E
353 EASTERN AVENUE, SUITE 206, TORONTO, CANADA M4M 1B7 TEL.(416) 461−2086

INTERIOR DESIGN CHOICE 3 © The Studio Store

Steelcase

P.O. Box 9, Don Mills, Ontario
M3C 2R7
Call 1-800-268-1121
In B.C. 112-800-268-1121

Sensor

Sensor designer Wolfgang Muller–Deisig:
"Office chairs should provide the same
kind of comfort as a favourite jacket
or a favourite pair of shoes — you
just slip them on and they fit. You
don't have to think about it. Sensor is
the same way. It just fits, and you
don't have to think about it. The
better a chair is designed, the better
people can forget about it."

Awards

Winner of a 1986 Institute of Business
Designers Award.

INTERIOR DESIGN CHOICE 3 © Steelcase

TEKNION J

Teknion Furniture Systems Inc.

607 Canarctic Drive
Downsview, Ontario
M3J 2P9
Head Office/Plant:
(416) 661-3370

Stow&Davis

A Division of Steelcase
P.O. Box 9, Don Mills, Ontario
M3C 2R7
Call 1-800-268-1121
In B.C. 112-800-268-1121

Edgewood
An unmistakably contemporary line of award-winning wood furniture designed for Stow & Davis by Robert Taylor Whalen. Simple yet sophisticated, the design brings out the natural beauty of carefully selected wood veneers while providing an aesthetic solution for the integration of electronic technology Elegant and affordable, providing outstanding quality and enduring value, Edgewood continues the century-old Stow & Davis tradition of combining fine craftsmanship and innovative design.

Awards

Winner of a 1986 Institute of Business Designers Award.
Winner of the 1986 ARIDO Award for Best New Product of Canadian Origin.

INTERIOR DESIGN CHOICE 3 © Stow & Davis

SunarHauserman

the integrated interiors company

1 Sunshine Avenue, Waterloo, Canada N2J 4K5
(519) 886-200

INTERIOR DESIGN CHOICE 3 © SunarHauserman, Ltd.

Tella Systems Inc.
Division of Patella Inc.

Head office:
161 Stirling Avenue
La Salle, Quebec
Canada H8R 3P3
(514) 364-0511

Showrooms in Montreal,
Toronto and Calgary

Manufacturers of
executive environments
and custom furniture.

Charly chairs
Design: Gerard van den Berg

From a collection that includes:
- crystal glass dinning and coffee tables
- marble and Pietra Serena tables
- showcases with wireless halogen lighting
- modular system of wall units and bookshelves
- chairs, sofas in leather and fabric
- floor and table halogen lamps

INTERIOR DESIGN CHOICE 3 © Tendex Silko Inc.

1

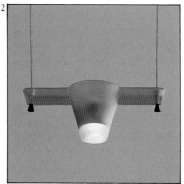
2

3

4

9

10

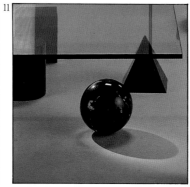
11

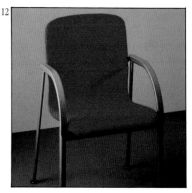
12

17

18

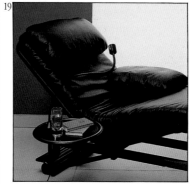
19

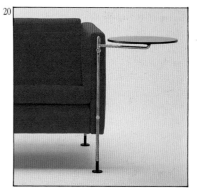
20

25

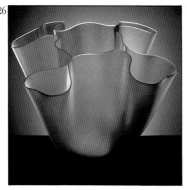
26

27

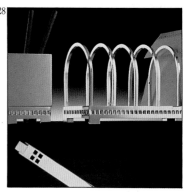
28

TRIEDE DESIGN

Triede Design Inc.
460 McGill
Montréal, Québec
H2Y 2H2
(514) 288-0063

254 King Street East
Toronto, Ontario
M5A 1K3
(416) 367-0667

Importer, manufacturer and distributor, TRIEDE DESIGN displays masterpieces of contemporary design from world-renowned architects in its Montreal and Toronto showrooms: enlightening advances in residential and contract furniture, lighting and accessories by Alessi, Arflex, Arteluce, Carlo Moretti, Casigliani, Danese, Flos, Flou, Fontana Arte (furniture and accessories only), Fritz Hansen, Goppion, Simon, Swid-Powell, Wittmann, Zanotta, and other prestigious firms dedicated to an approach that incorporates both distinctive design and functionalism. For the discerning specifier and dealer, the exclusive, inexhaustible Canadian source: TRIEDE

 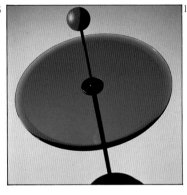  

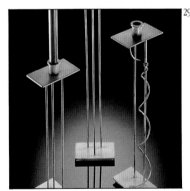  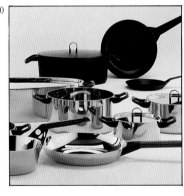 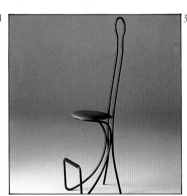

Row 1:
1. "FRISBI" Hanging Lamp
   Design: Achille Castiglioni, 1978
2. "CRISOL" Hanging Lamp
   Design: King, Miranda, Arnaldi, 1981
3. "WALL" Wall Sconce
   Design: King, Miranda, Arnaldi, 1979
4. "PAPILLONA" Floor Lamp
   Design: Tobia Scarpa, 1975
5. "TACCIA" Table Lamp
   Design: Achille & Pier G. Castiglioni, 1962
6. "AURORA" Hanging Lamp
   Design: King, Miranda, 1983
7. "GIBIGIANA" Table Lamp
   Design: Achille Castiglioni, 1981
8. "GIOVI" Wall Sconce
   Design: Achille Castiglioni, 1982

Row 2:
9. "CAFE" Chair
   Design: Pelikan, 1983
10. "T-LINE" Armchair
    Design: Burkhard Vogtherr, 1984
11. "METAFORA" Coffee Table
    Design: Lella & Massimo Vignelli, 1979
12. "SLIDE" Gliding Armchair
    Design: Burkhard Vogtherr, 1985
13. "L6" Table
    Design: Afra & Tobia Scarpa, 1984
14. "ORIO" Side Table
    Design: Pierluigi Cerri, 1985
15. "S1" Chair
    Design: Afra & Tobia Scarpa, 1986
16. "CARMEN" Armchair
    Design: Enzo Mari, 1985/1986

Row 3:
17. "PK24" Chaise Longue
    Design: Poul Kjaerholm, 1965
18. "NATHALIE" Bed
    Design: Vico Magistretti, 1980
19. "ITACA" Adjustable Lounge Chair
    Design: N. Gioacchini & L. Pettinari, 1985
20. "FELIX" Sofa Series
    Design: Burkhard Vogtherr, 1985
21. "LOSANNA" Sofa Series
    Design: Alessandro Mendini, 1986
22. "PACIFIC" Sofa Series
    Design: Cini Boeri, 1983
23. "MIXER" Office Series
    Design: Roberto Pamio
24. "BIACH INTERIEUR" Seating Series
    Design: Josef Hoffmann, 1905

Row 4:
25. "TWO-NOTE WHISTLING KETTLE"
    Design: Richard Sapper, 1983
26. "CARTOCCIO" Flower Vase
    Design: Pietro Chiesa, 1932
27. "KETTLE WITH WHISTLING BIRD"
    Design: Michael Graves, 1985
28. "DESK SET"
    Design: Richard Meier, 1986
29. "CANDLESTICKS"
    Design: Steven Holl, 1986
30. "KERGUELEN" Coat and Umbrella Stand
    Design: Enzo Mari, 1968
31. "LA CINTURA DI ORIONE" Cookware
    Design: Richard Sapper, 1986
32. "SPLUGA" Bar Stool
    Design: Achille & Pier G. Castiglioni, 1960

Wm. Whiteley

Wm. Whiteley Limited
214 Laird Drive, Toronto, Ontario M4G 3W4
Telephone: (416) 429-7503
special projects/murals/banners/signage/products for visual display/accessories/industrial and graphic design

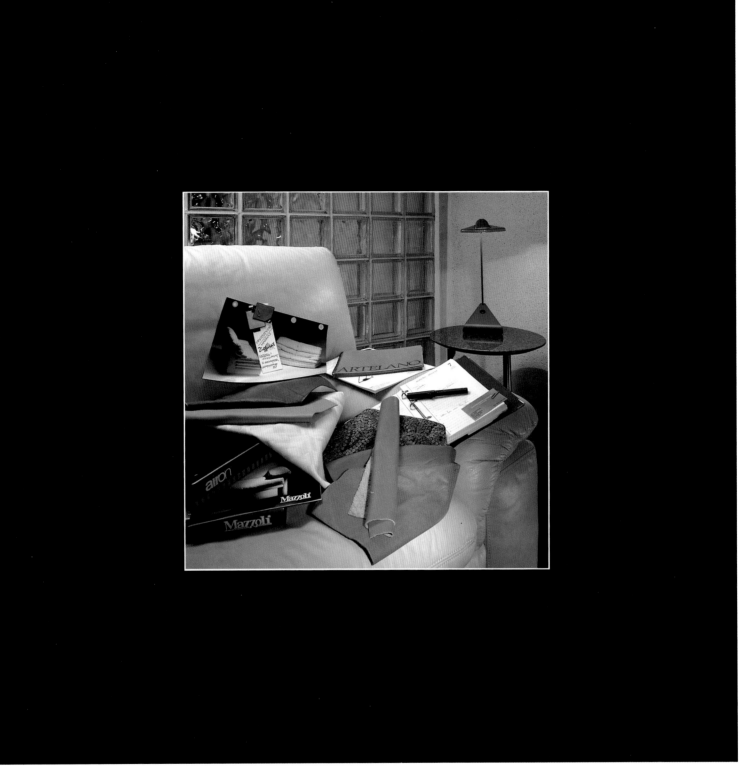

GMT INCORPORATED

Contemporary furniture, lighting and accessories

MAZZOLI • ARTELANO • AIRON • DESIGNWERKE
METALCO •INTERPROFIL •MICHEL MORIN •ICONOPLAST

Mobilier, luminaires et accessoires contemporains.

251 King Street East, Toronto, Ontario, Canada M5A 1K2
(416) 362-5900/362-6800 Telex: 06-218516

Ziggurat
CONCEPT INC.

INTERIOR DESIGN CHOICE 3 © Ziggurat Concept Inc.

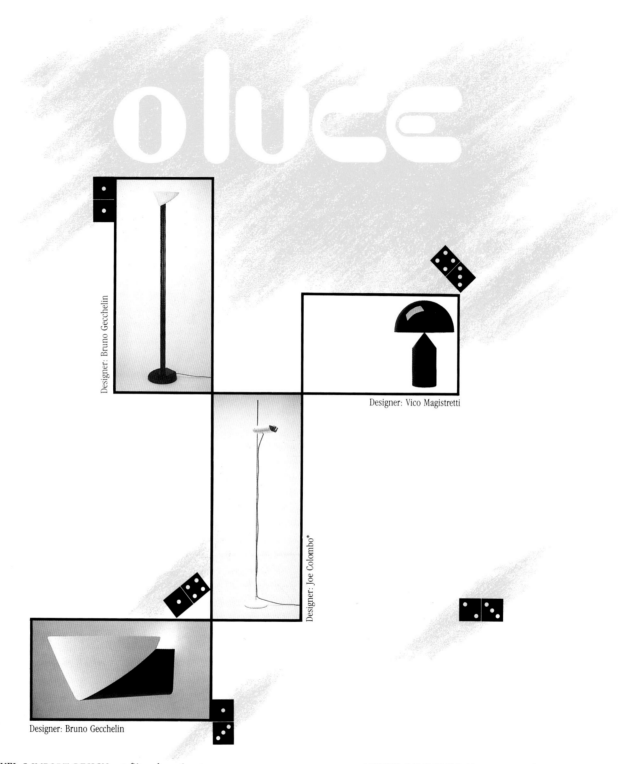

Designer: Bruno Gecchelin

Designer: Vico Magistretti

Designer: Joe Colombo*

Designer: Bruno Gecchelin

ACTUEL 5 IMPORT DESIGN est fière de présenter, enfin au Canada, la magnifique collection de luminaires halogènes **Oluce**.
Que des grands noms du design contemporain.
Cette maison de renom vient prendre sa place chez Actuel 5 Import Design aux côtés de manufacturiers italiens aussi prestigieux que INSA, OVER BBB, POLLUX, SKIPPER, VELCA, et YCAMI.
Pour le corps et l'esprit.

* Première lampe halogène spécialement conçue pour l'interieur.

ACTUEL 5

ACTUEL 5 IMPORT DESIGN is proud to present at last in Canada the magnificent **Oluce** collection of hallogen lights.
One of the great names in modern design.
This distinguished manufacturer has now found its place at Actuel 5 Import Design alongside of such prestigious Italian concerns as INSA, OVER BBB, POLLUX, SKIPPER, VELCA and YCAMI.
Pour le corps et l'esprit.

* First halogen lamp specially designed for interiors.

550, RUE SHERBROOKE OUEST, MONTRÉAL (QUÉBEC) H3A 1B9 842-1139

INTERIOR DESIGN CHOICE 3 © Actuel 5 Import Design Inc.

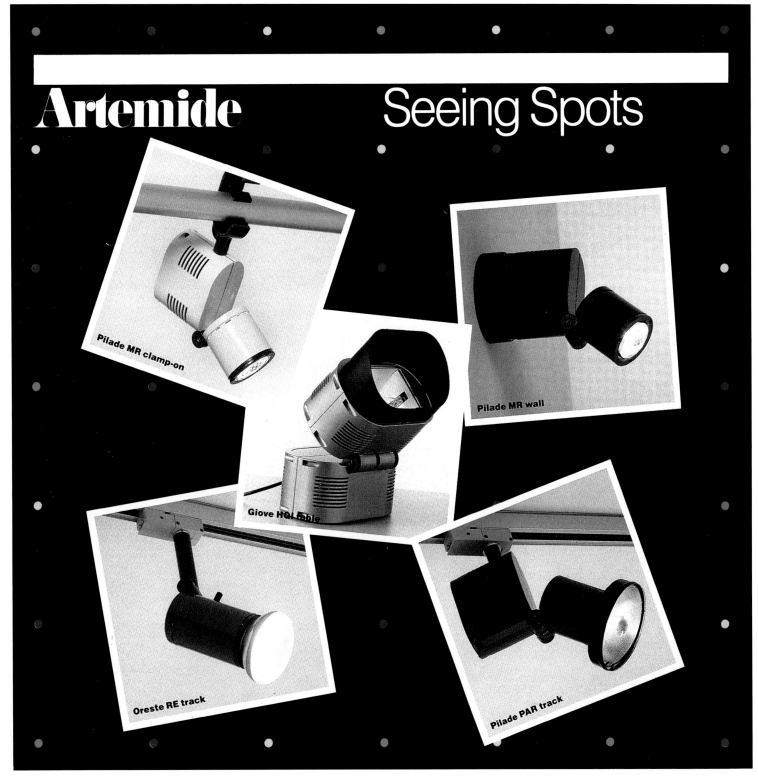

Artemide

Seeing Spots

Pilade MR clamp-on

Pilade MR wall

Giove HQI table

Oreste RE track

Pilade PAR track

Artemide Ltée
2408 de la Province
Longueuil, Quebec J4G 1G1
(514) 679-3717
Telex 055-60424

Artemide Ltd.
354 Davenport Road
Designers Walk (3rd floor)
Toronto, Ontario M5R 1K5
(416) 964-6234

Robert Sweep Inc.
400, 1501 1st Street SW
Calgary, Alberta T2R 0W1
(403) 237-9333

Gary Nerman Agencies
410-63 Albert Street
Winnipeg, Manitoba R2W 3R4
(204) 956-1214

Paul Binkley Associates
301 – 873 Beatty Street
Vancouver, B.C. V6B 2M6
(604) 687-4541

Pilade is a series of low voltage halogen spotlamps in die-cast aluminum with built-in transformers and adjustable diffusors. This series features table, wall/ceiling, clamp-on and track models and can be equipped with optional glass or wire mesh filters.

Oreste, a series of regular 120 Volt incandescent spotlamp fixtures, is available as a wall/ceiling, clamp-on, or track fixture.

Both series were designed by Ernesto Gismondi, as well as **Giove**, the newest series of spotlamps. It features the new Osram 150 Watt HQI metal halide lamp, one of the latest advances in energy efficient light sources. It provides consistent lamp color and superior color rendering in a wide variety of lighting applications. It also provides long lamp life (15,000 hours) and high lumen output (9,000 lumens average).

To receive more information about Giove, Pilade and Oreste, and Artemide's full line of lighting, furniture and accessories, write Artemide on your letterhead.

AU COURANT

354 Davenport Road
Toronto, Ontario
M5R 1K6
(416) 922-5611

Italy is embraced
and lighting comes of age
Attention turns
from function to form
Shape
Design
Daring
All part of the art
of lighting *au courant*

"Laser" by Nuova Lamperti
Design: Massimo Bagnara

THE ARCHITECTURE OF LIGHT

The ordering of space is the business of the architect and designer.

The illumination of this space is ours.

Head Office
149 Church Street
Toronto, Canada M5B 1Y4
(416) 863-1990
Telex: 06-23475

INTERIOR DESIGN CHOICE 3 © Raak of Canada Ltd.

Jeff Brown Fine Fabrics Limited

1785 Argentia Road, Mississauga, Ont. L5N 3A2 (416) 821-3666

Accessories International	Daphne Tyson	Hazelton House	Seven Continents
Alan Londin	Edelman	La Lune	Sirmos
Basset McNab	Gianni Versace	Orient Express	Textures & Company
China Seas	Gretchen Bellinger	Scalamandré	Unika Vaev
Craig Factories Inc.	Harrington	S. Harris	Yves Gonnet

HABERT ASSOCIATES LIMITED
321 Davenport Road, Toronto, Ontario   M5R 1K5   (416) 960-5323

INTERIOR DESIGN CHOICE 3 © Habert Associates Limited

TEXTILES

Designers Walk,	SHOWROOMS:	PRESENTING:	PHOTOGRAPHY:
354 Davenport Road,	Montreal (514) 933-0067	Jim Thomson Thai Silk	Andrew Regendanz
Toronto, Ontario, M5R 1K6	Ottawa (613) 235-8177	Boris Kroll Fabrics	
Tel.: (416) 922-5514	Toronto (416) 922-5514	Bayberry	FABRICS:
Telex: 06-217636 Laurii	Winnipeg (204) 885-6820	Karl Mann Associates	139-407 Cabernet
Head office: (416) 531-0788	Calgary (403) 228-7871	Silk Dynasty Inc.	139-603 Blue Coral
	Vancouver (604) 872-7667	Stratford Hall	Jim Thompson Thai Silk
		Silk Routs	
		Designtex	24K-12 Saphire
		Atlanta Architectural Textiles	Silk Dynasty Inc.

PRIMAVERA
INTERIOR ACCESSORIES LIMITED

300 King Street East
Toronto, Ontario M5A 1K4
(416) 368-3456 Telex 06-22367

Robin Vaile
President

Cowtan & Tout

Glant Fabrics

George W. Hansen Inc.

Jack Lenor Larsen Inc.

Primavera Lighting & Accessories

Randolph & Hein Inc.

INTERIOR DESIGN CHOICE 3 © Primavera Interior Accessories Limited

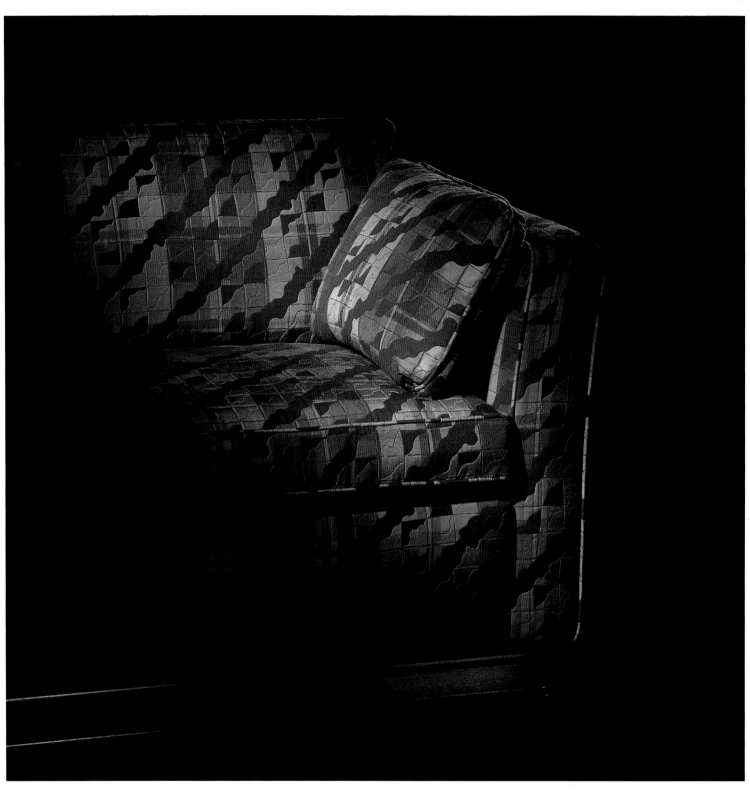

The European Collection
distributed by
Samo International Fabrics

Samo Textiles Ltd.
Downtown Showroom
Designers Walk
320 Davenport Road
Toronto, Ontario
M5R 1K6
(416) 920-3020

Head Office and Showroom
67 St. Regis Crescent North
Downsview, Ontario
M3J 1Y9
(416) 636-7273
Telex 06-23065

Quebec (514) 989-2944
Ottawa (613) 722-5343
Manitoba & Saskatchewan (204) 956-1214
Alberta (403) 282-9169
British Columbia (604) 872-7667

VESCOM 22

VINYL WANDBEKLEDING
VINYL WANDBEKLEIDUNG
TISSU-VINYLE MURAL
VINYL WALLCOVERING

Distributed by:

WALTER L. BROWN LIMITED wallcoverings

Toronto · Halifax · Montreal · Winnipeg · Calgary · Vancouver

17 Vickers Road, Toronto M9B 1C2 Canada (416) 231-4499 Telex 06-967659

INTERIOR DESIGN CHOICE 3 © Walter L. Brown Limited

STERLING PRINTS

Distributed by:

WALTER L. BROWN LIMITED wallcoverings

Toronto - Halifax - Montreal - Winnipeg - Calgary - Vancouver

17 Vickers Road, Toronto M9B 1C2 Canada (416) 231-4499 Telex 06-967659

BASF

fibre

Contract Directions

design

performance

selection

texture

colour

Design: Taehnne Associates Inc.

BASF Fibres is dedicated to technological advance in the field of carpet fibre. We are also dedicated to design, selection, and performance of contract carpet. As a major producer of fibres and yarns specially engineered for the contract market, BASF Fibres has always made a strong commitment to specifiers whose job it is to select suitable carpet for a variety of installations. In keeping with this ongoing commitment, we have located our Design Services office at Queen's Quay Terminal, Toronto. The office functions as a resource centre providing information pertinent to the understanding and specification of contract carpet. We invite your inquiries (416) 862-7762.

BASF Fibres Inc.
Design Services
Queen's Quay Terminal
207 Queen's Quay West
Suite 410, P.O. Box 111
Toronto M5J 1A7
Ontario, Canada

Zeftron ® is a registered trademark owned by BASF Corporation and is used under licence agreement.

Zeftron®nylon

INTERIOR DESIGN CHOICE 3 © BASF Fibres Inc.

Detail of Sistine Chapel by Michelangelo.

When it comes to great design, not all eyes are on the ceiling.

They're also on the floor. And on Du Pont Canada. Supplying the design community with leading carpet technology, we conduct extensive research and development into new, high performance fibres. Giving designers greater confidence and creative freedom. Du Pont certification requirements insure that carpets made of ANTRON® nylon manufactured by leading Canadian mills meet or exceed worldwide standards. Not only are we a member of the Canadian Carpet Institute,

but Du Pont keeps in touch with the design community by holding a number of informative seminars. By offering a consultant support service. Sponsoring the annual Du Pont ANTRON Design Awards. And by publishing a comprehensive manual entitled, "The Guide To Contract Carpeting." Bottom-lining it, no other company works as hard to meet the design industry's needs as Du Pont. Du Pont Canada and the ANTRON group of fibres.
Single source support at your feet.

Du Pont Canada Inc.
Contract Carpet Fibres
Box 26
Toronto-Dominion Centre
Toronto, Ontario, Canada
M5K 1B6
(416) 365-3555

®ANTRON is a Du Pont registered trade mark.

INTERIOR DESIGN CHOICE 3 © Dupont Canada

THOMAS E. DE JOURNO & ASSOCIATES

115 Dupont Street
Toronto, Ontario
M5R 1V4
(416) 967-0154

Providing the leading edge of
contract carpet technology to:
• Major Canadian Manufacturers
• The International Design Community
• Canadian and International Corporations

Our renowned carpet designers and
technological consultants provide the
tools for all phases of design,
development,   colouration,
specifications,   installation and
maintenance procedures for the industry
at large.

We develop, in co-operation with our
clients, a total   contract carpet design
package.
All phases of our industry are co-
ordinated to develop the highest
standard of end use product technology
available to our market-
place. As our position is
one of total support, it is
the architects, designers,   and
corporations who really represent us.
Our commitment to the industry with
over 20 years of exceptional service
is beyond reproach.

FRANCO BELGIAN COMPANY LIMITED
An exclusive commercial carpet showroom...

115 Dupont Street
Toronto, Ontario
M5R 1V4
(416) 967-0115

Franco Belgian Company Limited, Canada's foremost supplier of custom designed and manufactured commercial and residential carpet programs. After fifty years in business, the company offers renowned carpet designers and technological consultants to support the professional trade as well as a myriad of development and consulting services.

Emphasis on manufacturing is paramount. Over 1,000 stock carpet lines are merchandised, all under the manufacturer's own product labels. Cross reference indexing is available to assist the design, architectural, and decorating communities in the recognition and dissection of private labelled products.

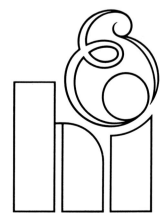

H & I Carpet Corporation
162 Bedford Road
Toronto, Ontario
M5R 2K9
(416) 961-6891

The Source for the designer's grandest inspirations…
□ Manufacturer's agents & distributors
□ Carpet designers
□ Consultants

Project: Hyatt Regency Hotel, Vancouver
Scope of work: 14,000 square yards
Product: 80% Wool/20% Nylon
         Axminster Weave

Designed and supplied by
H & I Carpet Corporation

INTERIOR DESIGN CHOICE 3 © H & I Carpet Corporation

heuga®

HEAD OFFICE/SIEGE SOCIAL

heuga canada limited/ltée,
P.O. Box/C.P. 1353,
14 Deauville, Mart D,
Place Bonaventure
Montréal, Québec
H5A 1H2

Tel: (514) 878-2785

REGIONAL HEAD QUARTERS

Ontario Region:
Tel: (416) 675-2410

Vancouver Region:
Tel: (604) 873-3651

BRANCH OFFICES:

Calgary:
Tel: (403) 229-2953
Ottawa:
Tel: (613) 564-0172
Quebec:
Tel: (418) 647-2179
Halifax:
Tel: (902) 443-1200

DESCRIPTION OF PHOTOGRAPHS:

1. U.N. Pavilion – Vancouver, Expo '86

2. La Laurentienne/Laurentian Insurance
   Montreal

3. V.I.P. Lounge – U.N. Pavilion
   Vancouver, Expo '86

INTERIOR DESIGN CHOICE 3 © Heuga Canada Limited/Ltée

INTERFACE®
FLOORING SYSTEMS CANADA

P.O. Box 1182
Lahr Drive
Belleville, Ontario
K8N 5E8
(613) 966-8090
Telex No. 06-62295

The Interface ingenuity that pioneered the only free-lay, no glue, modular carpet tile system, now brings an equally sensational innovation to the floorcovering market: Palette™ Plus.

To discover an exciting universe of design diversity within a cohesive colour logic system — delivered exclusively by the Palette™ Plus collection — contact your Interface representative for product presentation or for an appointment at one of our showrooms located throughout Canada, U.S., and worldwide. Call 1-800-267-2149.

Showrooms & Offices

CANADA	USA	INTERNATIONAL
Belleville	Atlanta	Hong Kong
Calgary	Chicago	Jedah, Saudi Arabia
Montreal	Houston	London, England
Toronto	Los Angeles	Paris, France
Vancouver	New York	Sydney, Australia
	San Francisco	Tokyo, Japan
	Washington, DC	

INTERIOR DESIGN CHOICE 3 © Interface Flooring Systems Canada

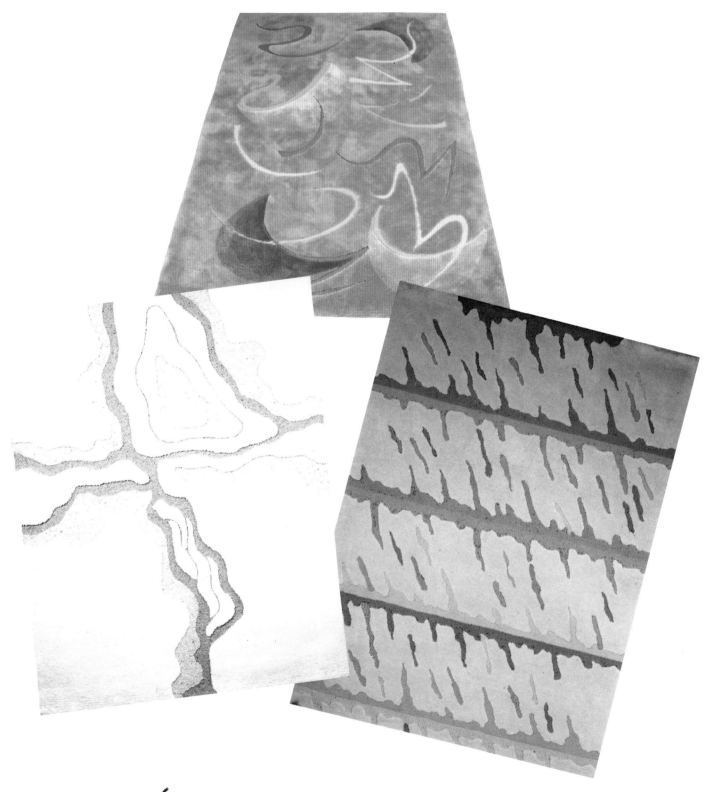

COLLECTION™

Tech-Style Rug G.A. Inc.
Centre International de Design
85, rue St-Paul ouest
Montréal, Québec H2Y 3V4
(514) 842-9272
Gita Ronn
Arleen Browman

Franco-Belgian Company Limited
115 Dupont Street
Toronto, Ontario
M5A 1V4
(416) 967-0115
Barbara McIntyre

Williams West
1516 West 3rd Avenue
Vancouver, B.C.
V6J 1J7
(604) 731-2172
Marlene Williams

Bill Knight Flooring Ltd.
895 Century Street
Winnipeg, Manitoba
R3H 0M3
(204) 237-3006
Dave Symonds

– Elegance and excellence in
  custom area rugs

– Various designs made to any size,
  shape and colour choice

– Create your own original design

– Commercial or residential

– Artist services provided in showrooms

INTERIOR DESIGN CHOICE 3 © Tangi Collection

FORMICA® BRAND products

THE COLOR GRID®, COLOR TRENDS, DESIGN CONCEPTS®, COLORCORE®, COLOR TIERS, STRIPES, NEW FORMICA BRAND METALS, NEW PATTERNS, H-125 FLOOR TILE, LAC MÉTALLIQUE, WOODGRAINS, MARBLES, LUSTRE – Have you discovered FORMICA brand products?

Toronto **(416) 498-9405**
Montreal **(514) 347-7501**

Photos (top to bottom)
1. Detail of COLOR TIERS used in "VIRIDIS" collection from "FORME-D". Design: Francine Couture
2. "FOREST OF TABLES" – Design: Michael Hosaluk, one of the winning designers in "COLOR & FORM" 1986. COLORCORE®, aluminum, glass, lacquered wood, plexiglass. Photo: Grant Kerman AK Photo.

3. "VITA BREVIS" student winner, "COLOR & FORM" competition, 1986 sponsored by FORMICA CANADA. COLORCORE® on plywood. Design: Stephane Laporte and Alain Daviault.

Background: FORMICA brand STRIPES 1885.

INTERIOR DESIGN CHOICE 3 © Formica Canada Inc.

Octopus Products Limited
200 Geary Avenue
Toronto, Ontario M6H 2B9
(416) 531-5051

Distributors of **Octolam**
and **Octolux** Laminates

Vancouver • Calgary • Edmonton
Winnipeg • Montreal • Ottawa
New York • Detroit • Cleveland

We shop the world market to offer the design community an unparalleled selection of specialty plastic and metallic laminates – all of which are stocked.

Call in an Octopus representative to introduce you to the finest the world has to offer.

1. Postformed elements produced with Octolam Grid & Granite laminates

2. Octolam Serigraphia laminate Armoire–Design by Richard Belanger

3. Octolux Mirror ceiling Metropolitan Toronto Convention Center Crang & Boake Architects

4. Octolam Gloss Laminate–Puressence Design by Pierette Claude ARIDO

INTERIOR DESIGN CHOICE 3 © Octopus Products Limited

WILSONART®

BRAND DECORATIVE LAMINATE

Corporate Headquarters:
Ralph Wilson Plastics Company
600 General Bruce Drive
Temple, TX 76501
TWX: (910) 890-5880

Hotline
When you need immediate response to
a question, or quick delivery (within
24 hours) of product samples and
literature, call toll free (within the
continental U.S.A.):
          1-800-433-3222
In Texas: 1-800-792-6000
In Canada: (817) 778-2711

Resource center, Las Colinas, Texas.
Reading table and cabinetry are
surfaced in (4590-15) Grey Millstone
with (1595-1) Black recessed accent
trim.

Designer: Stewart R. Skolnick, ASID,
IBD, Principal, Stewart R. Skolnick
Associates, Inc., New York, New York.

Photograph by: Peter Paige, Harrington
Park, New Jersey.

INTERIOR DESIGN CHOICE 3 © Wilsonart

MARBLE TREND

2050 Steeles Avenue West
Unit 4
Concord, Ontario
L4K 2V1
(416) 738-0400

Telex: 06-964759

MARBLE TREND LIMITED imports a dazzling array of exquisite and superbly crafted European marble tiles and ''designer'' products.
An investment in classic marble ensures timeless appeal and lasting value in any residential area or commercial project.

Whether you are a Developer, Builder, Architect/Specifier or Interior Designer, you will value the extensive marble selection marketed by MARBLE TREND.

A knowledgeable and experienced team of professionals is also on hand to coordinate your specific needs. Should you require additional technical data or are looking for that ''special'' marble, the Marble Trend team has the resources to supply you quickly and efficiently.

MARBLE TREND LIMITED offers you a distinctive line of executive desks, furnishings and accessories fashioned by top European designers to give you that unique look.

Create an atmosphere of excellence and sophistication with marble tile and products from MARBLE TREND LIMITED. We invite you to visit our showroom or call one of our regional representatives.

Brettons
The Promenade, Toronto
Interior Design: Petroff Jeruzalski
Kwok Shepherd Architects
Installation: York Marble

Photography: John Sherlock

E.J.B. Glassworks Ltd.
8731 General Currie Road
Richmond, B.C. V6Y 1M2

(604) 270-6032
Joel Berman
Architectural Glass

Joel Berman specializes in the design and fabrication of successful architectural glass art for commercial interior space with emphasis on corporate offices.

Our clients include:
Group 5 Design Associates
Musson Cattell MacKay Architects
Lignum Lumber Sales
Jim Pattison Group
Merrill Lynch Canada Inc.
Loewen Ondaatje McCutcheon & Co.
McDermot St. Lawrence Ltd.
Aetna Trust
Apple Canada Inc.
Ladner Downs

1. Curved leaded glass
conference room wall
Jim Pattison Group, Vancouver B.C.

2. Sandblast etched
conference room wall
Liddle, Burns, Beechwood & Baker
Law office, Vancouver, B.C.

3. Leaded boardroom wall for
Lignum Lumber Sales
Park Place, Vancouver, B.C.

Interiors by Group 5 Design
Associates Ltd.

INTERIOR DESIGN CHOICE 3 © E.J.B. Glassworks Ltd.

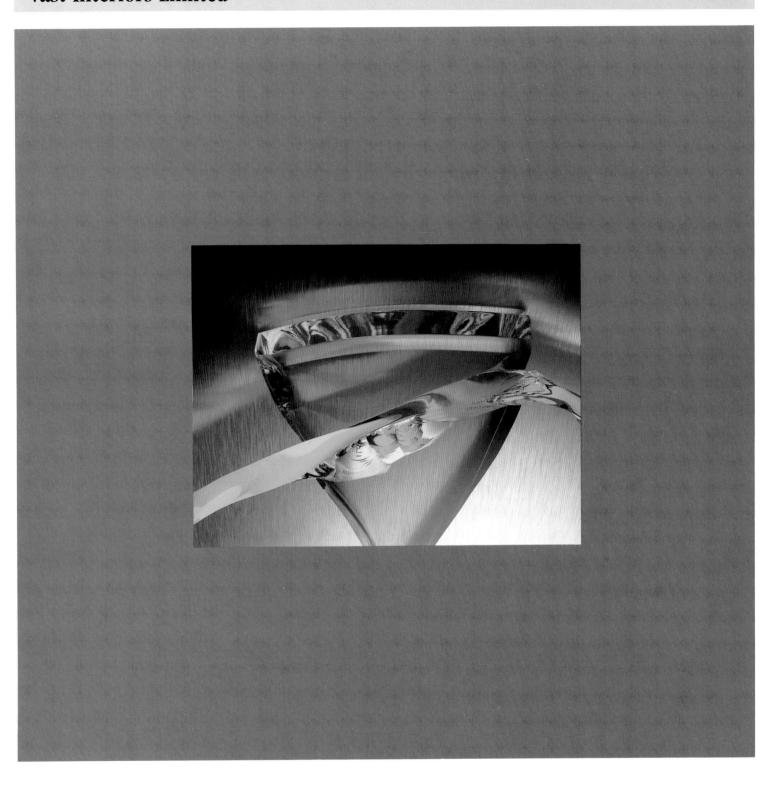

96 Bowes Road
Concord, Ontario
L4K 1J7
(416) 738-1170

Simply put, Vast Interiors is a company dedicated to providing innovative solutions in glass and mirror.

Over the years, we have worked with interior designers and architects, lending our creative expertise on projects of various sizes. From residential to commercial and corporate endeavors, Vast has enhanced interiors across the country.

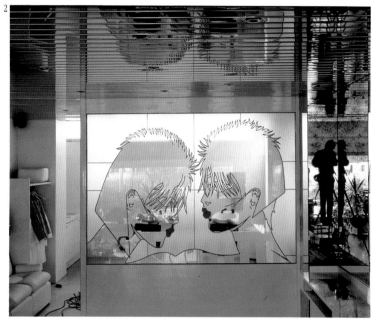

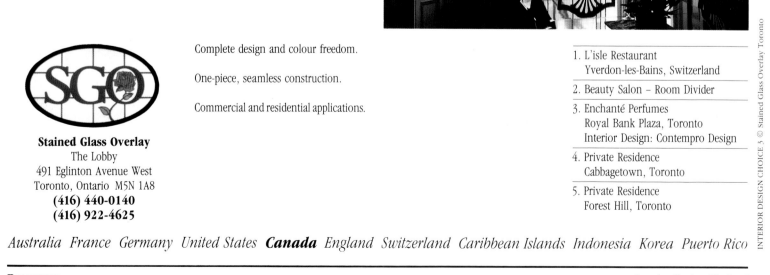

Complete design and colour freedom.

One-piece, seamless construction.

Commercial and residential applications.

Stained Glass Overlay
The Lobby
491 Eglinton Avenue West
Toronto, Ontario M5N 1A8
(416) 440-0140
(416) 922-4625

1. L'isle Restaurant
   Yverdon-les-Bains, Switzerland

2. Beauty Salon – Room Divider

3. Enchanté Perfumes
   Royal Bank Plaza, Toronto
   Interior Design: Contempro Design

4. Private Residence
   Cabbagetown, Toronto

5. Private Residence
   Forest Hill, Toronto

Australia France Germany United States **Canada** *England Switzerland Caribbean Islands Indonesia Korea Puerto Rico*

INTERIOR DESIGN CHOICE 3 © Stained Glass Overlay Toronto

HunterDouglas

Hunter Douglas Canada Ltd.
Architectural Products

7535 Bath Road
Mississauga, Ontario
L4T 4C1
(416) 678-1133

Hunter Douglas is the world's largest supplier of sun protection equipment. With a consistent record for innovation, the company has pioneered the introduction of blinds with aluminum slats in the 1940s. The world's first unique energy saving blind slat, and magnet powered between-glass-blinds are other recent firsts from Hunter Douglas.

The specification of window treatments has been raised to the level of a significant decision. Perhaps we could put our expertise to work for you.

Another Hunter Douglas product, the Luxalon Ceiling Systems are as exceptional as your ideas, as diverse as your imagination. They represent a simple, orderly approach to the art of interior design. Manufactured in North America, installed around the world, Hunter Douglas Luxalon Systems have proven themselves under a variety of conditions over a number of years. Offering unmatched simplicity and durability, the Luxalon Ceiling Systems are a truly sensible solution – the choice of today for tomorrow.

INTERIOR DESIGN CHOICE 3 © Hunter Douglas Canada Ltd.

Photo: Elaine Kilburn

2050 Ellesmere Road
Scarborough, Ontario
M1H 3A9
(416) 438-9640
Telex 065-26165

Metal Ceiling Systems

Sourcing the best suspended ceiling system whether acoustic, decorative or mechanical or any combination thereof, Dampa makes it easy through a wide range of standard and custom systems.

1. Ottawa International Airport
   Dampa 300

2. Ottawa Provincial Courthouse
   Dampa 100 Grid

3. The Promenade Mall-Toronto
   Dampa Light Beam

INTERIOR DESIGN CHOICE 3 © Dampa

© Peter Aaron/ESTO

B E N J A M I N
MOORE

15 Lloyd Avenue
Toronto, Ontario
M6N 1G9
(416) 766-1173

Texture. Color. Nuance. The subtleties
that define the designer's craft. The
critical difference that separate a job
that's merely complete from one that's
completely wonderful.

That's why the architectural firm of
Voorsanger & Mills Associates insists
on top quality coatings from Benjamin
Moore, and nothing less. Perhaps it's
this attention to detail that makes
Nightfalls Restaurant in Brooklyn,
New York as much a feast for the eyes,
as it is for the palate.

Finish it right from the start.

INTERIOR DESIGN CHOICE 3 © Benjamin Moore & Co. Limited

Golden Gate

One
of many
new
bathroom
faucets
from
Ginger's.

GINGER'S
BATHROOMS

945 Eglinton Avenue East (at Brentcliffe), Toronto, Ontario M4G 4B5 Telephone: (416) 429-3444

INTERIOR DESIGN CHOICE 3 © Ginger's Bathrooms

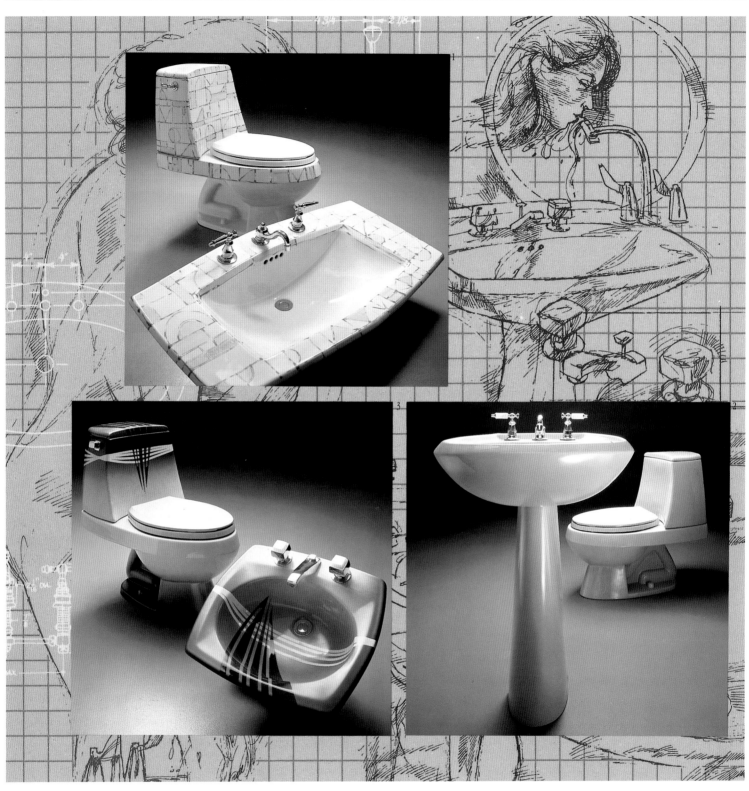

**Suncity Trading Co. Ltd./
Kohler Centre**
1979 Leslie Street
Don Mills, Ontario
M3B 2M3
(416) 449-3171

With 110 years experience in plumbing product, Kohler can manifest the imagination of any designer or architect. Our new catalogue is now available.

Kohler Artists Editions

1. Coloré™ – Christina Bertoni
2. Color Cloud™ – Karen Massaro
3. Solstice™ – Art Nelson

INTERIOR DESIGN CHOICE 3 © Suncity Trading Co. Ltd./Kohler Centre

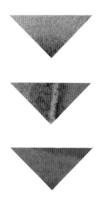

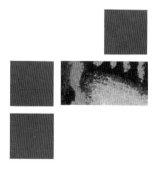

CONTRACTORS

British Columbia
Alberta
Saskatchewan
Manitoba
Ontario
Quebec
Nova Scotia
New Brunswick
Newfoundland

Alabama
Alaska
Arizona
Arkansas
California
Colorado
Connecticut
Delaware
Dist. of Columbia
Florida
Georgia
Hawaii
Idaho
Illinois
Indiana
Iowa
Kansas
Kentucky
Louisiana
Maine
Maryland
Massachusetts
Michigan

Minnesota
Mississippi
Missouri
Montana
Nebraska
Nevada
New Hampshire
New Jersey
New Mexico
New York
North Carolina
North Dakota
Ohio
Oklahoma
Oregon
Pennsylvania
Rhode Island
South Carolina
South Dakota
Tennessee
Texas
Utah
Vermont
Virginia
Washington
West Virginia
Wisconsin
Wyoming

Barbados
Bermuda
St. Martins
Trinidad

Contract Management.

One of the most successful established companies in North America offering Management & Technological expertise in the interior construction industry.

Manufacturing carpentry and millwork for office, retail and commercial interiors. The number one choice for quality construction.

Begg & Daigle
Store & Office Interiors
110 Milner Avenue
Scarborough, Ontario
M1S 3R2
(416) 298-8600
Fax: (416) 298-6453

Begg & Daigle Inc.
Store & Office Interiors
97 – 45 Queens Blvd.
Rego Park, New York
11374
(718) 997-6110
Fax: (718) 997-1088

INTERIOR DESIGN CHOICE 3 © Begg & Daigle

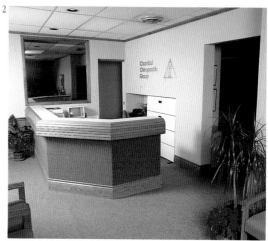

C.A.S. Interiors Inc.
549 Oakdale Road
Downsview, Ontario
M3N 1W7
(416) 743-6291

"From the beginning...hands on...day to day personal involvement in a company committed to making quality and service our cornerstone."

Steven McMahon
President

Elizabeth Morgan
Vice-President

Factors which ensure the satisfaction of our clients:
- Accurate budgets
- Ability to perform under pressure
- Completion of projects on schedule
- Quality workmanship
- Helpful and courteous personnel

1. Prudential Insurance
   Royal LePage Building
2. Chambul Chiropractic Clinic
3. Hamilton Computer
   33 Yonge Street

INTERIOR DESIGN CHOICE 3 © C.A.S. Interiors Inc.

Time for C.A.S. to look ahead:
To create a new direction, while continuing to
provide for the needs of our clients that got us here.
To this end we have created a new division of
C.A.S. Interiors.

MORGAN + McMAHON

Contract Planning & Construction

Morgan + McMahon
549 Oakdale Road
Downsview, Ontario
M3N 1W7
(416) 743-6291

Lease and purchasing negotiations have become so lengthy and complex that the actual time for the planned improvements and construction to take place has suffered.

Once the decision is made to proceed, Morgan + McMahon will take over, providing the important planning and precise execution required to ensure the desired results for our clients.

A wide selection of services and informative programs will be made available through Morgan + McMahon including...advice on leasehold construction...budget preparation... technical advice...complete contract planning...and full construction services to see the project through to completion.

With our aim to offer the ultimate in service, our vehicles are equipped with mobile phones, affording us the opportunity of immediate response.

Morgan + McMahon will work in concert with C.A.S. Interiors to provide the most comprehensive service possible to our clients and a program of expanding services as needs are identified.

INTERIOR DESIGN CHOICE 3 © C.A.S. Interiors Inc./Morgan + McMahon

Cameron-McIndoo Interiors Ltd.
20 Upjohn Road
Don Mills, Ontario
M3B 2V9
(416) 447-3301

General contractors specializing in
commercial interiors:
– Corporate
– Institutional
– Retail

McMillan Binch, Royal Bank Plaza
Interior Design:
Helen Moffet Associates Ltd.
■ Boardroom
● Reception Area

Walwyn Stodgell Cochran Murray Ltd.,
Walwyn Building
Interior Design:
Design Planning Associates
▶ Stairway

Suite 3306
Royal Trust Tower
Toronto Dominion Centre
(416) 363-6131

Project: Dome Mines
I.B.M. Tower, Toronto

Designer: Rice Brydone Ltd.
Toronto

Centre Leasehold Improvements

- The company with modern ideas and old fashioned quality

- The company formed in 1968 solely to handle leasehold improvements

- The company that is owned by the people involved in the day to day business

and

- The company where the employees take pride in their workmanship.

the experience creators

Forrec International Corporation
33 Britain Street
Toronto, Ontario Canada M5A 1R7
(416) 362-5782
Telefax: (416) 366-6848

Today's aggressive retail environment requires innovative and creative concepts to achieve market leadership.

Shopping has become a social and leisure experience best achieved in a total family entertainment environment. The key to tomorrow's profits is today's creative edge.

The Forrec International Corporation brings together a unique range of highly specialized skills and services to create exciting, unique concepts from entertainment facilities to speciality façades and marketing programmes for the retail market.

From conceptual design planning, through construction, to operations management the Forrec team gives you the creative edge no matter what scale of project you have in mind.

1. Fantasy Fair
   Woodbine Centre
2. Parisian Street
   West Edmonton Mall
3. Crystal Palace
   Canada's Wonderland
4. Fantasy Fair
   Woodbine Centre
5. Fantasy Fair
   Woodbine Centre

gillanders

33 Atomic Avenue
Toronto, Ontario
M8Z 5K8
(416) 259-5446

Boardrooms
Executive Suites
Professional Offices
Reception Desks
Financial Trading Rooms
Custom Quality Woodwork

What designers conceive
Gillanders make.

Excellent workmanship is
often rewarded with
future contracts.

Top: Bank of Bermuda
Hamilton, Bermuda
Bottom: Wittington Tower
Toronto, Ontario
Architect: Leslie Rebanks

INTERIOR DESIGN CHOICE 3 © Gillanders

Interior Dimensions
General Interior Contractors
980 Yonge Street, Suite 403
Toronto, Ontario
M4W 2J5
(416) 922-7165

Robert Horwitz, President
John Burns, VP Construction
Ron Cook, VP and Chief Estimator

Interior Dimensions are specialists in leasehold improvements of office space. We offer the following services to our clients:
- Pre-Budgeting and Project Scheduling assistance
- Completion of the project on schedule
- Competitive pricing
- Guaranteed workmanship

Our regular clients include:

- leading design firms and architects

- major building owners and managers

- major corporations, law firms, insurance companies, financial institutions

Affiliated members of ARIDO

1. Boardroom
Media Company

2. Reception Area
Petrochemical Corporation

3. Reception Area
Corporate Office Headquarters

INTERIOR DESIGN CHOICE 3 © Interior Dimensions

Photo: Shin Sugino

Photo: Shin Sugino

Photo: Steve Evans

Photo: David Whittaker

Photo: Shin Sugino

Photo: Steve Evans

Photo: David Whittaker

Photo: Sandy Mackay

Photo: Sandy Mackay

pancor
INDUSTRIES LIMITED

910 Westport Crescent
Mississauga, Ontario
L5T 1G1
(416) 673-2910

1 Client: CLUB MONACO	Designer: YABU PUSHELBERG
2 Client: YU FASHIONS	Designer: YABU PUSHELBERG
3 Client: LIPTON FASHIONS	Designer: SHIRO/ROBERTS + ASSOC.
4 Client: SIGNOR ANGELO	Designer: YABU PUSHELBERG
5 Client: RAPHAEL MACK	Designer: YABU PUSHELBERG
6 Client: GOODMAN MANTEAU	Designer: SHIRO/ROBERTS + ASSOC.
7 Client: MADAME ANGELO	Designer: YABU PUSHELBERG
8 Client: STUDIO 267	Designer: SHIRO/ROBERTS + ASSOC.
9 Client: HARRY ROSEN	Designer: SHIRO/ROBERTS + ASSOC.

INTERIOR DESIGN CHOICE 3 © Pancor Industries Limited

Client: The Pickle Barrel, Toronto
Designer: Gianna Design Associates

Client: Duncan Street Grill, Toronto
Designer: Gianna Design Associates

QUALITY GENERAL CONTRACTING CO.
140 Bentley Street, Markham, Ontario L3R 3L2 (416) 475-1315

INTERIOR DESIGN CHOICE 3 ©Quality General Contracting Co.

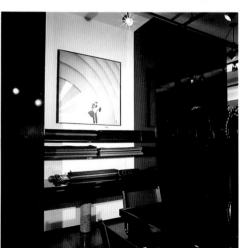

Client: T.H. Ross, Toronto
Designer: Shiro/Roberts + Associates

Client: Milli, New York
Designer: Yabu Pushelberg

Client: Correlli, Toronto
Designer: Shiro/Roberts + Associates

QUALITY GENERAL CONTRACTING CO.
140 Bentley Street, Markham, Ontario L3R 3L2 (416) 475-1315

Patella
construction

Patella Construction Inc.
161 Stirling Avenue
Lasalle, Quebec
H8R 3P3
(514) 364-1964
Telex: 055-66474

124 Bermondsey Road
Toronto, Ontario
M4A 1X5
(416) 752-7750
Telex: 069-63843

General contractor
Office interiors
Fine millwork
Commercial furniture

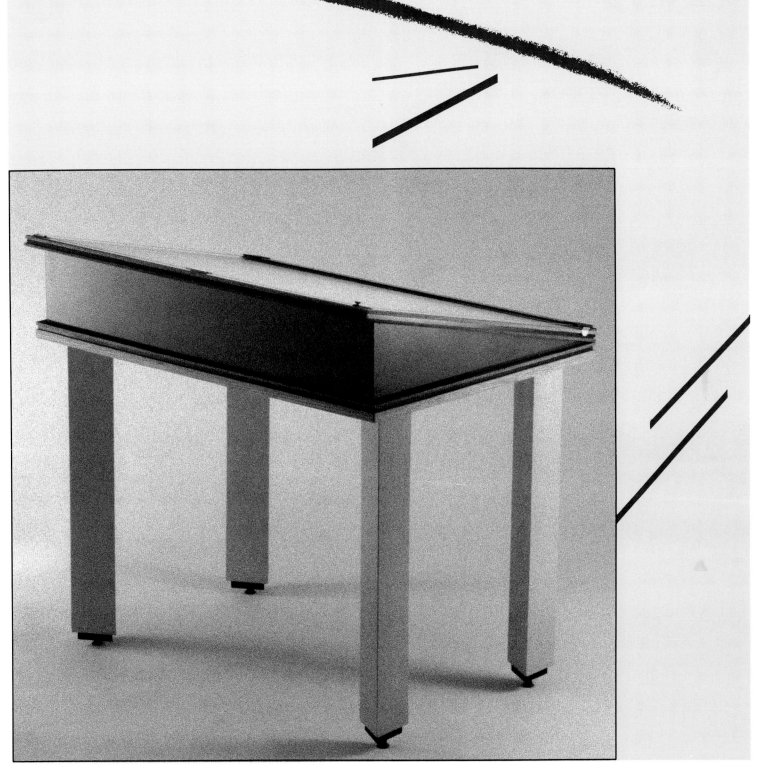

**Woodrites Custom Builders and
Renovators**
940 Queen Street West
Toronto, Ontario M6J 1G8
(416) 532-9621

Function and form:
Ideals that the Woodrites group affirms
in all our commissions.
Working with todays materials and
adhering to traditional values, we will
finely craft a single piece or make an
art of orchestrating large scale
renovations.

Recent commissions include supplying
work stations for Alias Research Inc.,
the reception area for Nightingale,
Quigley Makrimichalos Architects,

store fixtures, display units and
renovations for Venni Fashions.

A portfolio is available for your
further consideration.

Drafting table for design office.

INTERIOR DESIGN CHOICE 3 © Woodrites Custom Builders and Renovators

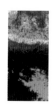

C O N S U L T A N T S

Photo: Tony Whibley

Photo: Jim D'Addio

H.H. Angus & Associates Ltd.
Consulting Engineers
1127 Leslie Street
Don Mills, Ontario
M3C 2J6
(416) 443-8200
Telex 06-986510
Fax 443-8290

H.H. Angus & Associates Ltd. is a diversified engineering company whose capabilities include engineering from the extraordinarily complex to the minor alteration.

Several years ago, the H.H. Angus Interior Design Engineering Group was formed to respond to the special needs and requirements of space planners and interior designers to meet the technical demands of today's business environment.

The mechanical and electrical engineering expertise of these individuals, whose talents are dedicated solely to this work, enable them to respond to the demands of their clients, ensuring the space is tuned to the user's needs and that such supplementary systems, as required, are in place.

Branch offices in:
Ottawa, Dallas, New York,
London (England)

Affiliates in:
Calgary, Winnipeg

1. Toronto Dominion Food Court
Toronto, Ontario
– Bregman + Hamann

2. Steelcase Canada Ltd.
Markham, Ontario
– Rice Brydone

3. Union Bank of Switzerland
New York, New York
– Mascioni & Behrmann

4. Sunnybrook Medical Centre
Toronto, Ontario
– Bregman + Hamann

1. Storwal International Inc. – Showroom, Toronto
Interior Design: Design Planning Associates

2. Xerox Canada Inc., North York
Interior Design: Marshall Cummings + Associates

3. Knox College Chapel, University of Toronto

4. The Gallery Building, The Consilium, Scarborough
The Prudential Insurance Co. of America and
The Equity Development Group Inc.
Bregman & Hamann Architects
Recipient of Award of Merit 1985-86
Illumination Engineering Society of North America

Crossey
Engineering LTD.

Consulting Engineers, 4141 Yonge St., North York, Ont. M2P 2A8 • (416) 221-3111 • FAX (416) 221-4354 • 332 Somerset St. W., Ottawa, Ont. K2P 0J9 • (613) 231-5812

Communication Systems

23 Prince Andrew Place
Don Mills, Ontario M3C 2H2
(416) 443-9300

A member of the
Southam Audio Visual Group

Rutherford Audio Visuals is a
full service company with equipment
sales – service and rental facilities.

Our Communication Systems
department specializes in consultation
with interior designers and architects
to design and create effective
communication environments for
training, conference and boardroom
facilities.

Burroughs Canada – UNISYS
Hall of Products Theatre
Interior Design by
Forest/Bodrug Partners Inc.

INTERIOR DESIGN CHOICE 3 © Rutherford Audio Visuals

E X H I B I T

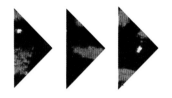

A N D

D I S P L A Y

BGM Colour Laboratories Ltd.
497 King Street East
Toronto, Ontario
M5A 1L9
(416) 947-1325

Successful exhibit or display design requires floor visibility and product or company identification. Display photography meets these requirements with cost effective flexibility.

Visual Marketing:
- Draws traffic at trade shows and conventions.
- Represents your products or any part of them. It can even detail how they are manufactured and how they may be used.

- Creates product and company identification immediately.
- Delivers your message in a language all people can understand.
- Adds a design element to your exhibit or display that is aesthetically appealing.

In addition to full photographic laboratory services, BGM offers display planning, project co-ordination and creative services.

Involve us in your projects early and maximize the benefits of Visual Marketing.
WE HAVE VISION

Special thanks to:

Towers Department Stores,
Store of the Future, Dartmouth
Paris Lites – A.G. Communications
General Motors of Canada Ltd.,
Display designed by Atlanta

INTERIOR DESIGN CHOICE 3 © BGM Colour Laboratories Ltd.

INTERIOR

LANDSCAPING

Dwarf Morru Boxwood 8 years old.

Juniper 15 years old.

THE INTERIOR LANDSCAPE GROUP INC.

80 Oakdale Road
Downsview, Ontario M3N 1V9
(416) 746-3765

Shimpaku Juniper 40 years old.

The Bonsai: An ancient tradition of the selection and transformation of seedlings into unique and exquisite miniature trees by dedicated horticultural artisans.

The Interior Landscape Group: A growing tradition in the creation of distinctive interior tropical plant installations that compliment and enhance architectural interior spaces.

The Bonsai symbolizes our dedication to the world of interior landscape design. Just like the Bonsai every creation unique unto itself…and just like the Bonsai, The Interior Landscape Group, has taken years of disciplined, practical and creative experience and used it towards making great interior spaces…even greater.

INTERIOR DESIGN CHOICE 3 © The Interior Landscape Group

What's this Jensen Green Team?
(and why isn't their display more serious?)
Hey! Lighten Up!
Plants and Trees, correctly placed
and cared for provide
THE FINAL JOYFUL TOUCH to any area:
Office, Atrium, Hotel, Home.
We believe this is a 'Team' effort.
Designer-specifiers
Selectors
Shippers
Installers
Tender Loving Care service
We do it all. We do it very well.
Let us supply that Final Joyful Touch.
Our skill and
your needs –
WHAT A TEAM!

Jensen International Inc.
140 Milner Avenue
Unit 44
Scarborough, Ontario
M1S 3R3
(416) 299-6466

INTERIOR DESIGN CHOICE 3 © Jensen International Inc.

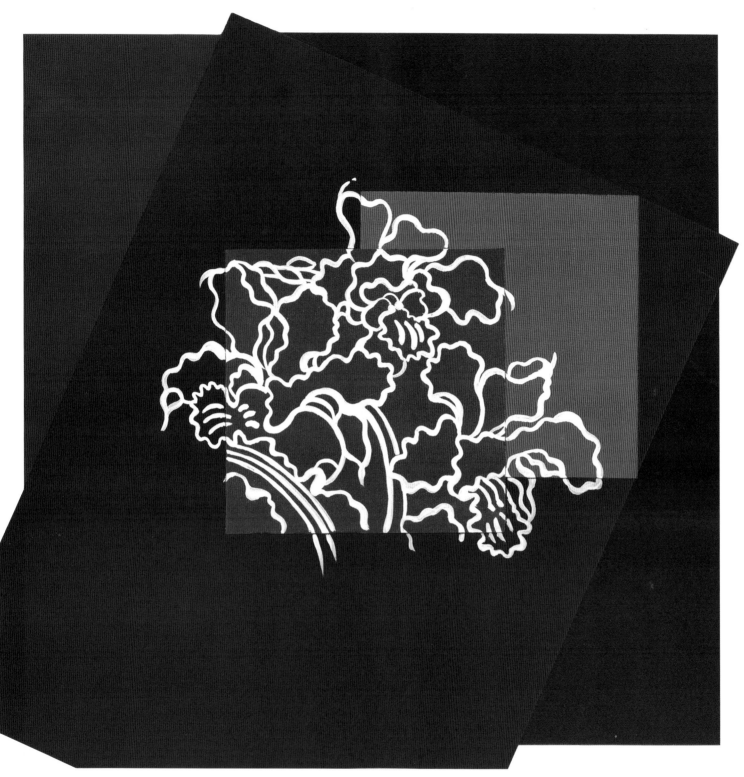

16 Lesmill Road
Don Mills, Ontario M3B 2T5
(416) 449-1974

The Final Touch brings to you the integrity, reputation and experience of Alfred and Shawn Dalgorf, Tom de Journo and Donna Matthews, together with Aberdeen Florists.

The world marketplace brings to us the most incredible sources of exotic fresh cut and silk flowers imaginable. The finest crystal and pottery is mated to arrangements that defy the imagination. Our consultants will meet with the designer, decorator, or architect on site to develop and create magnificent individual floral arrangements to suit the location. We specialize in the commercial, residential and hospitality marketplace.

A R T

A N D

A N T I Q U E S

**Contemporary Fine Art
Services Inc.**
411 Richmond Street East, Suite 103
Toronto, Ontario M5A 3S5
(416) 366-9770

For business and professional settings, we offer an in-office selection of Canadian works of art in every medium.

For designers of corporate, commercial and residential interiors, our showroom affords an opportunity to choose from a wide variety of original works and posters.

Additional services include
– lease-purchase and rental plans
– professional installation
– custom conservation framing
– inventory and valuation of existing collections
– special commissions

Joan Nicol, Alexandra Galbraith, Kathryn Minard, Karen Jacobson, Claire McKechnie

Photo: Jeff Nolte

**Design Collections
Gallery 400**
400 Summerhill Avenue
Toronto, Ontario M4W 2E4
(416) 920-1921

Eleanor Grant
President

Art is an important aspect in the development of any interior becoming an integral part of the design from the onset.

We work closely with designers, corporations and individuals to develop a continuing art program on a professional level.

We offer a diversity of established national and international artists and a full range of auxilliary art services.

Stow & Davis – Mississauga, Ontario
1. Reception – Don Bonham Sculpture
2. Lobby – Rita Letendre, Peter Banks, Don Bonham
3. Waiting Area – Nancy Hazelgrove
4. Corridor – Anton Cetin, Irene Kindness

Steelcase Canada Ltd. – Markham, Ontario
5. Reception – Peter Banks
6. Executive Hallway – Allan Shields

INTERIOR DESIGN CHOICE 3 © Design Collection/Gallery 400

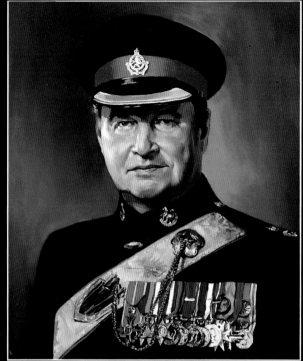

FIVE SIGNATURES

FINE ART · PORTRAITURE

111 Queen Street East
Suite 340
Toronto, Ontario
M5C 1S2
(416) 865-1803

A portrait painting by an accomplished artist is unsurpassed in expressing the full depth of appreciation for highly respected executives. There can be no finer or lasting tribute to honour them. Five Signatures presents the widest range of leading Canadian portrait artists. Let us assist you in selecting the artist most compatible with your executive's unique personality and in making the detailed arrangements when commissioning a portrait painting.

INTERIOR DESIGN CHOICE 3 © Five Signatures

Photo: Juan Amestoy

Marcus Enterprises Inc

294 Berkeley Street
Toronto, Ontario
M5A 2X5
(416) 967-7617

With the emphasis on individuality H.D. Marcus Enterprises Inc., in addition to its interior design service, provides a purchasing consulting service for country and formal antiques. This personalized service is extended to private and corporate sectors as well as to members of the design industry in Canada and the United States.

D E S I G N

A W A R D S

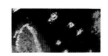

The Pantheon…for centuries it has stood as the perfect monument to man's design ingenuity. That's why we chose it as the basis for our 1986 Design Competition. The Challenge… to create conferencing, work, and relaxation areas for 60 people in the Pantheon using Haworth furniture systems. The Rewards…a trip for two to the Milan Furniture Show or $6,000, and a $4,000 donation in the winner's name to Interior Designers of Canada. The Results…Design Inspiration.

AWARD OF DISTINCTION
Awarded to the Winnipeg team of Grant Marshall, Leah Arnott-Peterson, Rob Everitt and Mark Pritchard for their design of a Haworth showroom within the Pantheon. Demonstrating the flexibility of Haworth systems, the spacial configurations and colour selection related directly to the rich lines and bold geometric patterning of the marble floor. Also receiving an Award of Distinction were Ted Maciurzynski and Esther Patzia.

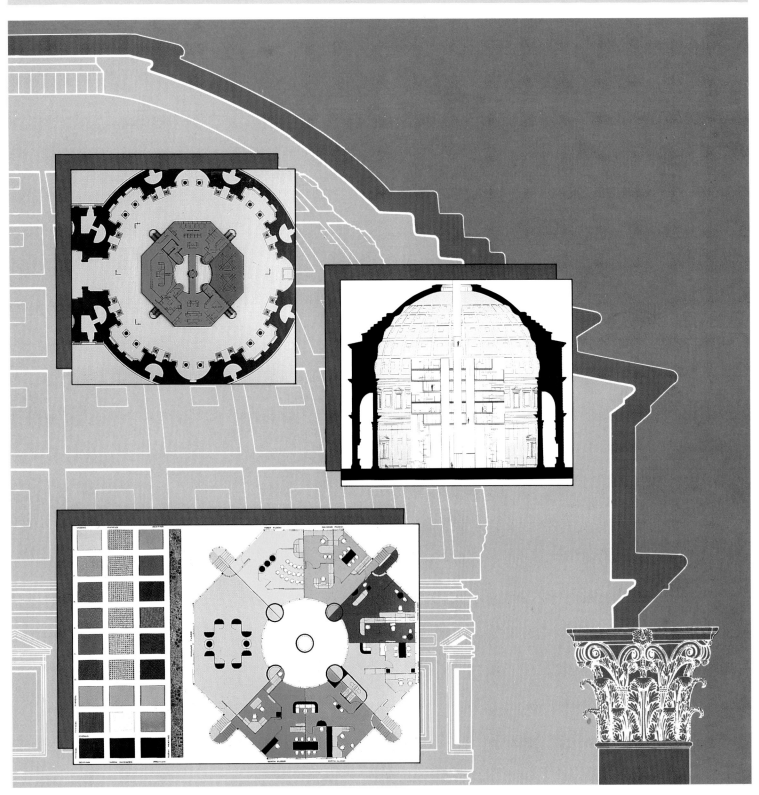

GRAND AWARD WINNER
Awarded to Toronto's Rice Brydone Limited Design Team for their magnificent fusion of past and present through Italesat…a satellite company within the Pantheon.

A sculpture within a sculpture, the breathtaking design expressed a sympathy for the space while providing unique and unobstructed vistas of the interior. A creative use of colour also served to heighten the sense of light penetration.

We would like to take this opportunity to thank the participants in the 1986 Haworth Design Competition. You have all succeeded in capturing and exemplifying the true spirit of design in Canada.
Original.
Creative.
Inspirational.

33 Yonge Street, Suite 270
Toronto, Ontario M5E 1G4
(416) 363-0702

2000 McGill College Ave., Suite 500
Montreal, Quebec H3A 3H3
(514) 842-2622

EXCELLENCE IN OFFICE FURNISHINGS

INTERIOR DESIGN CHOICE 3 © Haworth Office Systems, Ltd.

R E N D E R E R S

A N D

P H O T O G R A P H E R S

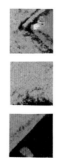

G.A. Design
31 Silverton Avenue
Toronto, Ontario
M3H 3E7
(416) 638-4933

Anna Gavrilescu

Design & architectural interior & exterior illustrations.

Techniques:
• Watercolour & gouache
• Black & white (ink)
• Markers

1. Kentucky Place Condominium
   Atlantic City, New Jersey

2. Photographic equipment store –
   proposal
   Toronto, Ontario

3. Crown West – Condominium
   Toronto, Ontario
   Design:
   David B. Margulis & Associates Inc.

4. Rosedale North – Toronto

INTERIOR DESIGN CHOICE 3 © G.A. Design

K E O G H
R E N D E R I N G

ARCHITECTURAL AND INTERIOR DESIGN RENDERING • PAUL KEOGH • TORONTO • (416) 423-2412

Morello Design & Co.
61 Marlborough Ave.
Toronto, Ontario
M5R 1X5
(416) 963-4315

Barb Morello D.I.D.

Interior and architectural renderings
for the commercial and residential
trade in the following medium:
- watercolour
- gouache
- marker
- airbrush
- pen & ink
- pencil

1. The Prince Condominiums
2. Lobby in the Prince
3. Bathroom
4. Used for Thornhill Design's ad

Client List:
Gabor & Popper Architects
Toronto Star
Freckles & Co.
G.L. Smith Designers & Planners
Media Buying Services Ltd.
Metric Properties
Stone Barn Estates
Inventure Developments Inc.
Country Heritage Homes
Thornhill Design
The Ron Paolone Group
Adcom
Atella Developments

Bilodeau/Preston
(communicating photographically) Ltd.
162 heston street n.w.
calgary alberta t2k 2c4
(403) 284-4400

An investment in quality –

Bilodeau/Preston Ltd. will ensure that your innovative designs, your attention to detail, and your quality craftsmanship are clearly depicted through artistic and distinctive photography.
Their expertise, their versatility, and their ability to listen and integrate your ideas, serve to present your work at its very best.

At your service across the country.

1. Max Bell Theatre –
   Calgary Centre for Performing Arts

2. Bonaventure Lounge –
   Hospitality Inn

3. Walsh Young –
   Domus Design Group Limited

4. Calgary Petroleum Club –
   Gilt Edge Carpets Inc.

INTERIOR DESIGN CHOICE 3 © Bilodeau/Preston

FRASER DAY PHOTOGRAPHY

34 Barbara Crescent
Toronto, Ontario
M4C 3B2
(416) 463-9052

For

Images

that are

out of this world.

We are

"Location Photography" Specialists

Who shoot for those that discern

the difference

between "Inventory" shooting

and creations

that sparkle with drama

Project: **Teleglobe Canada.**
Toronto International Centre

Thanks to: **Leslie Rebanks** of
Leslie Rebanks Architects

For the challenge

of capturing

the magic

of this dynamic space.

INTERIOR DESIGN CHOICE 3 © Fraser Day Photography

**TIM
HANRAHAN
PHOTOGRAPHER
INC.**

3717 Chesswood Drive
Downsview, Ontario
M3J 2P6
(416) 636-7263

Specializing in studio photography of
office and domestic furniture and
related products for 10 years.

INTERIOR DESIGN CHOICE 3 © Tim Hanrahan Photographer Inc.

Ian Leith & Associates Photography
1515 Matheson Blvd., C11
Mississauga, Ontario L4W 2P5
(416) 625-2410

Corporate photography
Annual Reports
Interiors and Architecture

1. **Nick Shulde**
Director of Marketing
Biltrite Nightingale Inc.

2. **Dean Dewey**
Director of Marketing
Irwin Seating Canada Ltd.

3. **Klaus Nienkamper**
President
Nienkamper

4. **Simha Fordsham**
V.P. & Director, Design & Communications
Olympia & York Developments Ltd.

INTERIOR DESIGN CHOICE 3 © Ian Leith & Associates Photography

Claude-Simon Langlois
Photographer

Les Productions Milnox
1573 Ducharme
Montréal, Québec
H2V 1G4
(514) 279-1352

Industrial, corporate, commercial and
advertising, on location assignments,
and additional services.

Prise de vue commerciale, industrielle,
corporative et publicitaire,
sur les lieux, et autres services
complementaires.

Clients:
 Alex Chapman Design Ltd.
 First Quebec Corp.
 Haworth Ltd.
 Innova Design Inc.
 Moureaux Hauspy Design Inc.
 Office Equipment Inc.
 Bernard Rosen & Associés
 Ultramar Canada
 Et plusieurs autres • And many others
 Montréal • Toronto

D E S I G N

S C H O O L S

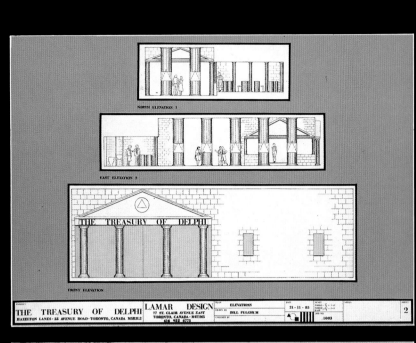

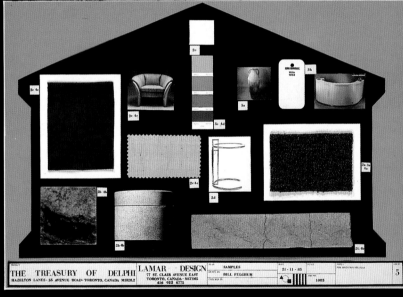

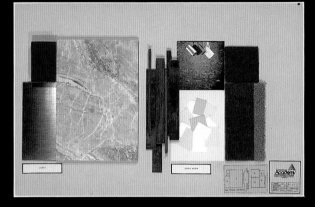

◄ **Bill Fulghum**

▲ ► **Moya McPhail**

► ► **Julie Law**

INTERNATIONAL

Academy
OF MERCHANDISING & DESIGN
TORONTO·MONTREAL·CHICAGO·TAMPA·KANSAS CITY

31 Wellesley Street East
Toronto, Ontario
M4Y 1G7
(416) 922-3666

The International Academy is dedicated to a new kind of college education – one which prepares its graduates for immediate entry into their chosen profession. The curriculum focuses on the development of marketable skills in an occupation oriented academic environment.

The Toronto Campus is located in the centre of the city for easy access to the design community, practising professionals, manufacturers showrooms, trade events, galleries, museums and the city's cultural

activities. Similar campuses are located in Chicago, Kansas City and Tampa in the United States, and a second Canadian Campus will open in the Place Bonaventure in Montreal in the fall of 1987.

The faculty is comprised of practising professionals drawn from the fields of Architecture, Interior Design, Graphic Design, Management, Marketing and the necessary academic areas of History, Art and Design.

The Academy is constantly in touch with the community and the professions

through the President's Advisory Board, a group of international leaders drawn from Business, Education and The Arts, who provide guidance for our ongoing commitment to innovative practical education. The Curriculum Advisory Council is a second group of outstanding Canadian professionals in the fields of Interior Design and Architecture, who work with the Chairman and the Faculty to recommend the most up to date curriculum to prepare the students for their professional careers. The Advisory

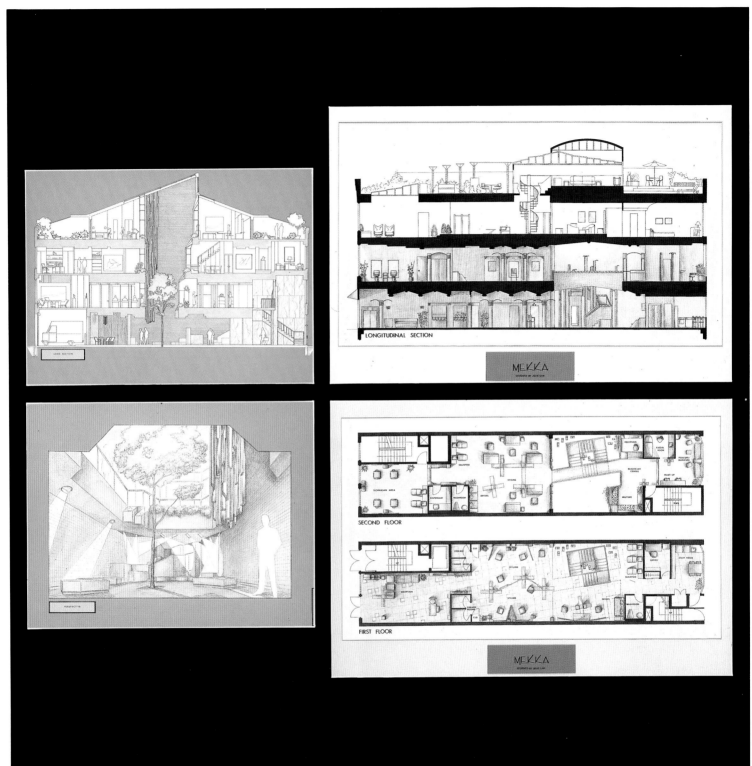

Board, the Curriculum Advisory Council and the professional faculty assist the students to attain the necessary work study experience, a requirement prior to graduation, and to maintain the Academy's 97% placement rate.

Interior Design is a creative and technically challenging field which requires both aesthetic sensitivity and the understanding of functional needs. The Academy's approach to interior design is to develop the student's talents and skills to their fullest

potential by exposure to all aspects of the discipline.

At present, the Academy offers both 2 Year Diploma and 3 Year professional programs in Interior Design which follow the guidelines established by F.I.D.E.R. (Foundation for Interior Design Education Research) the international accrediting organization of the profession. Academy graduates are prepared to enter any of the specialist areas of the field, including residential, commercial, hospitality or institutional work.

Jack W. Bell, F. ARIDO, I.D.C., A.S.I.D.
Chairman/Interior Design Department

Mr. Bell is a past president of the Association of Registered Interior Designers of Ontario, serves on ARIDO's Board of Governors, was a founder of the Interior Designers of Canada and is a member of the American Society of Interior Designers. During his professional career he has provided consulting services to all levels of government and corporate clients across Canada and the U.S. He has taught at O.C.A. and conducted seminars at universities and colleges across Canada and for the American Management Association and the Canadian Management Centre.

INTERIOR DESIGN CHOICE 3 © International Academy of Merchandising & Design

4

Q U I C K

C H O I C E

D I R E C T O R Y

I N D E X

▶ NEWFOUNDLAND

St. John's

BUTT, JUDY
INTERIOR DESIGN CONSULTANT
28 CRAIGMILLAR
ST. JOHN'S, NFLD. A1E 1Z8
(709) 579-6424

LIPPA & FUGGARD ASSOCIATES LTD.
718 WATER STREET
St.JOHN'S, NFLD. A1E 1C1
(709) 726-9672

MURPHY, ELIZABETH INTERIOR DESIGN
5 LORNE PLACE
ST. JOHN'S, NFLD. A1A 2V6
(709) 753-6161

MURPHY, LINDA INTERIOR DESIGN LTD.
16 GILLETT
ST. JOHN'S, NFLD.
(709) 368-0780

PARAB SARMENTO ASSOCIATES LTD.
21 PIPPY PLACE
ST. JOHN'S, NFLD. A1B 3X2
(709) 726-6798

SEAMAN-CROSS NEWFOUNDLAND
46 PIPPY PLACE
ST. JOHN'S, NFLD. A1B 3X4
(709) 753-1250

SQUIRES, ELAINE
INTERIOR DESIGN CONSULTANT
323 FRESHWATER
ST. JOHN'S, NFLD. A1B 1C3
(709) 579-0027

SUCLAR DESIGN
36 FARRELL DRIVE
ST. JOHN'S, NFLD
(709) 368-8213

▶ NOVA SCOTIA

Dartmouth

SEAMAN-CROSS LTD.
46 WRIGHT AVENUE
DARTMOUTH, NOVA SCOTIA B3B 1G6
(902) 469-8190

Halifax

BERARDINELLI DESIGN LTD.
16 BROOK STREET
HALIFAX, NOVA SCOTIA B3N 3A1
(902) 477-7706

BUSINESS FURNISHINGS LTD.
1564 ARGYLE
HALIFAX, NOVA SCOTIA B3J 2B3
(902) 425-7840

CONCEPT DESIGN
5162 DUKE STREET
HALIFAX, NOVA SCOTIA B3J 1N7
(902) 422-3421

CONTRACT DESIGN INCORPORATED
1874 BRUNSWICK STREET
HALIFAX, NOVA SCOTIA B3J 2G7
(902) 423-1339

CORE DESIGN GROUP
5251 DUKE STREET
HALIFAX, NOVA SCOTIA B3J 1P3
(902) 422-1486

DOUGLAS MCGRATH ENTERPRISES
2704 KING STREET
HALIFAX, NOVA SCOTIA B3K 4T8
(902) 454-0890

● **EATON'S CONTRACT INTERIORS**
3845 DUTCH VILLAGE RD., SUITE 101
HALIFAX, NOVA SCOTIA B3L 4H9
(902) 443-0610 **pg. 52, 108, 143**

INNERSPACE PLANNING & DESIGN
7071 BAYERS ROAD
HALIFAX, NOVA SCOTIA
(902) 455-9906

INTERPLAN – INTERNATIONAL PLANNING
& DESIGN ASSOC.
1127 BARRINGTON
HALIFAX, NOVA SCOTIA B3H 2P8
(902) 421-1967

KADESIGNS
5518 KANE PLACE
HALIFAX, NOVA SCOTIA B3K 2B3
(902) 454-9889

MATTINSON WHITE INTERIORS
1259 BARRINGTON
HALIFAX, NOVA SCOTIA B3J 1Y2
(902) 422-2275

MURRAY, JON
1359 BARRINGTON STREET
HALIFAX, NOVA SCOTIA B3J 1Y9
(902) 429-9551

ROBERTSON MACLEAN DESIGN LTD.
23 JAMES
HALIFAX, NOVA SCOTIA B3J 1T6
(902) 466-5511

SPACEWORKS
2409 GLADSTONE
HALIFAX, NOVA SCOTIA B3K 4V8
(902) 425-3519

THOMSON'S
OFFICE PRODUCTS & SYSTEMS LTD.
3695 BARRINGTON STREET
HALIFAX, NOVA SCOTIA B3K 2Y3
(902) 423-6381

TROUP, SUSAN DESIGN
1519 DRESDEN ROW
HALIFAX, NOVA SCOTIA B3J 2K3
(902) 425-4959

Sydney

SIGN DESIGN
70 PARKWOOD DRIVE
SYDNEY, NOVA SCOTIA B1S 1H7
(902) 562-5885

▶ QUEBEC

Hull

OFFICE EQUIPMENT CO. OF CANADA
75, RUE ST-RAYMOND
HULL, QUEBEC J8Y 1S4
(819) 770-0275

Montreal

ADD DESIGN INC.(LE GROUPE)
1255, BOUL. LAIRD
MONTREAL, QUEBEC H3P 2T1
(514) 733-5305

● **AMENAGEMENT COMMERCIAL**
ET DESIGN SIMPSON
P.O. BOX 1133, PLACE BONAVENTURE
MONTREAL, QUEBEC H5A 1G4
(514) 866-9991 **pg. 150**

ARBOUR, MADELEINE ET ASSOCIES
266, RUE ST-PAUL EST
MONTREAL, QUEBEC H2Y 1G9
(514) 878-3846

ATELIERS GAUTHIER, L'
1463, RUE PREFONTAINE
MONTREAL, QUEBEC H1W 2N6
(514) 523-1623

BEAULAC, HENRI
3851, AV. MARLOWE
MONTREAL, QUEBEC H4A 3L9
(514) 486-6442

BELANGER, JACQUES GROUPE DESIGN
2200 LE CORBUSIER
LAVAL, QUEBEC H7S 2C9
(514) 337-7074

BERNARD, CLAUDE DESIGN LTEE
451 RUE ST-SULPICE
MONTREAL, QUEBEC H2Y 2V9
(514) 287-9716

BOLTE, GABRIELLE DESIGN
3465, CHEMIN DE LA COTE-DES-NEIGES
MONTREAL, QUEBEC H3H 1T7
(514) 933-8493

BRAM GROUPE DESIGN INC.
103 MONTEE DU MOULIN
LAVAL, QUEBEC H7N 3Y7
(514) 667-1421

BRISSET-DES-NOS, FRANCINE
5055, AV. GATINEAU
MONTREAL, QUEBEC H3V 1E4
(514) 342-2496

BRUCE, BARBARA DESIGN INC.
1000, ST-ANTOINE OUEST
MONTREAL, QUEBEC H3C 3R7
(514) 875-5115

BURO DECOR INC.
7700 ROUTE TRANSCANADIENNE
MONTREAL, QUEBEC H4T 1A5
(514) 731-3385

BUROPLAN INC.
7945 ROUTE TRANSCANADIENNE
MONTREAL, QUEBEC H4S 1L3
(514) 337-6170

CAMPEAU & ASSOCIES INC.
4542, BOUL. DECARIE
MONTREAL, QUEBEC H3X 2H5
(514) 483-5440

**CARSLEY, JEAN INTERIEURS
& ASSOCIES**
1226, RUE BISHOP
MONTREAL, QUEBEC H3G 2E3
(514) 871-1643

**CHAMPALIMAUD, ALEXANDRA
ET ASSOCIES INC.**
32, CHEMIN RAMEZAY
MONTREAL, QUEBEC H3Y 3J9
(514) 931-2096

**CONCEPT DESIGN
FRANCOIS ROBIDAS LTEE**
1241, ST-HUBERT
MONTREAL, QUEBEC H2L 3Y8
(514) 843-7141

CONTINUUM DESIGN INC.
7881, BOUL. DECARIE
MONTREAL, QUEBEC H4P 2H2
(514) 739-7708

CORRIVEAU, JACQUES DESIGNER INC.
438, RUE ST-PIERRE
MONTREAL, QUEBEC H2Y 2M5
(514) 845-3233

D 3 GROUPE DESIGN INC.
136-A, ST-PAUL EST
MONTREAL, QUEBEC H2Y 1G6
(514) 861-5768

D PLUS 3
1050 MACKAY
MONTREAL, QUEBEC H3G 2H1
(514) 861-6487

• **PHILIPPE DAGENAIS DESIGN INC.**
1600 SHERBROOKE OUEST
MONTREAL, QUEBEC H3H 1C9
(514) 931-7294 **Pg. 134**

DECARIE, FRANCOIS
1573, AV. DU MONT-ROYAL EST
MONTREAL, QUEBEC H2J 1Z3
(514) 845-8446

DESIGN D.A.C. LTEE
2503 EST, BOUL. HENRI BOURASSA
MONTREAL, QUEBEC H2B 1V3
(514) 381-7497

• **DESIGN FORREST BODRUG**
1155, RUE METCALFE
MONTREAL, QUEBEC H3B 2V9
(514) 875-8507 **Pg. 58**

DESIGN NOVY INC.
1610, SHERBROOKE OUEST
MONTREAL, QUEBEC H3H 1E1
(514) 932-7870

DESIGN & PLANIFICATION PLUS INC.
5402, RUE RENTY
ST-LEONARD, QUEBEC H1R 1N7
(514) 324-6953

DESIGN 125
1255, RUE UNIVERSITY
MONTREAL, QUEBEC
(514) 866-9206

DESIGN SYLVIE NOISEUX
467 BONAVENTURE
TROIS RIVIERES, QUEBEC G9A 2B6
(514) 373-6749

DESJARDINS, BERNARD DESIGN LTEE
1134, RUE STE-CATHERINE OUEST
MONTREAL, QUEBEC H3B 1H4
(514) 879-1345

DIMENSIONS MJM INC.
5021, AV. GROSVENOR
MONTREAL, QUEBEC H3W 2M2
(514) 342-6121

**DUBOIS, ANDRE & ASSOCIES
DESIGNERS INC.**
1550 RUE DOCTEUR PENFIELD
MONTREAL, QUEBEC H3G 1C2
(514) 935-9303

DUCHARME, BENOIT & ASSOCIES INC.
65 RUE DE CASTELNAU OUEST
MONTREAL, QUEBEC H2R 2W3
(514) 495-1719

• **EATON'S CONTRACT INTERIORS**
32 RUE EIFFEL, BOX 285
MONTREAL, QUEBEC H5A 1B3
(514) 284-8960 **Pg. 52, 108, 143**

FAUCHER, PIERRE DESIGN LTEE
3468, RUE DRUMMOND
MONTREAL, QUEBEC H3G 1Y4
(514) 288-1188

GARNEAU, LEONARD
5318 BERRI
MONTREAL, QUEBEC H2V 3W1
(514) 271-7803

GOYETTE DUPLESSIS DESIGN
750 BOUL. LAURENTIEN
MONTREAL, QUEBEC H4M 2M4
(514) 744-4714

• **G S M DESIGN**
317, PLACE D'YOUVILLE
MONTREAL, QUEBEC H2Y 2B5
(514) 288-4233 **Pg. 54**

HAYART OUIMET & ASSOCIES
5150, RUE CHARLEROI
MONTREAL, QUEBEC H1G 3A1
(514) 327-3151

HICKS DESIGN
4800, AV. DU PARC
MONTREAL, QUEBEC H2V 4E6
(514) 271-1108

HINTON, CLAUDE INC.
912, AV. McEACHRAN
MONTREAL, QUEBEC H2V 3E2
(514) 277-7401

IDEE ENVIRONEMENT INC.
218 RUE ST-PAUL OUEST
MONTREAL, QUEBEC H2Y 1Z9
(514) 849-3205

INNOVA DESIGN INC.
1030, RUE ST-ALEXANDRE
MONTREAL, QUEBEC H2Z 1P3
(514) 875-5655

IRON CAT INC.
1225, AV. GREENE
MONTREAL, QUEBEC H3Z 2A4
(514) 933-1149

KINTOL ASSOCIATES INC.
5165, CHEMIN QUEEN MARY
MONTREAL, QUEBEC H3W 1X7
(514) 489-3245

LAMBERT & BONNEAU
1662, BOUL. ST-JOSEPH EST,
MONTREAL, QUEBEC H2J 1M9
(514) 521-1633

LARIVIERE & ASSOCIES INC.
2266, RUE ST-GERMAIN
MONTREAL, QUEBEC H4L 3T3
(514) 526-4636

LAUZON, MICHEL & ASSOCIES INC.
7265, RUE SAGARD
MONTREAL, QUEBEC H2E 2S6
(514) 722-8712

• **LERCH, MICHAEL INTERIORS INC.**
1448 SHERBROOKE STREET WEST
MONTREAL, QUEBEC H3G 1K4
(514) 287-0851 **Pg. 137**

LOCAS, BERNARD DESIGNERS LTEE
391, RUE ST-JACQUES
MONTREAL, QUEBEC H2Y 1N9
(514) 284-2288

LE STUDIO
740, RUE WILLIAMS
MONTREAL, QUEBEC H3C 1P1
(514) 878-9222

MAGNUS DESIGNS LTD.
5165, CHEMIN QUEEN MARY
MONTREAL, QUEBEC H3W 1X7
(514) 489-5578

MARCOVITZ, STEPHANIE
6969, ROUTE TRANSCANADIENNE
MONTREAL, QUEBEC H4T 1V8
(514) 931-2279

MARSHALL/MOORE DESIGN INC.
625, DORCHESTER OUEST
MONTREAL, QUEBEC H3B 1R2
(514) 875-8696

• **McCLINTOCK, PATRICIA ASSOCIES INC.**
1167, RUE ST-MARC
MONTREAL, QUEBEC H3H 2E4
(514) 932-1860 **Pg. 116**

MITCHELL-HOLLAND
2060, RUE DRUMMOND
MONTREAL, QUEBEC H3G 1W9
(514) 849-9165

• **MOUREAUX HAUSPY DESIGN INC.**
2140, RUE ST-MATHIEU
MONTREAL, QUEBEC H3H 2J4
(514) 935-4321 **Pg. 68**

OFFICE EQUIPMENT CO. OF CANADA
5990, CHEMIN COTE DE LIESSE
MONTREAL, QUEBEC H4T 1V7
(514) 342-5151

• **OSTROFF, LEONARD DESIGN ASSOCIES**
1200 DE LOUVAIN STREET WEST
MONTREAL, QUEBEC H4N 1G5
(514) 382-0571 **Pg. 96**

OUIMET VACHON & ASSOCIES
7393, 18e AVENUE
MONTREAL, QUEBEC H2A 2N4
(514) 376-1880

• **OVE DESIGN INTERIORS INC.**
356, RUE LE MOYNE
MONTREAL, QUEBEC H2Y 1Y3
(514) 844-8421 **Pg. 70**

PAGE, PIERRE ET ASSOCIES
354, RUE NOTRE DAME OUEST
MONTREAL, QUEBEC H2Y 1T9
(514) 849-8101

PARIZEAU, ROBERT & ASSOCIES LTEE
4542, BOUL. DECARIE
MONTREAL, QUEBEC H3X 2H5
(514) 483-5440

REED SAUDER DESIGN INC.
5103, BOUL. DE MAISONNEUVE OUEST
MONTREAL, QUEBEC H4A 1Z1
(514) 486-4292

**ROBILLARD, SENECAL HOUDE
DESIGNERS ENR.**
3575, BOUL. ST-LAURENT
MONTREAL, QUEBEC H2X 2T6
(514) 281-0088

RODRIGUE, MARC DESIGNER INC.
6650, METIVIER
MONTREAL, QUEBEC H4K 2L1
(514) 335-1233

ROSENBAUM INTERIORS INC
5025, RUE BUCHAN
MONTREAL, QUEBEC H2Y 2B6
(514) 738-1112

**ROY, JAQUES & ASSOCIES
DESIGNER INC.**
306, PLACE D'YOUVILLE
MONTREAL, QUEBEC H2Y 2B6
(514) 845-4587

ROY, PAUL DESIGNER
9580, BOUL. DE L'ACADIE
MONTREAL, QUEBEC H4N 1L8
(514) 382-9088

SHERIF DESIGN ASSOCIES
3704, RUE ST-DENNIS
MONTREAL, QUEBEC H2X 3L7
(514) 849-2864

SIGURDSON DESIGN
65, ST-PAUL OUEST
MONTREAL, QUEBEC H2Y 3S5
(514) 849-2367

SKEAN DESIGN INC.
P.O. BOX 574
MONTREAL, QUEBEC H3X 3T7

SODEPLAN INC.
1180, RUE DRUMMOND
MONTREAL, QUEBEC H3G 2S1
(514) 871-8833

SOUCY, RICHARD DESIGN
53, MILTON STREET
MONTREAL, QUEBEC H2X 1V2
(514) 489-4579

• **TDI ASSOCIATES DESIGN INC.**
363, RUE LEMOYNE
MONTREAL, QUEBEC H2Y 1Y3
(514) 288-8303 **Pg. 121**

VALENCAY, LE INC.
1621, RUE SHERBROOKE OUEST
MONTREAL, QUEBEC H3H 1E2
(514) 932-8131

WILLIAMS, EILEEN
200 DE GASPE, ILE DES SOEURS
MONTREAL, QUEBEC H3E 1E6
(514) 761-6344

Quebec

ATELIER AVANT-GARDE INC., L'
2646, CH. STE-FOY
STE-FOY, QUEBEC G1V 1V2
(418) 651-1616

BELLEY FORTIN & ASSOCIES INC.
908, 2200 CHAPDELAINE
STE-FOY, QUEBEC G1V 4G8
(418) 653-7248

BOUCHARD LAROCHELLE ET ASSOCIES
245 49 RUE OUEST
CHARLESBOURG, QUEBEC G1H 5E3
(418) 623-7293

CONCEPTION DESIGN INC.
8485 L'ESPERANCE
CHARLESBOURG OUEST, QUEBEC G2K 1M3
(418) 626-5080

**COTE CHRISTIANE RUEL
DESIGNER D'INTERIEUR**
820 ST-JEAN-BAPTISTE
LES SAULES, QUEBEC
(418) 872-5925

DECORATION ST-LOUIS ENR.
1648 CH. ST-LOUIS
SILLERY, QUEBEC G1S 1G8
(418) 687-0457

GROUPE CONCEPT ENR.
269, ST-PAUL
QUEBEC, QUEBEC G1K 3W6
(418) 692-0516

HOUDE GUAY GYSLAINE
253, RUE ST-PAUL
QUEBEC, QUEBEC G1K 8C1
(418) 692-3668

INTERIEUR DESIGN JLD INC.
519, 81 RUE OUEST
CHARLESBOURG, QUEBEC G1G 3B3
(418) 626-8315

**LAPLANTE, YVON ET ASSOCIES
DESIGNERS**
5, RUE DES SAULES EST
QUEBEC, QUEBEC G1L 1R5
(418) 628-4418

NORMAND JACQUES SDE INC.
115, 41 RUE OUEST
CHARLESBOURG, QUEBEC G1H 5M4
(418) 623-4004

SIMARD PAUL DESIGNER INC.
850 ST-VALLIER EST
QUEBEC, QUEBEC G1K 3R4
(418) 694-0398

▶ ONTARIO

Brampton

INTERIOR SPACE PLANNING
5 HEATHER PLACE,
BRAMPTON, ONTARIO L6S 1E7
(416) 459-4156

• **ISOMETRIC DESIGN GROUP INC.**
24 BEISEL COURT
BRAMPTON, ONTARIO L6Z 1P4
(416) 846-8675 **Pg. 89**

**JACQUELINE'S
HOUSE OF INTERIOR DESIGN**
109 ROYAL PALM DRIVE
BRAMPTON, ONTARIO L6Z 1P4
(416) 846-2233

NELSON HOFER ASSOC. INC.
1 BARTLEY BULL PKWY.
BRAMPTON, ONTARIO L6W 3T7
(416) 459-7263

OADBE ASSOCIATES LTD.
32 REGAN ROAD
BRAMPTON, ONTARIO L7A 1A7
(416) 846-5001

Burlington

ALMAS, PAUL R. & ASSOCIATES LTD.
760 BRANT
BURLINGTON, ONTARIO L7R 4B7
(416) 639-6310

• **DESIGN WEST/
THE ULTIMATE SOURCE GROUP INC.**
855 HARRINGTON COURT
BURLINGTON, ONTARIO L7N 3P3
(416) 639-7474 **Pg. 152**

OGINO, JEFFREY R. DESIGNS
961 FRASER DRIVE
BURLINGTON, ONTARIO L7L 4X8
(416) 681-0711

KINGSTON

• **SIMPSONS**
COMMERCIAL INTERIORS & DESIGN
945 GARDINERS ROAD
KINGSTON, ONTARIO K7M 7H4
(613) 389-5750 **Pg. 150**

STONE, DAVID & ASSOCIATES LTD.
24 CHATMAN STREET
KINGSTON, ONTARIO K7K 4G5
(613) 546-0207

Hamilton

BECK, A.W. DESIGN
921 SCENIC DRIVE
HAMILTON, ONTARIO L9C 1H7
(416) 383-5557

COOPER'S THE OFFICE PEOPLE
673 KING EAST
HAMILTON, ONTARIO L8M 1A1
(416) 522-7651

CREATIVE DESIGN CONSULTANTS
775 KING WEST
HAMILTON, ONTARIO L8S 1K2
(416) 525-4140

DAVIS, PATRICIA PLANNING & DESIGN
52 HAROLD COURT
HAMILTON, ONTARIO L8S 2R8
(416) 525-2238

FENNELL DESIGN
718 MAIN STREET EAST
HAMILTON, ONTARIO L8M 1K9
(416) 547-6046

NIEUWLAND ASSOCIATES INC.
187 HERKIMER STREET
HAMILTON, ONTARIO L8P 2H7
(416) 523-5945

SOBEL HARVEY AUGUSTA HOUSE
283 MAIN WEST
HAMILTON, ONTARIO L8P 1J7
(416) 528-7973

London

AD HOC DESIGN
189 COLLEGE AVENUE
LONDON, ONTARIO N6A 1X9
(519) 663-9048

BROWN, THORNTON K. INTERIORS INC.
131 WYCHWOOD PLACE
LONDON, ONTARIO N6G 1S7
(519) 473-9566

COMMON MARKET, THE
339 TALBOT STREET
LONDON, ONTARIO N6A 2R5
(519) 679-0390

DAWSON, R.C. COMPANY LTD.
DAWSON GROUP DESIGN
544 EGERTON STREET
LONDON, ONTARIO N5W 3Z8
(519) 451-1980

DECISION PLANNING ASSOCIATES
627 CENTRAL AVENUE
LONDON, ONTARIO N5W 3P7
(519) 438-9967

FDC DESIGN SERVICES
373 TALBOT STREET
LONDON, ONTARIO N6A 2R7
(519) 663-8276

GIELEN DESIGN LINES INC.
116 MILL STREET
LONDON, ONTARIO N6A 1P6
(519) 432-2238

GILL, DOUGLAS LIMITED
479 RICHMOND STREET
LONDON, ONTARIO N6A 3E4
(519) 672-6001

INNERSPACE BUSINESS INTERIORS
200 QUEENS AVENUE
LONDON, ONTARIO N6A 1J3
(519) 679-0165

INTERIO OF LONDON LTD.
240 RICHMOND STREET
LONDON, ONTARIO N6B 2H6
(519) 433-5113

LONDON BUSINESS INTERIORS INC.
200 QUEENS AVENUE
LONDON, ONTARIO N6A 1J3
(519) 438-2324

SHERIDAN, PATRICIA
273 EVERGLADE CRESCENT
LONDON, ONTARIO N6H 4M7
(519) 472-0195

• **SIMPSONS**
COMMERCIAL INTERIORS & DESIGN
400 YORK STREET, SUITE 200
LONDON, ONTARIO N6B 3N2
(519) 679-4811 **Pg. 150**

Niagara On The Lake

JOHN DOWNTON INTERIORS LTD.
363 SIMCOE
NIAGARA ON THE LAKE, ONTARIO L0S 1J0
(416) 468-3163

• **DEL McMILLAN DESIGN GROUP**
GLENDALE AVE., AT Q.E.W., P.O. BOX 566
NIAGARA ON THE LAKE, ONTARIO L0S 1J0
(416) 688-1165 **Pg. 117**

Oakville

• **BARBARA ANGELA INTERIORS**
145 TRAFALGAR ROAD
OAKVILLE, ONTARIO L6J 3G7
(416) 842-2103 **Pg. 132**

HELLER, F. DESIGN SERVICES
1570 BAYVIEW ROAD
OAKVILLE, ONTARIO L6L 1A1
(416) 827-6882

McCARTHY & SHERRY ASSOCIATES
128 LAKESHORE ROAD EAST
OAKVILLE, ONTARIO L6J 1H4
(416) 844-4806

PRAYSNER, ANNE
156 RANDALL
OAKVILLE, ONTARIO L6J 1P4
(416) 845-9248

• **SIL AND ASSOCIATES**
333 WYECROFT ROAD
OAKVILLE, ONTARIO L6K 2H2
(416) 842-5183 **Pg. 78**

Orillia

DOUGLAS HAMILTON DESIGN
11 COLDWATER STREET EAST
ORILLIA, ONTARIO L3V 1W4
(705) 325-4545

WENDY SUTHERLAND INTERIORS
15 BRANT EAST
ORILLIA, ONTARIO L3V 1Y7
(705) 325-6230

Ottawa

ACCENTS INCORPORATED
338 SOMERSET WEST
OTTAWA, ONTARIO K2P 0J9
(613) 233-7435

• **BENITZ & BENITZ DESIGNS LTD.**
OTTAWA, ONTARIO
(613) 564-0208 **Pg. 39**

BOBROW FIELDMAN GROUP INC., THE
46 ELGIN STREET
OTTAWA, ONTARIO K1P 5K8
(613) 238-4091

BUSINESS ENVIRONMENTS
FURNITURE LTD.
130 ALBERT, SUITE 202
OTTAWA, ONTARIO K1P 5G4
(613) 238-7651

CAPITAL OFFICE INTERIORS LTD.
17 AURIGA DRIVE
NEPEAN, ONTARIO K2E 7T9
(613) 723-2000

CLAUDE DESIGN & ASSOCIATES
1312 BANK
OTTAWA, ONTARIO K1S 5H7
(613) 523-6707

COLVIN DESIGN CANADA LTD.
33 IVY CRESCENT
OTTAWA, ONTARIO K1M 1Y1
(613) 744-1534

CORUSH LAROCQUE SUNDERLAND
& PARTNERS LTD.
15 AURIGA DRIVE
NEPEAN, ONTARIO K2E 7T9
(613) 723-1611

COURDIN, MICHAEL DESIGN
45 BLACKBURN AVENUE
OTTAWA, ONTARIO K1N 8A4
(613) 233-3570

CREATIVE DESIGN ALTERNATIVES
77 METCALFE
OTTAWA, ONTARIO K1P 5L6
(613) 230-5622

DG INTERIORS
28 MEADOWBANK DRIVE
NEPEAN, ONTARIO K2G 0N9
(613) 820-7202

DESIGN ASSOCIATES LTD., THE
332 SOMERSET STREET WEST
OTTAWA, ONTARIO K2P 0J9
(613) 230-3850

DISEGNO INTERIOR CONSULTANTS
46 ELGIN
OTTAWA, ONTARIO K1P 5K6
(613) 232-2449

ELITE DESIGN STUDIOS INC.
323 SOMERSET STREET WEST
OTTAWA, ONTARIO K2P 0J8
(613) 238-7979

• **FORREST-BODRUG & ASSOCIATES**
130 ALBERT
OTTAWA, ONTARIO K1P 5G4
(613) 236-9473 **Pg. 58**

GABRIEL DESIGN
109 MURRAY STREET
OTTAWA, ONTARIO K1N 5M5
(613) 230-1822

HALLMARK INTERIORS
325 DALHOUSIE STREET
OTTAWA, ONTARIO K1N 7G1
(613) 230-5666

KALIL, ANITA DESIGNS INC.
53 QUEEN STREET
OTTAWA, ONTARIO K1P 5C5
(613) 238-2565

KOMAR DESIGNS
2581 HOBSON ROAD
OTTAWA, ONTARIO K1V 8M7
(613) 738-4479

LOATES, W. & ASSOCIATES
260 HEARST WAY, SUITE 606
KANATA, ONTARIO K2L 3H1
(613) 592-3153

MOBILIA LTD.
1723 CARLING AVENUE
OTTAWA, ONTARIO K3A 1C8
(613) 729-9100

NATER, THOMAS CONSULTANTS INC.
344 FRANK STREET
OTTAWA, ONTARIO K2P 0Y1
(613) 235-7355

NOLAN, LINDA INTERIORS
190 BRONSON AVENUE
OTTAWA, ONTARIO K1R 6H4
(613) 238-4447

**OFFICE EQUIPMENT
CO. OF CANADA (OE INC.)**
768 BELFAST ROAD
OTTAWA, ONTARIO K1G 0Z5
(613) 236-7281

OTTAWA BUSINESS INTERIORS LTD.
183 COLONADE ROAD
NEPEAN, ONTARIO K2E 7J4
(613) 226-4090

OTTAWA CABINET CO. LTD.
24 FLORENCE
OTTAWA, ONTARIO K2P 0W7
(613) 234-0552

• **PRESTON**
310 SOMERSET STREET WEST
OTTAWA, ONTARIO K2P 0J9
(613) 232-7175 **Pg. 72, 148**

REISMAN, CARIN C. DESIGN
146 ROGER ROAD
OTTAWA, ONTARIO K1H 5C8
(613) 733-5441

ROLLIN, MICHEL INTERIORS
5 ARLINGTON AVENUE
OTTAWA, ONTARIO K2P 1C1
(613) 233-3408

S & H PLANNING ASSOCIATES LTD.
148 BANK STREET
OTTAWA, ONTARIO K1P 5N8
(613) 235-1165

**SAUNDERS-McFARLANE
DESIGN CONSULTANTS INC.**
157 GILMOUR
OTTAWA, ONTARIO K2P 0N8
(613) 237-4481

• **SIMPSONS
COMMERCIAL INTERIORS & DESIGN**
275 SLATER STREET
OTTAWA, ONTARIO K1P 5H9
(613) 237-3996 **Pg. 150**

SPACESCAPES INTERIORS INC.
53 QUEEN STREET
OTTAWA, ONTARIO K1P 5C5
(613) 235-4677

**SMIT–BOURTON CORPORATE
DESIGN & PLANNING LTD.**
379 METCALFE
OTTAWA, ONTARIO K2P 1S7
(613) 233-1945

TAYLOR-IRVING & ASSOCIATES
325 DALHOUSIE
OTTAWA, ONTARIO K1N 7G2
(613) 236-7702

THATCHER, CARROLL DESIGN INC.
311 RICHMOND ROAD
OTTAWA, ONTARIO K1Z 6X3
(613) 729-2646

TIMM ROBINSON INTERIORS
193 BANK STREET
OTTAWA, ONTARIO K2P 1W7
(613) 232-2649

TREASURES DECORATIVE ARTS STUDIO
145 YORK STREET
OTTAWA, ONTARIO K1N 5Y3
(613) 235-3015

VAN LEUWEN BOOMKAMP LTD.
430 HIGHWAY 7
KANATA, ONTARIO K2L 1T9
(613) 836-1400

VILLENEUVE, MICHELE INTERIOR DESIGN
50 FLORENCE STREET
OTTAWA, ONTARIO K2P 0W7
(613) 234-4323

**WATSON, TED
INTERIOR DESIGNER & CONSULTANT**
316 DALHOUSIE
OTTAWA, ONTARIO K1N 7E7
(613) 232-4295

WOZNIAK, J. DESIGN INC.
98 LEOPOLDS DRIVE
OTTAWA, ONTARIO K1V 7E3
(613) 233-9379

Pickering

• **HOLMES & BRAKEL LIMITED**
935 BROCK ROAD SOUTH
PICKERING, ONTARIO L1W 2X9
(416) 683-6222 **Pg. 144**

JPN PLANNING ASSOCIATES LTD.
824 ELVIRA COURT SOUTH
PICKERING, ONTARIO L1W 2L1
(416) 839-7557

• **OMNIPLAN DESIGN GROUP LIMITED**
92 CHURCH STREET SOUTH
PICKERING, ONTARIO L1V 2S6
(416) 427-2902 **Pg. 94**

Stratford

BROCK, JOHN ARCHITECTS
151 NILE STREET
STRATFORD, ONTARIO N5A 4E1
(519) 271-4603

WAYSIDE INTERIORS
150 HURON
STRATFORD, ONTARIO N5A 5S8
(519) 273-0880

Sudbury

CALLINGHAM CONTRACT INTERIORS
1535 PARIS
SUDBURY, ONTARIO P3E 3B7
(705) 522-5227

MANOR HOUSE INTERIOR DESIGNS
251 ELM WEST
SUDBURY, ONTARIO P3C 1V5
(705) 673-1773

PARAMOUNT HOME FURNISHINGS LTD.
327 ELM WEST
SUDBURY, ONTARIO P3C 1V7
(705) 674-6427

• **SIMPSONS
COMMERCIAL INTERIORS & DESIGN**
96 LARCH STREET
SUDBURY, ONTARIO P3E 1C1
(705) 673-4181 **Pg. 150**

Including: Concord, Don Mills, Etobicoke, Islington, Markham, Mississauga, Rexdale, Richmond Hill, Scarborough, Thornhill, Toronto, Weston.

ACCETTE, GUY INTERIORS LTD.
55 YORK STREET
TORONTO, ONTARIO M5J 1R7
(416) 368-9287

ADAMS, LEONARD INC.
65 HIGH PARK AVENUE
TORONTO, ONTARIO M6P 2R7
(416) 769-2814

ADAMS, RON S.
2 AUSTIN CR.
TORONTO, ONTARIO M5R 3E3
(416) 533-7772

AGENDA LTD.
1125B LESLIE STREET
DON MILLS, ONTARIO M3C 2J6
(416) 445-7429

• **AGNELLI-ORSINI DESIGN INC.**
2 PHOEBE STREET
TORONTO, ONTARIO M5T 1A7
(416) 593-0633 **Pg. 37**

• **AID 2000 INC.**
101 FRESHWAY DRIVE, UNIT 66D
CONCORD, ONTARIO L9K 1R9
(416) 661-6433 **Pg. 36**

ALBERTINE DESIGN CENTRE, THE
225 MACPHERSON AVENUE
TORONTO, ONTARIO M4V 1A1
(416) 964-0600

• **ALEXANDER'S FINE FURNITURE**
717 KIPLING AVENUE
TORONTO, ONTARIO M8Z 5G4
(416) 252-9347 **Pg. 166**

ALLEN, BEVERLEY INTERIORS
160 BEDFORD
TORONTO, ONTARIO M5R 2K9
(416) 927-8720

**ALLEN, PATRICK JOHN
INTERIOR DESIGN**
53 BEACHVIEW CRESCENT
TORONTO, ONTARIO M4E 2L6
(416) 699-0273

AMES, DOROTHY DESIGN STUDIO LTD.
145 ROXBOROUGH WEST
TORONTO, ONTARIO M5R 1T9
(416) 922-4769

ART SHOPPE
2131 YONGE STREET
TORONTO, ONTARIO M4S 2A6
(416) 487-3211

ASHMOUNT INTERIOR ENTERPRISES LTD.
1451 ROYAL YORK
WESTON, ONTARIO M9P 3B2
(416) 248-4275

**ATKINSON McLEOD DESIGN
CONSULTANTS LTD.**
211 YONGE STREET
TORONTO, ONTARIO M5B 1M4
(416) 362-2311

ATWOOD'S EXECUTIVE OFFICE INTERIORS
110 BLOOR STREET WEST, SUITE 304
TORONTO, ONTARIO M5S 2W7
(416) 968-0820

AYLWIN, E.D.
83 HOWLAND AVENUE
TORONTO, ONTARIO M5R 3B2
(416) 925-6295

**B & H INTERIORS
A DIVISION OF BREGMAN & HAMANN
ARCHITECTS & ENGINEERS**
481 UNIVERSITY AVENUE
TORONTO, ONTARIO M5G 2H4
(416) 596-2299

BABCOCK ZANNER INCORPORATED
118 AVENUE ROAD
TORONTO, ONTARIO M5R 2H4
(416) 920-8162

BAKER, LAURA INTERIOR DESIGN
95 THORNCLIFFE PARK DRIVE
TORONTO, ONTARIO M4H 1L6
(416) 425-0016

BANCLIFFE INTERIORS
2014 QUEEN STREAT EAST
TORONTO, ONTARIO M4L 1J3
(416) 694-3423

**SONIA BANGAY
INTERIOR DESIGN CONSULTANT**
165 KINGSWOOD ROAD
TORONTO, ONTARIO M4E 3N4
(416) 698-3159

BANRI & ASSOCIATES
173 MARGUERETTA STREET
TORONTO, ONTARIO M6H 3S4
(416) 535-5933

BARONE, MICHAEL & ASSOCIATES
393 NUGGET AVENUE
TORONTO, ONTARIO M1S 4G3
(416) 299-1090

BARTELLO'S
2 BERNARD AVENUE
TORONTO, ONTARIO M5R 1R2
(416) 967-6311

• **BARTLETT INGER & ASSOCIATES**
2A GIBSON AVENUE
TORONTO, ONTARIO M5R 1T5
(416) 926-8247 **Pg. 40**

BEATON FLOY LTD.
212 ROSE PARK DRIVE
TORONTO, ONTARIO M4T 1R5
(416) 483-2487

BELL, LEE INTERIORS LTD.
47 THORNCLIFFE PARK DRIVE
TORONTO, ONTARIO M4H 1J5
(416) 421-0825

• **BENITZ & BENITZ LTD.**
355 BERKELEY STREET
TORONTO, ONTARIO M5A 2X6
(416) 926-1632 **Pg. 39**

BERKELEY INTERIOR DESIGN LTD.
55 BERKELEY
TORONTO, ONTARIO M5A 2W5
(416) 368-4676

BERLONI DESIGN ASSOCIATES
1778 WESTON ROAD
TORONTO, ONTARIO M9N 1V8
(416) 241-6408

BERNARD & ASSOCIATES
144 FRONT STREET WEST
TORONTO, ONTARIO M5J 1G2
(416) 979-1100

• **BIGIO, JOSEPH INTERIOR DESIGN INC.**
600 EGLINTON AVENUE WEST
TORONTO, ONTARIO M5N 1C1
(416) 481-5423 **Pg. 84**

BLAIN, CHRISTOPHER INC.
221 AVENUE ROAD
TORONTO, ONTARIO M5R 2J3
(416) 923-2458

BLEAKLEY LABBETT LTD.
25 HAYDEN STREET
TORONTO, ONTARIO M4Y 2P2
(416) 923-2442

BOORMAN, LINDA INTERIORS LTD.
23 CASTLE KNOCK
TORONTO, ONTARIO M5N 2J3
(416) 483-8447

BRADMAN, DON ASSOCIATES
56 THE ESPLANADE
TORONTO, ONTARIO M5E 1A6
(416) 368-0054

BRAEM & MINNETTI INTERIORS
1262 YONGE STREET
TORONTO, ONTARIO M4T 1W5
(416) 923-7437

BRAY, HAROLD INTERIORS LTD.
1790 ALBION
REXDALE, ONTARIO M9V 4J8
(416) 749-7811

BRISLAND, WILLIAM DESIGN INC.
27 DAVIES AVENUE
TORONTO, ONTARIO M4M 2A9
(416) 469-5208

BRITACAN BUSINESS INTERIORS LTD.
505 CONSUMMERS ROAD
WILLOWDALE, ONTARIO M2J 4V8
(416) 494-2007

BROCK, JOHN C,
81A FRONT STREET EAST
TORONTO, ONTARIO M5E 1B8
(416) 366-1333

BROWN, GERRY & ASSOCIATES INC.
50 GERVAIS DRIVE
DON MILLS, ONTARIO M3C 1W2
(416) 449-6444

BURANDT INTERIORS LTD.
63 BERKELEY
TORONTO, ONTARIO M5A 2W5
(416) 864-1331

BURKE, CATHERINE
DESIGN CONSULTANTS
72 BALMORAL AVENUE
TORONTO, ONTARIO M4V 1J4
(416) 923-6562

• **BURNELL, DAVID/BY DESIGN ONLY**
3015 QUEEN STREET EAST
SCARBOROUGH, ONTARIO M1N 1A5
(416) 699-0352 **Pg. 133**

BURO DECOR INC.
3 CHURCH STREET
TORONTO, ONTARIO M5E 1M2
(416) 860-1400

BUSAT DESIGN ASSOCIATES
298 MERTON STREET
TORONTO, ONTARIO M4S 1A9
(416) 487-4191

CWD INTERIORS & CONSULTANTS LTD.
151 CARLINGVIEW DRIVE
REXDALE, ONTARIO M9W 5S4
(416) 675-2225

• **CABRERA, RAFAELL INTERNATIONAL**
914 YONGE STREET
TORONTO, ONTARIO M4W 3C8
(416) 964-6947 **Pg. 119**

CAMPAIS DESIGN
77 PROGRESS
SCARBOROUGH, ONTARIO M1P 2Y7
(416) 298-0320

CAMPBELL – ALLEN DESIGN
2300 YONGE STREET
TORONTO, ONTARIO M4P 1E4
(416) 482-5292

CANTU DISEGNO
71 McCAUL
TORONTO, ONTARIO M5T 2X1
(416) 977-7273

CAVILLA DESIGNS INC.
23 ROSEMONT AVENUE
THORNHILL, ONTARIO L3T 6E5
(416) 889-8896

• **CECCONI EPPSTADT SIMONE**
663 QUEEN STREET EAST
TORONTO, ONTARIO M4M 1G4
(416) 462-1445 **Pg. 44**

• **CHABAN, ROBERT J. AND ASSOCIATES**
268 LAKESHORE ROAD EAST
PORT CREDIT, ONTARIO L5G 1H1
(416) 274-1510 **Pg. 106**

CHAMI DESIGN ASSOCIATES
264 SPRING GARDEN AVENUE
WILLOWDALE, ONTARIO M2N 3G9
(416) 222-4198

• **CHAPMAN, ALEX DESIGN LTD.**
49 SPADINA AVENUE
TORONTO, ONTARIO M5V 2J1
(416) 597-1576 **Pg. 124**

• **CHENIER, D. ASSOCIATES LTD.**
263 AVENUE ROAD
TORONTO, ONTARIO M5R 2J4
(416) 964-1545 **Pg. 46**

CHENG, JOSEPH INTERIOR DESIGN INC.
22 HOUSTON CRESCENT
WILLOWDALE, ONTARIO M2J 3H8
(416) 497-0556

CHILDREN'S DESIGN CENTRE INC.
549 EGLINTON AVENUE WEST
TORONTO, ONTARIO M5N 1B5
(416) 488-6666

CHRISTENSEN, RANDY & ASSOCIATES LTD.
229 MACPHERSON AVENUE
TORONTO, ONTARIO M4V 1A1
(416) 928-9024

• **CITIWORKS DESIGN INC.**
296 RICHMOND STREET WEST
TORONTO, ONTARIO M5V 1X2
(416) 531-5749 **Pg. 42, 87**

COLLINS DESIGN GROUP
INTERNATIONAL
550 ALDEN ROAD
MARKHAM, ONTARIO L3R 6A8
(416) 479-4919

COMFIND
2350 BRIDLETOWNE CIR.
TORONTO, ONTARIO M1W 3R8
(416) 498-7920

COMMERCESPACE DESIGN LTD.
85 EGLINTON AVENUE EAST
TORONTO, ONTARIO M4P 1H5
(416) 489-6936

COMMERCIAL DESIGN GROUP
505 EGLINTON AVENUE WEST
TORONTO, ONTARIO M5N 3A2
(416) 488-7554

CORPORATE BUSINESS INTERIORS
562 EGLINTON AVENUE EAST
TORONTO, ONTARIO M4P 1B6
(416) 485-5111

CONCEPTS INTERIOR DESIGN
117 MANVILLE
SCARBOROUGH, ONTARIO M1L 4J7
(416) 752-4559

CONNOISSEUR, THE
194 DAVENPORT
TORONTO, ONTARIO M5R 1J2
(416) 925-1020

CORPLAN DESIGN INC.
69 SHERBOURNE STREET
TORONTO, ONTARIO M5A 3X7
(416) 863-6630

CORPORATE OFFICE DESIGN INC.
1903 LESLIE STREET
TORONTO, ONTARIO M3B 2M3
(416) 447-8507

• **COTTON, PETER C. INC.**
56 THE ESPLANADE
TORONTO, ONTARIO M5E 1A7
(416) 863-6743 **Pg. 103**

CSAGOLY ASSOCIATES INC.
35 ANNESLEY AVENUE
TORONTO, ONTARIO M4G 2T5
(416) 482-0002

CURR DESIGN CORPORATION
464 KING STREET EAST
TORONTO, ONTARIO M5A 1L7
(416) 366-2234

DI DESIGN AND DEVELOPMENT
CONSULTANTS LTD.
110 BOND STREET
TORONTO, ONTARIO M5B 1X8
(416) 595-9598

DANA CONSULTANTS LTD.
19 YORKVILLE
TORONTO, ONTARIO M4W 1L1
(416) 924-8453

DANN DUNN DESIGNS INC.
3240A YONGE STREET
TORONTO, ONTARIO M4N 2L4
(416) 483-0629

DARRAGH DESIGN ASSOCIATES LTD.
77 MOWAT AVENUE
TORONTO, ONTARIO M6K 3E3
(416) 534-7519

DEBRA'S DESIGN INTERIORS
66 HOWLAND AVENUE
TORONTO, ONTARIO M5R 2B3
(416) 537-2631

DESICON PLUS
146 WEST BEAVER CREER ROAD
RICHMOND HILL, ONTARIO L4B 1C2
(416) 731-7151

DESIGN GROUP CONSULTANTS LTD.
2 GLOUCESTER
TORONTO, ONTARIO M4Y 1L5
(416) 967-1500

• **DESIGN PLANNING ASSOCIATES**
322 KING STREET WEST
TORONTO, ONTARIO M5V 1J2
(416) 977-2355 **Pg. 43**

DESIGN TEAM PLUS LTD.
111 RAILSIDE ROAD
DON MILLS, ONTARIO M3A 1B2
(416) 443-1516

DESIGNCORP LTD.
48 SHERBOURNE
TORONTO, ONTARIO M5A 2P7
(416) 263-4622

DESIGNING WOMEN
112 MERTON STREET
TORONTO, ONTARIO M4S 2Z8
(416) 489-2470

DESMOND INTERIORS
79 HAZELTON
TORONTO, ONTARIO M5R 2E4
(416) 922-8087

DESTAR DESIGN LTD.
284 KING STREET WEST
TORONTO, ONTARIO M5V 1J2
(416) 596-0486

DIRSTEIN ROBERTSON LTD.
77 YORKVILLE
TORONTO, ONTARIO M5R 1C1
(416) 961-6211

DIRSTEIN & WEALE INTERIORS LTD.
369 EGLINTON AVENUE WEST
TORONTO, ONTARIO M5N 1A2
(416) 481-1155

DOWNTON, JOHN INTERIORS LTD.
50 PRINCE ARTHUR
TORONTO, ONTARIO M5R 1B5
(416) 964-8819

DOWNER, ERIC INTERIORS LTD.
116 PURVIS CRESCENT
SCARBOROUGH, ONTARIO M1B 1H9
(416) 291-3155

• **DUNCAN, CHERYL L. AND ASOCIATES**
80 FRONT STREET EAST
TORONTO, ONTARIO M4E 1T4
(416) 967-6090 **Pg. 126**

• **EATON'S CONTRACT INTERIORS**
2130 LAWRENCE AVENUE EAST
SCARBOROUGH, ONTARIO M1R 3A6
(416) 752-4900 **Pg. 52, 108, 143**

ELLIS, MICHAEL & ASSOCIATES
82 ARUNDEL
TORONTO, ONTARIO M4K 3A4
(416) 465-5698

ELLMAN DESIGN CONSULTANTS LTD.
67 MOWAT AVENUE
TORONTO, ONTARIO M6K 3E3
(416) 531-3569

ERDOS-POLLAK DESIGN CONSULTANTS
194 WILSON AVENUE
TORONTO, ONTARIO M5M 3A7
(416) 489-5128

ARTHUR ERICKSON
80 BLOOR STREET WEST
TORONTO, ONTARIO M5S 2V1
(416) 967-4477

• **FIELDING & ASSOCIATES**
300 NORTH QUEEN STREET
ETOBICOKE, ONTARIO M9C 5K4
(416) 626-6727 **Pg. 51**

FLETCHER, SHEILAGH
DESIGN CONSULTANTS
431 RICHMOND STREET EAST
TORONTO, ONTARIO M5A 1R1
(416) 864-9146

• **FORREST/BODRUG PARTNERS INC.**
439 UNIVERSITY AVENUE
TORONTO, ONTARIO M5G 1Y8
(416) 598-2965 **Pg. 58**

FRANKLAND RUSZNYAK
ASSOCIATES LTD.
228 GERRARD STREET EAST
TORONTO, ONTARIO M5A 2E8
(416) 928-7422

FRENCKLES AND CO.
18 BELMONT
TORONTO, ONTARIO M5R 1P8
(416) 920-2763

FREUND, FRANCES R.
DESIGN CONSULTANTS
94 CUMBERLAND
TORONTO, ONTARIO M5R 1A3
(416) 964-6540

FUTURIC OFFICE SYSTEM AND DESIGN
410 CONSUMERS ROAD
WILLOWDALE, ONTARIO M2J 1P9
(416) 494-7902

FUTURIC SPACE PLANNING SYSTEMS
361 SUPERTEST ROAD
DOWNSVIEW, ONTARIO M3J 2M4
(416) 667-1006

GALEA, ELLIS CONSULTANTS LTD.
329 ST. GEORGE STREET
TORONTO, ONTARIO M5R 2R2
(416) 922-8848

GALLIVANT INC.
181 GLENROSE AVENUE
TORONTO, ONTARIO M4T 1K7
(416) 482-8668

GEDDES, ELISABETH
DESIGN CONSULTANT
79 BERKELEY
TORONTO, ONTARIO M5A 2W7
(416) 364-1260

• **GIANNA DESIGN ASSOCIATES**
593 YONGE STREET
TORONTO, ONTARIO M4Y 1Z4
(416) 967-1761 **Pg. 109**

GILES & ASSOCIATES
2 MAGNOLIA
SCARBOROUGH, ONTARIO M1K 3K1
(416) 261-7010

• **GIO TAN DESIGN ASSOCIATES INC.**
169 CARLTON STREET
TORONTO, ONTARIO M5A 2K3
(416) 926-1937 **Pg. 56**

GIRARD ROGERS DESIGN
86 ROSELAWN
TORONTO, ONTARIO M4R 1E6
(416) 534-7004

GLUCKSTEIN DESIGN PLANNING INC.
321 DAVENPORT ROAD
TORONTO, ONTARIO M5R 1K5
(416) 928-2067

GUILD, JOHN INTERIOR DESIGN LTD.
310 DAVENPORT ROAD
TORONTO, ONTARIO M5R 1K6
(416) 922-3700

GUTHRIL, W.J. PLANNING ASSOCIATES
797 DON MILLS ROAD
DON MILLS, ONTARIO M3C 1V1
(416) 429-3230

HAHN, D. ASSOCIATES
PLANNERS & DESIGNERS
107 SCOLLARD
TORONTO, ONTARIO M5R 1G4
(416) 967-3718

HAMILTON DESIGN
874 MAGNETIC DRIVE
DOWNSVIEW, ONTARIO M3J 2C4
(416) 661-3927

HANNA, DOROTHY DESIGN
25 PRICE
TORONTO, ONTARIO M4W 1Z1
(416) 964-4821

HARRISON/BLACK
PARTNERSHIP ARCHITECTS
1681 BAYVIEW AVENUE, SUITE 200
TORONTO, ONTARIO M4G 3C1
(416) 489-0893

HEFELE MAKOWKA
87 MOWAT AVENUE
TORONTO, ONTARIO M6K 3E3
(416) 534-6666

• **HELENA INTERIORS**
103 AVA ROAD
TORONTO, ONTARIO M6C 1V9
(416) 787-7595 **Pg. 136**

• **HERCZEGH, INGRID INC.**
54 AUSTIN TERRACE
TORONTO, ONTARIO M5R 1Y6
(416) 533-7034 **Pg. 110**

HERITAGE INTERIORS
224 DAVENPORT
TORONTO, ONTARIO M5R 1J7
(416) 922-6448

HEYBURN LIEBERMAN LTD.
40 KODIAK CRESCENT
DOWNSVIEW, ONTARIO M3J 3G5
(416) 633-9933

• **HIRSCHBERG, MARTIN**
DESIGN ASSOCIATES LTD.
334 QUEEN STREET EAST
TORONTO, ONTARIO M5A 1S8
(416) 868-1210 **Pg. 112**

HOLMAN DESIGN
21 KERN ROAD
DON MILLS, ONTARIO M3B 1S9
(416) 441-1877

• **HOLMBERG AULD INC.**
260 RICHMOND STREET EAST
TORONTO, ONTARIO M5A 1P4
(416) 364-2950 **Pg. 57**

HOLMES, BRIAN G. LTD.
BUSINESS INTERIORS
81 McPHERSON STREET
MARKHAM, ONTARIO L3R 3L3
(416) 475-0166

HOUGHTON DESIGNS LTD.
81-A LOWTHER
TORONTO, ONTARIO M5R 1C9
(416) 967-5246

HOWLETT DESIGN CONSULTANTS LTD.
144 FRONT STREET WEST
TORONTO, ONTARIO M5J 2L7
(416) 977-5281

• **HUI, ALBERT DESIGN ASSOCIATES**
742 QUEEN STREET WEST
TORONTO, ONTARIO M6J 1E9
(416) 869-0894 **Pg. 111**

HYMAS, ALISON
DESIGN ASSOCIATES INC.
322 KING STREET WEST
TORONTO, ONTARIO M5V 1J2
(416) 977-8387

IDACA ARCHITECTURAL INTERIORS
270 AVENUE ROAD
TORONTO, ONTARIO M4V 2G7
(416) 964-6264

• **IDEA CONSULTANTS INC.**
250 THE ESPLANADE
TORONTO, ONTARIO M5A 1J2
(416) 860-1679 **Pg. 114**

IMPRIMUS DESIGN CONSULTANTS
78 HUMBER CREST BLVD
TORONTO, ONTARIO M6S 4L1
(416) 762-8076

• **INTEFAC INC.**
5420 TIMBERLEA BLVD.
MISSISSAUGA, ONTARIO L4W 2T7
(416) 624-6700 **Pg. 61, 145**

• **INTER-DESIGN**
30 RIDLEY GARDENS
TORONTO, ONTARIO M6R 2T8
(416) 532-9435 **Pg. 88**

INTERCEDE FACILITY MANAGEMENT LTD.
1220 ELLESMERE
SCARBOROUGH, ONTARIO M1P 2X5
(416) 292-1997

INTERIORS BY OLGA MACLELLAN
14 VICTOR
TORONTO, ONTARIO M4K 1A8
(416) 465-8824

INTERIORS PLUS INC.
50 GALAXY BLVD.
REXDALE, ONTARIO M9W 4Y4
(416) 675-7993

INTERNATIONAL DESIGN GROUP INC., THE
188 AVENUE ROAD
TORONTO, ONTARIO M5R 2J1
(416) 961-1811

INTERSPACE
151 NASHDENE ROAD
SCARBOROUGH, ONTARIO M1V 2T3
(416) 299-7788

**IRVINE, HERBERT & JULIE LOMBARD
INTERIOR DESIGN**
9 ROSEMARY LANE
TORONTO, ONTARIO M5P 3E7
(416) 781-7229

IVEY DESIGN CONCEPTS LTD.
139 SPRUCE
TORONTO, ONTARIO M5A 2J6
(416) 961-7153

JD DESIGN
285 MACPHERSON AVENUE
TORONTO, ONTARIO M4V 1A4
(416) 928-6766

• **JEFFREY/BULLOCK
DESIGN CONSULTANTS INC.**
55 UNIVERSITY AVENUE
TORONTO, ONTARIO M5J 2H7
(416) 868-1616 **Pg. 60**

JOHNSTON DESIGN ASSOCIATES LTD.
406 KING STREET EAST
TORONTO, ONTARIO M5A 1L4
(416) 362-0703

JOHNSTON, ROBERT DESIGNS INC.
25 LIBERTY STREET
TORONTO, ONTARIO M6K 1A6
(416) 535-6077

JOLANDA INTERIORS
2368 BLOOR STREET WEST
TORONTO, ONTARIO M6S 1P5
(416) 762-9638

KEARNS MANCINI ARCHITECTS
269 RICHMOND STREET WEST
TORONTO, ONTARIO M5V 1X1
(416) 585-2332

• **KETCHESON, DONALD LTD.**
13 CLARENCE SQUARE
TORONTO, ONTARIO M5V 1H1
(416) 593-0744 **Pg. 62**

KING, DALE K. INTERIOR DESIGN
456 PAPE AVENUE
TORONTO, ONTARIO M4K 3P7
(416) 469-0507

• **KING, NORMA DESIGN INC.**
114A SACKVILLE STREET
TORONTO, ONTARIO M5A 3E7
(416) 862-9180 **Pg. 128**

KIRK, A.G. CONSULTANTS LTD.
205 RICHMOND STREET WEST
TORONTO, ONTARIO M5V 1V5
(416) 595-1737

KNOX, RANDY INTERIOR DESIGN INC.
65 CASTLE FRANK ROAD
TORONTO, ONTARIO M4W 2Z9
(416) 961-7133

• **KURTZ MANN DESIGN**
390 DUPONT STREET
TORONTO, ONTARIO M5R 1V9
(416) 927-0353 **Pg. 154**

• **KYRANIS, CHRIS & ASSOCIATES LTD.**
5233 DUNDAS STREET WEST
ISLINGTON, ONTARIO M9B 1A6
(416) 239-0549 **Pg. 90**

LAUMANN, GERRARD LTD.
154 DAVENPORT ROAD
TORONTO, ONTARIO M5R 1J2
(416) 964-2323

LAURENCE, ROBERT DESIGNS
267½ QUEEN STREET EAST
TORONTO, ONTARIO M5A 1S6
(416) 363-1157

LEE, W. INTERIOR DESIGN INC.
523 THE QUEENSWAY
TORONTO, ONTARIO M8Y 1J7
(416) 252-7115

LEMPICKI, B. INTERIORS
50 PRINCE ARHUR
TORONTO, ONTARIO M5R 1B5
(416) 925-1194

LETT-SMITH ARCHITECTS
1170-R YONGE STREET
TORONTO, ONTARIO M4W 2L9
(416) 968-6990

L'IMAGE DESIGN
7100 WARDEN AVENUE
MARKHAM, ONTARIO L3R 5M7
(416) 475-7703

LINEATION LTD.
352 MELROSE AVENUE
TORONTO, ONTARIO M5M 1Z4
(416) 789-3232

LISKA, HENRY G. AND ASSOCIATES INC.
26 TRANBY AVENUE
TORONTO, ONTARIO M5R 1N5
(416) 928-0074

LOATES, W. & ASSOCIATES
819 YONGE STREET
TORONTO, ONTARIO M4W 2G9
(416) 964-6335

**LOVETT, DAVID
DESIGN CONSULTANTS INC.**
366 ADELAIDE STREET WEST
TORONTO, ONTARIO M5A 1X3
(416) 368-0072

LUNA PARK
67 MOWAT AVENUE
TORONTO, ONTARIO M6K 3E3
(416) 536-3807

LYONS, CECILY INTERIOR DESIGN
444 ST. GERMAIN
TORONTO, ONTARIO M5M 1X1
(416) 789-0413

• **MDI DESIGN CONSULTANTS INC.**
72 FRASER AVENUE
TORONTO, ONTARIO M6K 3E1
(416) 533-4642 **Pg. 91**

MJ DESIGN CONSULTANTS
373 QUEEN STREET EAST
TORONTO, ONTARIO M5A 1T2
(416) 364-0494

MACKAY DESIGN ASSOCIATES
1701 BATHURST STREET
TORONTO, ONTARIO M5P 3K2
(416) 481-7917

MACLELLAN & ASSOCIATES
401 RICHMOND STREET WEST
TORONTO, ONTARIO M5V 1X3
(416) 232-0306

MAJ DESIGN ASSOCIATES
1248 AVENUE ROAD
TORONTO, ONTARIO M5N 2G7
(416) 489-0793

MM INTERIORS LTD.
7315 WOODBINE AVENUE
MARKHAM, ONTARIO L3R 3V7
(416) 475-9181

• **MANION, BURT INTERIOR DESIGN LTD.**
283 MACPHERSON AVENUE
TORONTO, ONTARIO M4V 1A4
(416) 923-6611 **Pg. 138**

MANNING MARTIN LIMITED
406 SUMMERHILL AVENUE
TORONTO, ONTARIO M4W 2E4
(416) 963-4311

**MANOLIU, MARIA & ASSOCIATES
DESIGN CONSULTANTS LTD.**
372 BAY STREET
TORONTO, ONTARIO M5H 2W9
(416) 860-1511

• **MARCUS, H.D. ENTERPRISES INC.**
294 BERKELEY STREET
TORONTO, ONTARIO M5A 2X5
(416) 967-7617 **Pg. 276**

MARGULIS, DAVID B. & ASSOCIATES INC.
413 DUNDAS STREET EAST
TORONTO, ONTARIO M5A 2A9
(416) 363-3303

MARKSON JEROME ARCHITECTS
161 DAVENPORT
TORONTO, ONTARIO M5R 1J1
(416) 920-3131

• **MAROUHOS, SAM AND ASSOCIATES**
17 ST. JOSEPH STREET
TORONTO, ONTARIO M4Y 1J8
(416) 923-4074 **Pg. 92**

• **MARSHALL CUMMINGS & ASSOCIATES LTD.**
43 DAVIES AVENUE
TORONTO, ONTARIO M4M 2A9
(416) 461-3563 **Pg. 64**

MARSHALL, ROBERT
597 CONCORD
TORONTO, ONTARIO M6H 2R2
(416) 532-8181

MASTER DESIGN GROUP
550 ALDEN ROAD
MARKHAM, ONTARIO L3R 6A8
(416) 479-4466

MARZOTTO-RUBB ASSOCIATES
875 EGLINTON AVENUE WEST
TORONTO, ONTARIO M6C 2B9
(416) 782-8902

MASTRANGELI, GINO & ASSOCIATES LTD.
28 OAKLEY BLVD.
SCARBOROUGH, ONTARIO M1P 3P3
(416) 755-9419

MATHESON-WILSON LTD.
108 QUEEN STREET EAST
TORONTO, ONTARIO M5C 1S6
(416) 366-9951

MATTHEW DESIGN ASSOCIATES
46 STEPHENSON AVENUE
TORONTO, ONTARIO M4C 1G1
(416) 699-6725

MAYHEW AND PETERSON INC.
64 PRINCE ARTHUR PLACE
DON MILLS, ONTARIO M3C 2H4
(416) 444-7315

McBURNEY A. MARK
76 BERKELEY STREET
TORONTO, ONTARIO M5A 2W7
(416) 863-1980

• **McWATT ANDERSON
DESIGN CONSULTANTS INC.**
67 MOWAT AVENUE
TORONTO, ONTARIO M6K 3E3
(416) 530-4800 **Pg. 66**

MEICKLE, BETTY INTERIORS
46 ELGIN
TORONTO, ONTARIO M5B 1G6
(416) 881-2227

**MEICKEJOHN, ROBERT
DESIGN ASSOCIATES**
133 LOWTHER
TORONTO, ONTARIO M5R 1E4
(416) 964-2081

MELFORD DESIGNS
31 MELFORD DRIVE
SCARBOROUGH, ONTARIO M1B 2G6
(416) 299-4333

• **MICHAUD DESIGN CONSULTANTS**
24 KEW BEACH AVENUE
TORONTO, ONTARIO M4L 1B7
(416) 690-6422 **Pg. 93**

**MILNE-MAUREEN MILNE
INTERIOR DESIGN LTD.**
73-A ROXBOROUGH WEST
TORONTO, ONTARIO M5R 1T9
(416) 960-3811

MOFFET, HELEN ASSOCIATES LTD.
45-A HAZELTON AVENUE
TORONTO, ONTARIO M5R 2E3
(416) 925-3831

• **MOLE WHITE & ASSOCIATES LTD.**
260 KING STREET EAST 4TH FLOOR
TORONTO, ONTARIO M5V 1H9
(416) 867-1414 **Pg. 63**

MONO THOUGHT INC.
2466 DUNDAS STREET WEST
TORONTO, ONTARIO M6P 1W9
(416) 530-0859

**MOORHEAD FLEMING
CORBAN McCARTHY**
33 BRITAIN STREET
TORONTO, ONTARIO M5A 1R7
(416) 366-9238

MORDEN, JACQUELINE INTERIORS LTD.
4192 DUNDAS STREET WEST
TORONTO, ONTARIO M8X 1X3
(416) 233-3636

• **MOREL INTERIORS**
162 CUMBERLAND STREET
TORONTO, ONTARIO M5R 3N5
(416) 961-3385 **Pg. 139**

**NEWBIGGING, MARGARET
INTERIORS INC.**
99 NORTON
WILLOWDALE, ONTARIO M2N 4A4
(416) 221-8883

**NICHOLS, RONALD A.
ENVIRONMENTAL DESIGN**
110 BLOOR STREET WEST
TORONTO, ONTARIO M5S 1P7
(416) 923-5648

NOAKES COHEN LTD.
1250 BAY STREET
TORONTO, ONTARIO M5R 2B1
(416) 967-2800

NOFFKE, EDGAR W. INTERIORS
27 MACLENNAN
TORONTO, ONTARIO M4W 2Y5
(416) 922-8366

NORTH, JOHN S. DESIGNERS INC.
4 HILLHOLM ROAD
TORONTO, ONTARIO M5P 1M2
(416) 485-3323

OLIVER, MURRAY W. LTD.
19 EDGEWOOD CRESCENT
TORONTO, ONTARIO M4W 3A8
(416) 923-6240

**O.E. INC.
(OFFICE EQUIPMENT CO. OF CANADA)**
525 DENISON
MARKHAM, ONTARIO L3R 1B8
(416) 491-9330

OMEGA DESIGN TEAM, THE
11 C LAIDLAW ROAD
MARKHAM, ONTARIO L3P 1W5
(416) 294-3931

OMNISPACE ENVIRONMENTS INC.
260 RICHMOND STREET WEST
TORONTO, ONTARIO M5V 1W5
(416) 591-7000

• **OVE DESIGN INTERIORS INC.**
29 COMMERCIAL ROAD
TORONTO, ONTARIO M4G 1Z3
(416) 423-6228 **Pg. 70**

PANACHE DESIGN LIMITED
361 KING STREET EAST
TORONTO, ONTARIO M5A 1L1
(416) 369-0084

• **POI DESIGN CONSULTANTS**
120 VALLEYWOOD DRIVE
MARKHAM, ONTARIO L3R 6A7
(416) 479-1123 **Pg. 146**

PEGGIE–JOYCE INTERIORS LTD.
1742 AVENUE ROAD
TORONTO, ONTARIO M5N 2G7
(416) 787-1100

PELLOW ARCHITECT
214 KING STREET WEST
TORONTO, ONTARIO M5M 1K4
(416) 593-5660

PLUS 5 INTERIORS
1230 YONGE STREET
TORONTO, ONTARIO M4T 1W3
(416) 923-5231

• **PRESTON**
500 UNIVERSITY AVENUE, 10TH FLOOR
TORONTO, ONTARIO M5G 1V7
(416) 598-3540 **Pg. 72, 148**

• **PULSANN**
111 QUEEN STREET EAST
TORONTO, ONTARIO M5C 1S2
(416) 865-1196 **Pg. 71**

RDL DESIGN CONSULTANTS
8 BIRCH AVENUE
TORONTO, ONTARIO M4V 1G8
(416) 968-0133

RGS DESIGNS
360 BLOOR STREET EAST
TORONTO, ONTARIO M4W 3M3
(416) 960-0488

• **RAITT, LYNN INTERIORS**
190 ST. GEORGE STREET
TORONTO, ONTARIO M5R 2N4
(416) 723-1244 **Pg. 95**

REBANKS, LESLIE ARCHITECTS
22 ST. CLAIR AVENUE EAST
TORONTO, ONTARIO M4T 2S3
(416) 964-7163

RENTON, E.S. DESIGN INTERIORS
5128 DUNDAS STREET WEST
TORONTO, ONTARIO M9A 1C2
(416) 233-3690

RETAIL ENVIRONMENTS LTD.
2382 DUNDAS STREET WEST
TORONTO, ONTARIO M6P 1W9
(416) 536-2204

RICE, VALERIE & ASSOCIATES
43 ALVIN AVENUE
TORONTO, ONTARIO M4T 2A7
(416) 323-9914

RICE, WARREN ASSOCIATES LTD.
67 MOWAT AVENUE
TORONTO, ONTARIO M6K 3E3
(416) 537-5597

• **RICE BRYDONE LTD.**
635 QUEEN STREET EAST
TORONTO, ONTARIO M4M 1G4
(416) 466-4446 **Pg. 74, 76, 118**

RICHMOND HEIGHTS INTERIORS LTD.
11645 YONGE STREET,
RICHMOND HILL, ONTARIO L4C 4K7
(416) 884-5931

RIDPATH'S INTERIOR DESIGN
906 YONGE STREET
TORONTO, ONTARIO M4W 2J2
(416) 920-4441

• **ROBINSON GROUP LTD., THE**
263 DAVENPORT ROAD
TORONTO, ONTARIO M5R 1J9
(416) 960-2444 **Pg. 141**

ROLLINS RAEBURN INTERIOR DESIGN INC.
146 DAVENPORT ROAD
TORONTO, ONTARIO M5S 1J1
(416) 923-5676

ROBB STEWART DESIGN INC.
521 KING STREET WEST
TORONTO, ONTARIO M5V 1K4
(416) 596-8301

RUTHERFORD, S. GRANT DESIGN INC.
285 VICTORIA
TORONTO, ONTARIO M5B 1W1
(416) 598-3413

RYAN, WILLIAM DESIGN ASSOCIATES
114 BEDFORD
TORONTO, ONTARIO M5R 2K2
(416) 923-0015

SAVEIN, LORRAINE
INTERIORS LTD.
44 St. CLAIR AVENUE EAST
TORONTO, ONTARIO M4T 1M9
(416) 964-3933

SCHOFIELD, MANUEL J. LTD.
74 HAZELTON
TORONTO, ONTARIO M5R 2E2
(416) 962-3190

SEARS & RUSSELL CONSULTANTS
147 DAVENPORT ROAD
TORONTO, ONTARIO M5R 1J1
(416) 926-8242

• **SHELAGH'S OF CANADA LTD.**
354 DAVENPORT ROAD
TORONTO, ONTARIO M5R 1K6
(416) 924-7331 **Pg. 200**

• **SHIRO/ROBERTS & ASSOCIATES**
15 GERVAIS DRIVE
DON MILLS, ONTAIO M3C 1Y8
(416) 449-1529 **Pg. 98**

• **SIMPSONS**
COMMERCIAL INTERIORS AND DESIGN
49 GERVAIS DRIVE
DON MILLS, ONTARIO M3C 1Y9
(416) 449-0110 **Pg. 150**

SMALL, NEAL DESIGN LTD.
94 AVENUE ROAD
TORONTO, ONTARIO M5R 2H2
(416) 964-3396

• **SMITH, G.L. PLANNING & DESIGN INC.**
1111 FINCH AVENUE WEST
DOWNSVIEW, ONTARIO M3J 2E5
(416) 736-1290 **Pg. 101**

SOEGANDI, ADRIAN
DESIGN ASSOCIATES
338 DUNDAS STREET EAST
TORONTO, ONTARIO M5A 2A1
(416) 960-6193

SOMMERVILLE HATTIE DRURY
INTERIOR DESIGN
138 IMPERIAL
TORONTO, ONTARIO M5P 1C6
(416) 483-6924

SOREN, MEL INTERIOR DESIGN
355 MT. PLEASANT
TORONTO, ONTARIO M4T 2G7
(416) 483-1190

SPACE TIME PLANNING
10 BRITAIN
TORONTO, ONTARIO M5A 1R6
(416) 868-0111

STAHMER, MAIKE
INTERIOR DESIGN LTD.
176 MACPHERSON
TORONTO, ONTARIO M5R 1W8
(416) 923-2364

STAPLES, RAY INTERIORS
114 BIRCH AVENUE
TORONTO, ONTARIO M4V 1C8
(416) 922-4218

STARK, JAMES GARY
862 MANNING AVENUE
TORONTO, ONTARIO M6G 2W8
(416) 535-6357

STEER, SUZANNE LTD.
111 MACPHERSON
TORONTO, ONTARIO M5R 1W9
(416) 967-0267

STEIN, BETTY INTERIORS
19 GLENGROVE EAST
TORONTO, ONTARIO M4N 1E6
(416) 487-9153

STERLING, M. DESIGN GROUP INC.
146 FRONT STREET WEST
TORONTO, ONTARIO M5J 1G2
(416) 596-1279

STEVENSON, JOHN INTERIORS LTD.
110 RICHMOND STREET EAST
TORONTO, ONTARIO M5C 2P9
(416) 860-0010

STICKS & STONES INCORPORATED
15 HILLSBORO AVENUE
TORONTO, ONTARIO M5R 1S6
(416) 928-0587

• **STOCKS, PAUL A. LTD.**
35 COLDWATER ROAD
DON MILLS, ONTARIO M3B 1Y8
(416) 449-9733 **Pg. 79**

STRATFORD & COMEAU ARCHITECTS
404 KING STREET EAST
TORONTO, ONTARIO M5A 1L4
(416) 362-9811

STRONG ASSOCIATES ARCHITECTS
111 AVENUE ROAD
TORONTO, ONTARIO M5R 2G3
(416) 961-6911

STUDIO NINETY THREE INTERIORS
93 COLLIER
TORONTO, ONTARIO M4W 1M1
(416) 928-0509

STUDIO 85 INTERIOR PLANNING
85 THE EAST MALL
TORONTO, ONTARIO M8Z 5W4
(416) 253-4629

SUTTON + VESKA INC.
1216 YONGE STREET
TORONTO, ONTARIO M4T 1W1
(416) 924-9295

SWAIN, ANNE
INTERIOR DESIGN INC.
585-A MT. PLEASANT
TORONTO, ONTARIO M4S 2M5
(416) 485-0244

SWEENEY ASSOCIATES
501 QUEEN STREET EAST
TORONTO, ONTARIO M5A 1V1
(416) 361-0822

SYNFORM DESIGN GROUP
74 SCOLLARD STREET
TORONTO, ONTARIO M5R 1G2
(416) 921-8717

● **TANNER HILL ASSOCIATES INC.**
25 OVERLEA BLVD.
TORONTO, ONTARIO M4H 1B1
(416) 429-1600 **Pg. 127**

● **STUDIO STORE, THE**
353 EASTERN AVENUE
TORONTO, ONTARIO M4M 1B7
(416) 461-2086 **Pg. 204**

TAYLOR, ARLENE ASSOCIATES
73 LAIRD DRIVE
TORONTO, ONTARIO M4G 3T4
(416) 422-4283

**THORNE, GRANT
INTERIOR DESIGN LTD.**
116 YORKVILLE
TORONTO, ONTARIO M5R 1C2
(416) 923-7777

● **TODAY'S BUSINESS INTERIORS**
393 NUGGET AVENUE
SCARBOROUGH, ONTARIO M1S 4G3
(416) 292-5155 **Pg. 80**

TOLIAS, BILL CONSULTING INC.
15 McMURRICH
TORONTO, ONTARIO M5R 2A3
(416) 924-6562

TOMCZYK & ASSOCIATES LTD.
52 TALLWOOD DRIVE
TORONTO, ONTARIO M3B 2P5
(416) 443-8660

● **TOTAL ENVIRONMENTAL PLANNING**
265 HOOD ROAD
MARKHAM, ONTARIO L3R 4N3
(416) 474-0510 **Pg. 81, 102**

TOTAL OFFICE PLANNING
2 BLOOR STREET EAST
TORONTO, ONTARIO M4W 1A7
(416) 924-7121

URBAN SHOWCASE, THE
160 BEDFORD
TORONTO, ONTARIO M5R 2K9
(416) 923-9690

VELME, SYLVIA DESIGN
45-B HAZELTON
TORONTO, ONTARIO M5R 2E3
(416) 927-8361

VOGLER AHN DESIGN ASSOCIATES
169 GERRARD STREET EAST
TORONTO, ONTARIO M5A 2E4
(416) 963-9577

WTC DESIGNS
27 DAVIES AVENUE
TORONTO, ONTARIO M4M 2A9
(416) 469-4196

**WACHSMITH, C.
DESIGN CONSULTANT**
20 ROWLEY
TORONTO, ONTARIO M4P 2S6
(416) 485-3312

**WARSON, MARIKA
INTERIOR DESIGN**
548 MERTON
TORONTO, ONTARIO M4S 1B3
(416) 489-1360

WARD, ERIC
238 DAVENPORT ROAD
TORONTO, ONTARIO M5R 1J6
(416) 665-4375

WATSON, ROBERT INTERIORS
17 ROBIN HOOD ROAD
ISLINGTON, ONTARIO M9A 2W6
(416) 964-6682

WATT, AUDREY LTD.
50 ROXBOROUGH WEST
TORONTO, ONTARIO M4W 1K1
(416) 920-3017

WELKER, EDWARD INTERIORS LTD.
1964 AVENUE ROAD
TORONTO, ONTARIO M5M 4A1
(416) 787-9531

WILLIAM BUSINESS INTERIORS
2465 CAWTHRA ROAD
MISSISSAUGA, ONTARIO L5A 3P2
(416) 277-1463

**WILSON, DOROTHY
INTERIOR DESIGN**
53 BALMORAL AVENUE
TORONTO, ONTARIO M4V 1J5
(416) 923-6722

WILSON AND TURNER
15A CLARENCE SQUARE
TORONTO, ONTARIO M5V 1H1
(416) 598-3397

WINNICK, M.J. INTERIOR DESIGNERS LTD.
2 BLOOR STREET WEST, SUITE 2008
TORONTO, ONTARIO M4W 3E2
(416) 964-8808

WINTERS DESIGN PLANNING
130 YONGE STREET
TORONTO, ONTARIO M5C 1X4
(416) 364-4520

WINTZEN, LUC DESIGN INC.
62 BELMONT STREET
TORONTO, ONTARIO M5R 1P8
(416) 961-3760

WINSTON, JACK DESIGNS INC.
234 DAVENPORT ROAD
TORONTO, ONTARIO M5R 1J6
(416) 968-6511

● **WOOD WILKINGS LTD.**
65 FRONT STREET EAST
TORONTO, ONTARIO M5E 1B5
(416) 865-9980 **Pg. 120**

● **YABU PUSHELBERG**
359 KING STREET EAST
TORONTO, ONTARIO M5A 1L1
(416) 362-1414 **Pg. 17**

YEN, CHRIS DESIGNS INC.
378 QUEEN STREET EAST
TORONTO, ONTARIO M5A 1T1
(416) 868-6669

Windsor

**ARMADA, JAN
DESIGN CONSULTANTS**
3694 ASKIN BLVD.
WINDSOR, ONTARIO N9E 3J9
(519) 969-7313

BASIC TWO DESIGNS LIMITED
108 McDOUGALL
WINDSOR, ONTARIO N9A 1K8
(519) 254-0880

BENNING INTERIORS LIMITED
3203 WALKER
WINDSOR, ONTARIO N8W 3B7
(519) 966-6226

BUCKNER, DOUGLAS W. LTD.
4769 WYANDOTTE EAST
WINDSOR, ONTARIO N8Y 1H9
(519) 945-1951

**FONTANA, M.
DESIGNS & WOODWORK INC.**
5145 HALFORD STREET
RR NO. 1, WINDSOR, ONTARIO N9A 6J3
(519) 737-6550

INTEGRATED DESIGNS
2260 UNIVERSITY WEST
WINDSOR, ONTARIO N9B 1B5
(519) 256-9061

JAMIESON, NEIL INTERIORS LTD.
322 PELISSIER
WINDSOR, ONTARIO N9A 4K7
(519) 253-6670

McLEAN, GREGORY M.
5161 TECUMSEH ROAD EAST
WINDSOR, ONTARIO N8T 1C3
(519) 944-4744

NADALIN DESIGN DEPARTMENT
2525 JEFFERSON
WINDSOR, ONTARIO N8T 2W5
(519) 944-2294

O'NEILL, JAMES D. LTD.
1574 LINCOLN
WINDSOR, ONTARIO N8V 2J4
(519) 258-5501

RYAN, PETER K. LTD.
256 PELISSIER
WINDSOR, ONTARIO N9A 4K2
(519) 253-7471

▶ M A N I T O B A

Winnipeg

ARNOTT & ASSOCIATES
115 BANNATYNE
WINNIPEG, MANITOBA R3B 0R3
(204) 943-8844

AUSTEN GERALD INTERIOR DESIGN LTD.
585 RIVER
WINNIPEG, MANITOBA R2M 2R3
(204) 284-9964

BLANKSTEIN DESIGN INC.
1129 EMPRESS STREET
WINNIPEG, MANITOBA R3E 3H1
(204) 775-2559

CALNITSKY HESHKA ASSOCIATES
110 OSBORNE S.
WINNIPEG, MANITOBA R3L 1Y5
(204) 453-6441

COREY SMITH DESIGN LTD.
685 PEMBINA HWY.
WINNIPEG, MANITOBA R3M 2L6
(204) 453-7306

COUNTERPOINT DESIGN INC.
120 FORT STREET
WINNIPEG, MANITOBA R3C 1C7
(204) 956-0542

CUNNINGHAM BUSINESS INTERIORS
1680 ELLICE AVENUE
WINNIPEG, MANITOBA R3H 0Z2
(204) 774-1624

DC DESIGN CONCEPT
46 MONTCLAIR BAY
WINNIPEG, MANITOBA R3T 4B3
(204) 269-7253

DECOR 8
2 DONALD STREET
WINNIPEG, MANITOBA R3L 0K5
(204) 475-6193

DECORAGE
850 KEEVATIN
WINNIPEG, MANITOBA R2R 0Z5
(204) 633-6085

DESIGN IDEAS INC.
932 ST. JAMES STREET
WINNIPEG, MANITOBA R3H 0K3
(204) 775-2540

DESIGN MANITOBA
433 RIVER
WINNIPEG, MANITOBA R3L 0C3
(204) 453-2390

DESIGN PROFILE
100 OSBORNE STREET
WINNIPEG, MANITOBA
(204) 475-3588

• **DESIGNWORKS INC.**
90 ALBERT STREET
WINNIPEG, MANITOBA R3B 1G2
(204) 942-2129 **Pg. 50**

DOJACK, TOM DESIGN INC.
88 SPENCE STREET
WINNIPEG, MANITOBA R3C 1Y3
(204) 772-1600

ENVIRONMENTAL SPACE PLANNING
290 VAUGHAN
WINNIPEG, MANITOBA R3B 2N8
(204) 944-9292

• **EATON'S CONTRACT INTERIORS**
69 MUIR ROAD
WINNIPEG, MANITOBA R2X 2X7
(204) 633-8530 **Pg. 52, 108, 143**

ENVIRONMENTAL SPACE PLANNING
290 VAUGHAN
WINNIPEG, MANITOBA R3B 2N8
(204) 944-9292

FINGOLD ENTERPRISES LTD.
93 LOMBARD AVENUE
WINNIPEG, MANITOBA R3B 3B1
(204) 942-5578

GIRLING, L.F. & ASSOCIATES
8 DONALD STREET
WINNIPEG, MANITOBA R3L 2T8
(204) 477-0218

GREGORY – CARTWRIGHT
812 WALL STREET
WINNIPEG, MANITOBA R3G 2T8
(204) 786-8601

INSITE DESIGN CONSULTANTS
240 GRAHAM AVENUE
WINNIPEG, MANITOBA R3C 0J7
(204) 942-3583

INTERPLANNING ASSOCIATES
93 LOMBARD AVENUE
WINNIPEG, MANITOBA R3B 3B1
(204) 942-5578

JAMES DUGUAY ASSOCIATES
930 – 360 MAIN STREET
WINNIPEG, MANITOBA R3C 3Z3
(204) 947-2843

**JOHNSON, STELLA
DESIGN CONSULTANTS**
67 MONTCLAIR BAY
WINNIPEG, MANITOBA R3T 4B4
(204) 261-7538

MARSHALL, GRANT INTERIORS
158 SPENCE STREET
WINNIPEG, MANITOBA R3L 1Y3
(204) 774-0211

McLACHLAN & McLACHLAN
130 SCOTT STREET
WINNIPEG, MANITOBA R3L 0K9
(204 284-1860

MITCHELL, MARK & ASSOCIATES INC.
749 WALL STREET
WINNIPEG, MANITOBA R3G 2T6
(204) 775-1025

NUMBER TEN DESIGN GROUP
310-115 BANNATYNE AVENUE EAST
WINNIPEG, MANITOBA R3B 0R3
(204) 942-0981

PANACHE, THE LTD.
1129 EMPRESS
WINNIPEG, MANITOBA R3E 3H1
(204) 786-1427

PARCOR LTD.
464 HARGRAVE STREET
WINNIPEG, MANITOBA R3A 0X5
(204) 943-3438

PARTNERS BY DESIGN
222 OSBORNE STREET
WINNIPEG, MANITOBA R3L 1Z3
(204) 452-7638

**RADCLIFFE, AYALA
DESIGN CONSULTANTS**
4-222 OSBORNE SOUTH
WINNIPEG, MANITOBA R3L 0K9
(204) 475-3969

SMITH CARTER PARTNERS LTD.
1601 BUFFALO PLACE
WINNIPEG, MANITOBA R3T 3K7
(204) 477-1260

VEITCH, RONALD M.
57 MIDDLEGATE
WINNIPEG, MANITOBA R3C 2C5
(204) 783-1059

WIEBE, KAREN
513 HELMSDALE AVENUE
WINNIPEG, MANITOBA R2K 0W7
(204) 669-6914

YOUNG SNOW DESIGN ASSOCIATES
1183 MARKHAM ROAD
WINNIPEG, MANITOBA R3T 3Z9
(204) 269-0333

▶ S A S K A T C H E W A N

R e g i n a

ALFORD'S
1500 4TH AVENUE
REGINA, SASKATCHEWAN S4R 8G8
(306) 522-5651

**BOWERING CARBONNEAU &
ASSOCIATES LTD.**
2353 SMITH
REGINA, SASKATCHEWAN S4P 2P7
(306) 757-0145

CITE DESIGN
1316 RAE STREET
REGINA, SASKATCHEWAN S4T 2C3
(306) 525-1991

• **EATON'S CONTRACT INTERIORS**
641 PARK STREET
REGINA, SASKATCHEVAN S4N 5N1
(306) 352-6636 **Pg. 52, 108, 143**

INNER DIMENSIONS DESIGN ASSOCIATES
2347B CORNWALL STREET
REGINA, SASKATCHEWAN S4P 2L4
(306) 359-3101

KUPCHANKO DESIGN
312 McDONALD
REGINA, SASKATCHEWAN S4N 5V9
(306) 924-0762

MARKWARTS' HOUSE OF DECOR LTD.
3806 ALBERT STREET
REGINA, SASKATCHEWAN S4S 3R2
(306) 584-8454

McDONALD, JANETTE INTERIORS
2398 SCARTH
REGINA, SASKATCHEWAN S4P 2J7
(306) 757-6781

OGGI INTERIORS
2429 11TH AVENUE
REGINA, SASKATCHEWAN S4P 0K4
(306) 352-2645

REGINA DESIGNWORKS LTD.
312 MACDONALD
REGINA, SASKATCHEWAN
(306) 924-0762

RELIABLE STATIONERS LTD.
106 LEONARD STREET NORTH
REGINA, SASKATCHEWAN S4N 5V7
(306) 924-0555

• **SIMPSONS**
COMMERCIAL INTERIORS & DESIGN
240 LEONARD STREET NORTH
REGINA, SASKATCHEWAN S4N 5V7
(306) 775-1955 **Pg. 150**

SUPREME OFFICE PRODUCTS LTD.
1916 DEWDNEY
REGINA, SASKATCHEWAN S4R 1G9
(306) 757-8651

TAYLOR PATERSON INTERIORS
2176 7TH AVENUE
REGINA, SASKATCHEWAN S4R 1C4
(306) 525-6161

ZURICH DESIGN CONSULTANTS
2500 – 13TH AVENUE
REGINA, SASKATCHEWAN S4P 0W2
(306) 757-2542

Saskatoon

BAY, THE
205 2ND AVENUE NORTH
SASKATOON, SASKATCHEWAN S7K 2B7
(306) 242-7611

BONLI INTERIORS LTD.
GROSVENOR PARK SHOPPING CENTRE
SASKATOON, SASKATCHEWAN
(306) 373-3113

DAYS DESIGN CONSULTANTS
740 1ST AVENUE NORTH
SASKATOON, SASKATCHEWAN S7K 1Y1
(306) 244-6500

DESIGN SHOPE LTD.
2313 HANSELMAN PLACE
SASKATOON, SASKATCHEWAN S7L 6A9
(306) 653-3246

DUDDRIDGE INTERIOR DESIGN INC.
613 9TH STREET EAST
SASKATOON, SASKATCHEWAN S7H 0M4
(306) 652-1612

• **EATON'S CONTRACT INTERIORS**
1802A QUEBEC AVENUE
SASKATOON, SASKATCHEWAN S7K 1W2
(306) 242-1905 **Pg. 52, 108, 143**

HOLLIDAY-SCOTT INTERIORS LTD.
1026 LOUISE AVENUE
SASKATOON, SASKATCHEWAN S7H 2P6
(306) 477-1556

PLANNED COMMERCIAL INTERIORS
626 BROADWAY AVENUE
SASKATOON, SASKATCHEWAN S7N 1A9
(306) 244-8314

• **SIMPSONS**
COMMERCIAL INTERIORS & DESIGN
3040 MINERS AVENUE NORTH
SASKATOON, SASKATCHEWAN S7K 5V1
(306) 933-4311 **Pg. 150**

WELLS STUDIO OF DESIGN
617 MAIN STREET
SASKATOON, SASKATCHEWAN S7H 0J8
(306) 653-1012

WESTERN RETAIL INTERIORS LTD.
208 JESSOB
SASKATOON, SASKATCHEWAN S7N 1Y4
(306) 477-2244

▶ ALBERTA

Calgary

• **ANGUS WRIGHT**
DESIGN CONSULTANTS LTD.
306 MOUNT ROYAL VILLAGE
1550 – 8TH STREET SW
CALGARY, ALBERTA T2R 1K1
(403) 229-2717 **Pg. 38**

ASSOCIATED DESIGN GROUP
8947 BAYLOR CT. SW
CALGARY, ALBERTA T2V 3N5
(403) 281-6637

BALTZAN FURNISHINGS & INTERIORS
2115 4TH STREET SW
CALGARY, ALBERTA T2S 1W8
(403) 228-4682

BERGMEISTER B. & ASSOCIATES LTD.
2916 19TH STREET NE, NO. 204
CALGARY, ALBERTA T2E 6Y9
(403) 250-2807

BOND & MOGRIDGE ARCHITECTS LTD.
926 5TH AVENUE SW, NO. 500
CALGARY, ALBERTA T2P 0N7
(403) 228-4712

BONDAR INTERIORS
1451 14TH STREET SW
CALGARY, ALBERTA T3C 1C8
(403) 229-2005

BRAND E.H. INTERIOR DESIGN
CONSULTANT LTD.
2424 4TH STREET SW, NO 400
CALGARY, ALBERTA T2S 2T4
(403) 228-0000

BURNS, ROBERT INTERIORS
1223, RANCHVIEW ROAD NW
CALGARY, ALBERTA T3G 2C2
(403) 238-6042

BUSBY KERRY INTERIOR DESIGNER
1802 BOWNESS ROAD NW
CALGARY, ALBERTA T2N 3K4
(403) 270-3767

BUSINESS INTERIORS LIMITED
926 5TH AVENUE SW
CALGARY, ALBERTA T2P 0N7
(403) 269-7303

CALETO INTERIORS
1040 THORNEYCROFT DRIVE NW
CALGARY, ALBERTA T2K 3K8
(403) 274-1941

• **CAMPBELL, STEPHEN DESIGN LTD.**
224 11TH AVENUE SW, 2ND FLR.
CALGARY, ALBERTA T2R 0C3
(403) 262-7416 **Pg. 86**

CBL DESIGN GROUP LTD.
222 – 3RD STREET SW
CALGARY, ALBERTA T2P 1P9
(403) 233-2585

CWA INTERIOR SYSTEMS LTD.
2608 43RD STREET SE
CALGARY, ALBERTA
(403) 235-2277

• **COHOS EVAMY PARTNERSHIP, THE**
902 11TH AVENUE SW, NO. 200
CALGARY, ALBERTA T2R 0E7
(403) 245-5501 **Pg. 48**

CONSTRUCTION CONCEPTS
1509 CENTRE STREET SW, NO. 230
CALGARY, ALBERTA T2G 2E6
(403) 232-6353

COOK CULHAM PEDERSEN &
VALENTINE
1011 GLENMORE TRAIL SW, 4TH FLR.
CALGARY, ALBERTA T2V 4R6
(403) 253-6459

CRIDLAND, DOUGLAS
INTERIOR DESIGN LTD.
908 17TH AVENUE SW
CALGARY, ALBERTA T2T 0A3
(403) 228-0636

CRKVENAC & ASSOCIATES
INTERIOR DESIGN
831 7TH AVENUE SW
CALGARY, ALBERTA T2P 1A2
(403) 265-4427

DAVANTI
CONTEMPORARY INTERIORS LTD.
708 11TH AVENUE SW
CALGARY, ALBERTA T2R 0E4
(403) 264-1316

DESIGN 28 LTD.
618 18TH AVENUE NW
CALGARY, ALBERTA T2M 0T8
(403) 289-7979

DESIGN TEXTURES LTD.
416 MERIDIAN ROAD SE, BAY A19
CALGARY, ALBERTA T2A 1X2
(403) 248-7770

DESIGN WORK
3932 EDMONTON TRAIL NE.
CALGARY, ALBERTA T2E 3P6
(403) 230-9464

INTERIOR
DESIGNERS

308

DEUCE INTERIOR & DESIGN INC.
1700 VARSITY ESTATES DR. NW
CALGARY, ALBERTA T3B 2W9
(403) 288-9297

**DOBBYN SHELAGH
INTERIOR DESIGN LTD.**
10 MEADOWLARK CR. SW
CALGARY, ALBERTA T2V 1Z1
(403) 255-0464

DOMUS DESIGN GROUP LTD.
239 10TH AVENUE SE, NO. 103
CALGARY, ALBERTA T2G 0V9
(403) 234-9090

DRAWING BOARD
224 11TH AVENUE SW, MN.FLR.
CALGARY, ALBERTA T2R 0C3
(403) 233-8448

• **EATON'S CONTRACT INTERIORS**
1122 4TH STREET SW
CALGARY, ALBERTA T2R 1M1
(403) 266-3006 **Pg. 52, 108, 143**

ETHAN ALLEN GALLERY
GLENMORE TRAIL & ELBOW DRIVE SW
CALGARY, ALBERTA
(403) 258-2346

FELDBERG DESIGNS LTD.
1815 BAYSHORE ROAD SW
CALGARY, ALBERTA T2V 3M2
(403) 281-0835

FINAL TOUCH INTERIORS
9203 MACLEOD TRAIL SW
CALGARY, ALBERTA T2H 0M2
(403) 258-2720

FISHMAN, ARTHUR & ASSOCIATES
2424 4TH STREET SW, NO. 720
CALGARY, ALBERTA T2S 2T4
(403) 229-3590

FORM 3 DESIGNS LTD.
2215 27TH AVENUE NE
CALGARY, ALBERTA T2E 7M4
(403) 250-1470

• **FORREST BODRUG & ASSOCIATES LTD.**
602 11TH AVENUE SW
CALGARY, ALBERTA T2R 1J8
(403) 266-6612 **Pg. 58**

GRAHAM McCOURT ARCHITECTS
602 12TH AVENUE SW, LWR. FLR.
CALGARY, ALBERTA T2R 1J3
(403) 264-7760

GREENWOOD, EV INTERIOR DESIGN
40 ABINGDON CR. NE
CALGARY, ALBERTA T2A 6S5
(403) 272-8192

HARDING & ASSOCIATES
808 4TH AVENUE SW, NO. 260
CALGARY, ALBERTA T2P 3E8
(403) 266-0811

HAYASHI & ASSOCIATES LTD.
404 6TH AVENUE SW, NO. 350
CALGARY, ALBERTA T2P 0R9
(403) 261-2601

HEMMING, JAMES DESIGN LTD.
1057 20TH AVENUE NW
CALGARY, ALBERTA T2M 1E7
(403) 284-3488

**HOWELL ASSOCIATES
INTERIOR DESIGN LTD.**
116A 8TH AVENUE SE
CALGARY, ALBERTA T2G 0K6
(403) 269-8267

**HUGHES, BABOUSHKIN
& ASSOCIATES LTD.**
309 2ND AVENUE SW, NO. 105
CALGARY, ALBERTA T2P 0C5
(403) 262-3930

HUTCHISON, KEN ARCHITECT LTD.
1518A 7TH STREET SW, 2ND FLR.
CALGARY, ALBERTA T2R 1A7
(403) 228-9307

**INTERIORS BY DM SIMONE MAC RAE
& ASSOCIATES LTD.**
CALGARY, ALBERTA
(403) 242-2994

INTERIOR EXPRESSIONS
908 17TH AVENUE SW, NO. 100
CALGARY, ALBERTA T2T 0A3
(403) 229-4484

**IRELAND, SHIRLEY
INNER-VISION DESIGN**
3838 ELBOW DRIVE SW
CALGARY, ALBERTA T2S 2J8
(403) 243-0120

JACOBS, KATHLEEN DESIGN CONSULTANT
63 QUEEN ISABELLA CLOSE SE
CALGARY, ALBERTA T2J 3R2
(403) 278-1831

JANET DESIGN
300 17TH AVENUE SW
CALGARY, ALBERTA T2S 0A8
(403) 228-3029

KPL DESIGN ASSOCIATES LTD.
2835 19TH STREET NE, BAY 2A
CALGARY, ALBERTA T2E 7A2
(403) 250-1411

KRAEMER, TAIPALE & ASSOCIATES LTD.
112 4TH AVENUE SW, NO. 1210
CALGARY, ALBERTA T2P 0H3
(403) 237-7890

LOCKHART DESIGN LTD.
3707 54TH AVENUE SW
CALGARY, ALBERTA T3E 5H5
(403) 242-2644

• **MARSHALL CUMMINGS &
ASSOCIATES LTD.**
221 10TH AVENUE SW
CALGARY, ALBERTA T2R 0A4
(403) 233-8423 **Pg. 64**

McARTHUR FINE FURNITURE
67 GLENBROOK PLACE SW
CALGARY, ALBERTA T3E 6W4
(403) 246-6266

McEVOY, MARY INTERIORS LTD.
614A 17TH AVENUE SW
CALGARY, ALBERTA T2S 0B4
(403) 228-1330

MARIHOF INTERIORS LTD.
CALGARY, ALBERTA
(403) 282-9516

MILLER, RON DESIGN CONSULTANT LTD.
639 5TH AVENUE SW, NO. 220
CALGARY, ALBERTA T2P 0M9
(403) 265-0974

MORTENSEN'S, KAI
1235 11TH AVENUE SW
CALGARY, ALBERTA T3C 0M5
(403) 245-5751

NELSON MACDONALD DESIGN LTD.
2424 4TH STREET SW, NO. 470
CALGARY, ALBERTA T2S 2T4
(403) 228-9010

MOLYNEAUX INTERIORS LTD.
604 1ST STREET SW, NO. 307
CALGARY, ALBERTA T2P 1M7
(403) 264-8878

OLLIVER INTERIORS
188 BRACEWOOD ROAD SW
CALGARY, ALBERTA T2W 3C1
(403) 238-0559

PENTHOUSE
6020 2ND STREET SW
CALGARY, ALBERTA T2H 0H2
(403) 253-7835

PRESTUPA, NOPLE INTERIOR DESIGN LTD.
815 17TH AVENUE SW, NO. 203
CALGARY, ALBERTA T2T 0A1
(403) 229-2826

PROJECT INTERIORS
BOX 4484 STN. C
CALGARY, ALBERTA
(403) 277-3321

**RAINES, BARRET PARTNERSHIP
CONSULTANTS**
714 1ST STREET SE
CALGARY, ALBERTA T2G 2G8
(403) 269-4961

RHODES & DUNCAN INTERIOR DESIGN
321 10TH AVENUE SW, 2ND FLOOR
CALGARY, ALBERTA T2R 0A5
(403) 266-7222

• **RICE BRYDONE LTD.**
706 7TH AVENUE SW
CALGARY, ALBERTA T2P 0Z1
(403) 233-8865 **Pg. 74, 76, 118**

RICHARDSON HARRADANCE ASSOCIATES LTD.
908-17TH AVENUE SW, NO. 313-315
CALGARY, ALBERTA T2T 0A3
(403) 228-1212

SHOE STRINGS
312 WEST PALLISER SQUARE
CALGARY, ALBERTA T2P 2G8
(403) 271-0526

STAGE II INTERIORS LTD.
908 17TH AVENUE SW, NO. 202
CALGARY, ALBERTA T2T 0A3
(403) 245-5546

STEF DESIGN SOFT ART STUDIOS
2845 23RD STREET NE, NO. 112
CALGARY, ALBERTA T2E 7A4
(403) 250 5669

STYLEX INTERIORS LTD.
3504 66 TH AVENUE SE, BAY 3
CALGARY, ALBERTA T2C 1P3
(403) 279-3739

TAVENDER, CAROLYN ASSOCIATES
709 11TH AVENUE SW, NO. 204
CALGARY, ALBERTA T2R 0E3
(403) 264-7400

TIMM ROBINSON INTERIORS LTD.
2500 4TH STREET SW
CALGARY, ALBERTA T2S 1X6
(403) 228-5644

TURNER, G.E. CONSULTING LTD.
3607 ELBOW DRIVE SW
CALGARY, ALBERTA T2S 2J6
(403) 243-8906

TURVEY, BOB DESIGN INC.
3016 19TH STREET NE
CALGARY, ALBERTA T2E 6Y9
(403) 250-1655

UNICA DESIGN STUDIO LTD.
75 GLENDEER DRIVE SW
CALGARY, ALBERTA T2H 2S8
(403) 259-4040

VAN BUREN DESIGN
6024 LEWIS DRIVE SE
CALGARY, ALBERTA T2E 5Z3
(403) 240-1119

VAN ELLENBERG DESIGNS LTD.
129 WOODFERN PLACE SW
CALGARY, ALBERTA T2W 4R7
(403) 281-1700

WALLACE & ASSOCIATES DESIGNERS & PLANNERS
260 SCENIC WAY NW
CALGARY, ALBERTA T3L 1B8
(403) 239-2967

WILLIAMS, L.A. INTERIOR DESIGNER
1518 7TH STREET SW, 2ND FLR.
CALGARY, ALBERTA T2R 1A7
(403) 229-0177

WINNICK, M.J. INTERIOR DESIGNERS LTD.
202 6TH AVENUE SW, NO. 330
CALGARY, ALBERTA T2P 2R9
(403) 265-7040

WOODBINE INTERIORS LTD.
1416 107TH AVENUE SW
CALGARY, ALBERTA T2W 0B9
(403) 258-2535

ZUL, BOGA ARCHITECT LTD.
338 15TH AVENUE SW
CALGARY, ALBERTA T2R 0P8
(403) 228-4177

Edmonton

ARCHIMAGE DESIGN GROUP INC.
10357 109TH STREET
EDMONTON, ALBERTA T5J 1N3
(403) 428-6120

ARDEN WHITE DESIGN GROUP
11221 79TH AVENUE
EDMONTON, ALBERTA T6G 0P2
(403) 437-7339

ARRINGTON, SHELLY DESIGN CONTRACTOR
15221 104TH AVENUE
EDMONTON, ALBERTA T5P 0R6
(403) 489-7210

BALTZAN FURNISHINGS & INTERIORS
10815 103RD AVENUE
EDMONTON, ALBERTA T5J 0J4
(403) 424-7351

BARRIGAN FRANK – DESIGNS
5 WESTVIEW PLACE
ST. ALBERT, ALBERTA T8N 3J8
(403) 459-0423

BERNWARD DESIGN LTD.
10134 87TH STREET
EDMONTON, ALBERTA T5H 1N4
(403) 429-0392

BILINSKE, KAREN DESIGN & PROJECT CONSULTANTS LTD.
9908 109TH STREET, NO. 2
EDMONTON, ALBERTA T5K 1H5
(403) 424-9666

BRAND, EDITH H. INTERIOR DESIGN CONSULTANT LTD.
8525 ARGYLL ROAD
EDMONTON, ALBERTA T6C 4B2
(403) 468-4853

CAMERON INTERIORS
284 SADDLEBACK ROAD
EDMONTON, ALBERTA T6J 4R7
(403) 453-4357

CARTER, DONNA DESIGN CONSULTANT
10402 28A AVENUE
EDMONTON, ALBERTA T6J 4J6
(403) 438-4098

CHANCELLOR INTERIORS
14234 98TH AVENUE
EDMONTON, ALBERTA T5N 0C3
(403) 451-0441

CHERIDEA DESIGN CONSULTATION
6710 93RD STREET
EDMONTON, ALBERTA T6E 3B4
(403) 439-0611

CHRISTENSEN, MARILYN
10803 12TH STREET
EDMONTON, ALBERTA T5M 0H4
(403) 452-8201

• COHOS, EVAMY PARTNERSHIP
10130 112TH STREET, NO. 300
EDMONTON, ALBERTA T5K 2K4
(403) 429-1580 **Pg. 48**

CORPORATE ENVIRONMENT CONSULTANTS INC.
9945 – 50TH STREET, NO. 518
CALGARY, ALBERTA T6A 3X5
(403) 468-2464

DESIGNER'S TOUCH
14107 58TH AVENUE
EDMONTON, ALBERTA T6H 1C8
(403) 437-3061

DIGIUSEPPE INTERIOR DESIGN LTD.
ST. ALBERT, ALBERTA
(403) 459-2135

DINGMAN, ROBERT & ASSOCIATES LTD.
10050 117TH STREET
EDMONTON, ALBERTA T5K 1W7
(403) 482-6368

DOMA DESIGN CONSULTANTS LTD.
10235 101ST STREET, NO. 908
EDMONTON, ALBERTA T5J 3G1
(403) 424-2229

DUGGAN, B INTERIOR DESIGN LTD.
10345 – 133RD STREET
EDMONTON, ALBERTA T5N 1Z8
(403) 451-0696

• EATON'S CONTRACT INTERIORS
114683 – 14TH STREET
EDMONTON, ALBERTA T5M 1W7
(403) 452-7385 **Pg. 52, 108, 143**

FROST, EMILY & ASSOCIATES LTD.
10431 140TH STREET
EDMONTON, ALBERTA T5N 2L8
(403) 452-7603

GLENORA ANTIQUES & INTERIORS
12415 STONY PLAIN ROAD, NO. 3
EDMONTON, ALBERTA T5N 3N3
(403) 482-2266

GRUNDAU'S FURNITURE LTD.
9938 70TH AVENUE
EDMONTON, ALBERTA T6E 0V7
(403) 439-4618

HAHN, R.F. DESIGNS LIMITED
9327 74TH AVENUE
EDMONTON, ALBERTA T6E 1E3
(403) 433-7453

HOLZ-STRACHAN INTERIOR DESIGN LTD.
10110 107 STREET, NO. 203
EDMONTON, ALBERTA T5J 1J4
(403) 424-0911

**HUGH C. WENDY
INTERIOR DESIGN CONSULTANT LTD.**
14026 101A AVENUE
EDMONTON, ALBERTA T5N 0L2
(403) 453-3062

INNERTECH DESIGN CONSULTANTS
10711 181ST STREET
EDMONTON, ALBERTA T5S 1N3
(403) 489-4645

INTERFORM FURNITURE LTD.
6912 76TH AVENUE
EDMONTON, ALBERTA T6B 2R2
(403) 466-1269

INTERIORS BY JANE
10014 109TH STREET, NO. 8
EDMONTON, ALBERTA T5J 1M4
(403) 428-1323

INTERPLAN LTD.
10567 109TH STREET
EDMONTON, ALBERTA T5H 3B1
(403) 423-6785

JOSTAR INTERIORS LTD.
5204 86TH STREET
EDMONTON, ALBERTA T6E 5J6
(403) 468-1727

KASIAN DESIGN GROUP
9707 110TH STREET, NO. 800
EDMONTON, ALBERTA T5K 2L9
(403) 482-6912

LE BELLE ARTI
12722 ST. ALBERT TRAIL
EDMONTON, ALBERTA T5L 4S5
(403) 452-4111

McMURRAY STORE FIXTURES LTD.
11315 154TH STREET
EDMONTON, ALBERTA T5M 1X8
(403) 451-3476

MILLER OFFICE GROUP
4990 92ND AVENUE
EDMONTON, ALBERTA T6B 2S2
(403) 468-4990

**NOYCE, DOUG & ASSOCIATES
INTERIOR DESIGN LTD.**
11158 65TH STREET
EDMONTON, ALBERTA T5W 4K1
(403) 474-0473

OMNI DESIGN LIMITED
10852 97TH STREET, NO. 203
EDMONTON, ALBERTA T5H 2M5
(403) 421-4869

PALEY, ROBERT L. ARCHITECT
14448 118TH AVENUE, 2ND FLR.
EDMONTON, ALBERTA T5L 2M5
(403) 453-6855

PLUS GROUP LTD., THE
10024 JASPER AVENUE, NO. 300
EDMONTON, ALBERTA T5J 1R9
(403) 420-1133

PROTZ, ALICE INTERIOR DESIGN
11220 99TH AVENUE, NO. 319
EDMONTON, ALBERTA T5K 2K6
(403) 488-9581

RGO OFFICE PRODUCTS LTD.
10733 104TH AVENUE
EDMONTON, ALBERTA T5J 3K1
(403) 426-6063

ROMAN INTERIOR DESIGN LTD.
1632 42ND STREET
EDMONTON, ALBERTA T6L 5P4
(403) 461-6117

SANDE'S INTERIOR DECORATING
14804 STONY PLAIN ROAD
EDMONTON, ALBERTA T5N 3S5
(403) 452-5246

SCOTT-CALVIN INTERIORS
9540 104TH AVENUE
EDMONTON, ALBERTA T5H 3X3
(403) 424-1233

SPRAGUE FURNITURE LTD.
9947 109TH STREET
EDMONTON, ALBERTA T5K 1H6
(403) 423-3196

SUROWIAK, J.I. INTERIOR DESIGNS
14120 80TH STREET, NO. 11
EDMONTON, ALBERTA T5C 1L6
(403) 476-9291

**TANNER & ASSOCIATES
INTERIOR DESIGN LTD.**
10822 – 123RD STREET
EDMONTON, ALBERTA T5M 0C6
(403) 452-9667

**UNIGROUP ARCHITECTS AND
INTERIOR DESIGNERS INC.**
10408 124TH STREET, NO. 2202
EDMONTON, ALBERTA T5N 1R5
(403) 488-7271

**WALTERS & WRIGHT
DESIGN CONSULTANTS**
15968 – 109TH AVENUE
EDMONTON, ALBERTA T5P 1B7
(403) 489-5914

WILKIN, R.L. ARCHITECT
10545 87TH AVENUE
EDMONTON, ALBERTA T6E 2P6
(403) 432-7491

WOLSKI, M.B. INTERIOR DESIGN LTD.
10132 105TH STREET, NO. 200
EDMONTON, ALBERTA T5J 1C9
(403) 423-1811

WOODWARD STORES (ALBERTA) LTD.
SOUTHGATE SHOPPING CENTER
EDMONTON, ALBERTA T6H 4M6
(403) 435-0511

WOODWARD STORES (ALBERTA) LTD.
10205 101ST STREET
EDMONTON, ALBERTA T5J 3E8
(403) 424-0151

ZUBYK DESIGN SERVICES
10361 82ND AVENUE, NO. 200
EDMONTON, ALBERTA T6E 1Z8
(403) 461-6091

▶ B R I T I S H   C O L U M B I A

B u r n a b y

CITYSCAPE INTERIORS
4142 RUMBLE
BURNABY, B.C. V5J 1Z8
(604) 434-7174

COLLINS FURNITURE GALLERY LTD.
4240 MANOR
BURNABY, B.C. V5G 1B2
(604) 435-5566

GRAY, PATRICIA INTERIORS INC.
5801 MAYVIEW CIRCLE
BURNABY, B.C. V5E 4B7
(604) 522-9141

INTERPLAN DESIGN ASSOCIATES
4695 HASTINGS EAST
BURNABY, B.C. V5C 2K6
(604) 299-2324

PRESTON'S INTERIORS LTD.
3135 GRANVILLE
BURNABY, B.C. V6H 3K1
(604) 733-8345

Richmond

Richmond

D & L DESIGN
7560 BRIDGE
RICHMOND, B.C. V6Y 2S7
(604) 273-4711

GERRARD DESIGNS INC.
132-3031 WILLIAMS
RICHMOND, B.C. V7E 4G1
(604) 272-5414

IPL INTEGRA PLANNING WESTERN
11140 MELLIS
RICHMOND, B.C. V6X 1L7
(604) 273-7197

PBI DESIGN CONSULTANTS LTD.
7520 RIVER ROAD
RICHMOND, B.C. V6X 1X6
(604) 278-0225

TANDA DESIGN GROUP
200 – 12640 BRIDGEPORT ROAD
RICHMOND, B.C. V6V 1J5
(604) 270-9958

WOODWARD'S
5300 No. 3 ROAD
RICHMOND, B.C. V6X 2X9
(604) 270-3322

Vancouver

ABBA DESIGN LTD.
555 W. HASTINGS, 7TH FLOOR
VANCOUVER, B.C. V6B 4N6
(604) 669-6204

ARCHIPELAGO DESIGN LTD.
101 – 1290 HOMER STREET
VANCOUVER, B.C. V6B 2Y5
(604) 685-8011

ASHLEY – PRYCE, JOHN
32 – 1386 NICOLA STREET
VANCOUVER, B.C. V6G 2G2
(604) 685-2910

ATELIER DESIGN CONSULTANTS LTD.
202 – 1089 W. BROADWAY
VANCOUVER, B.C. V6H 1E2
(604) 738-7250

BBA DESIGN CONSULTANTS INC.
1065 HOWE ST.
VANCOUVER, B.C. V6Z 1P6
(604) 688-4551

BEKKE DESIGN ASSOCIATES LTD.
1555 W. 7TH
VANCOUVER, B.C. V6J 1S1
(604) 732-7696

BERTUZZI, GEORGI DESIGNS LTD.
911 HOMER STREET
VANCOUVER, B.C. V6B 2W6
(604) 669-1846

BIKADI INTERIOR DESIGN LTD.
312 – 674 LEG IN BOOT SQUARE
VANCOUVER, B.C. V5Z 4B3
(604) 872-2431

BLUEBIRD INTERIORS LTD.
1718 MARINE
VANCOUVER, B.C. V7V 1J3
(604) 922-6968

CANWEST MARKETING SYSTEMS LTD.
1038 HOMER STREET
VANCOUVER, B.C. V6B 2W9
(604) 681-5070

CHACHKAS DESIGN LTD.
1070 ROBSON STREET
VANCOUVER, B.C. V6E 1A7
(604) 688-6417

CITY INTERIORS LTD.
P.O. BOX 49208
2373 – 595 BURRARD STREET
VANCOUVER, B.C. V7X 1K8
(604) 661-5010

CLOSE, SUSAN & ASSOCIATES LTD.
203 – 1836 W. 5TH
VANCOUVER, B.C. V6J 1P3
(604) 733-2716

**COLLABORATIVE DESIGN
CONSULTANTS INC.**
301 – 1028 HAMILTON STREET
VANCOUVER, B.C. V6B 2R9
(604) 669-4606

CO-ORDINATED HOTEL INTERIORS LTD.
626 BUTE STREET
VANCOUVER, B.C. V6E 3M1
(604) 688-8571

DESIGN 21
21 WATER STREET
VANCOUVER, B.C. V6B 1A1
(604) 682-6871

DESIGNCORP
405 – 550 BURRARD STREET
VANCOUVER, B.C. V6C 2J6
(604) 687-2888

DESIGN WEST INTERIORS
3396 MARINE DRIVE
WEST VANCOUVER, B.C. V7V 1M9
(604) 922-9550

• **EATON'S CONTRACT INTERIORS**
701 GRANVILLE STREET
VANCOUVER, B.C. V6B 4E5
(604) 661-4600 **Pg. 52, 108, 143**

EXECUTIVE OFFICE INTERIORS LTD.
500 – 73 WATER STREET
VANCOUVER, B.C. V6B 1A1
(604) 685-6331

GLADWIN, ALIKI & ASSOCIATES INC.
112 – 12 WATER STREET
VANCOUVER, B.C. V6B 1A5
(604) 687-7411

GOLDENROD DESIGNS
1455 WEST 10TH AVENUE
VANCOUVER, B.C. V6H 1J8
(604) 734-8383

• **GROUP 5 DESIGN ASSOCIATES LTD.**
1305 W. GEORGIA STREET
VANCOUVER, B.C. V6E 3K6
(604) 681-8155 **Pg. 55**

H & S DESIGN
1672 WEST 2ND AVENUE
VANCOUVER, B.C. V6J 1H4
(604) 733-4818

HIGGINS, DARRELL
1103 – 2077 NELSON STREET
VANCOUVER, B.C. V6G 2Y2
(604) 689-7032

**HOPPING KOVACH GRINNELL
DESIGN CONSULTANTS**
81 CORDOVA WEST
VANCOUVER, B.C. V6B 1C8
(604) 684-6438

HUISH, DON & ASSOCIATES LTD.
946 MAIN
VANCOUVER, B.C. V6A 2W3
(604) 684-7211

HURRELL, ROBIN ASSOCIATES LTD.
3561 DUVAL ROAD
VANCOUVER, B.C. V7J 3E8
(604) 734-8212

IDEAL INTERIORS LTD.
1036 MAINLAND STREET
VANCOUVER, B.C. V6B 2T4
(604) 685-4207

**INTEGRATED DESIGN SERVICES
VANCOUVER LTD.**
353 WATER STREET
VANCOUVER, B.C. V6B 1B8
(604) 685-1719

JONES, LYN T. ASSOCIATES LTD.
P.O. BOX 46354, STATION G
VANCOUVER, B.C. V6R 4G6
(604) 327-8898

JORDANS INTERIORS LTD.
1470 WEST BROADWAY
VANCOUVER, B.C. V6H 1H4
(604) 733-1174

KBD ASSOCIATES
400 – 744 WEST HASTINGS STREET
VANCOUVER, B.C. V6C 1A5
(604) 688-3893

KAVANAUGH, DON & ASSOCIATES LTD.
2050 CARDINAL CRESCENT
DEEP COVE, B.C. V7G 1Y4
(604) 929-7623

KEATE & CO. DESIGNERS
2554 VINE STREET
VANCOUVER, B.C. V6K 3L1
(604) 736-5491

KEETLEY DESIGN CONSULTANTS INC.
744 HASTINGS WEST
VANCOUVER, B.C. V6C 1A5
(604) 689-7222

KENNEDY, PATRICK INTERIOR DESIGN
527 – 119 WEST PENDER STREET
VANCOUVER, B.C. V6B 1S4
(604) 682-2024

KIDDO WORKS DESIGN INC.
22 EAST 2ND AVENUE
VANCOUVER, B.C. V5T 1B1
(604) 874-3384

KOEMAN DESIGN CONSULTANTS LTD.
800 PENDER WEST
VANCOUVER, B.C. V6C 2V6
(604) 688-9988

LECHTZIER, MERTON R. INC.
4675 HUDSON
VANCOUVER, B.C. V6H 3B9
(604) 733-2873

• **LEDINGHAM, ROBERT M. INC.**
2327 YEW
VANCOUVER, B.C. V6K 3H1
(604) 734-1281 **Pg. 115**

**McCUTCHEON & ARNDT
DESIGN CONSULTANTS LTD.**
108 – 1365 HOWE STREET
VANCOUVER, B.C. V6Z 1R7
(604) 669-3211

MAGNUSON INTERIORS
6020 FLEMING STREET
VANCOUVER, B.C. V5P 3G6
(604) 327-6979

MAY, DENNIS INTERNATIONAL
4011 WEST 33RD AVENUE
VANCOUVER, B.C. V6N 2H9
(604) 224-7607

MIRICH, SHELLY DESIGN INC.
1290 HOMER STREET
VANCOUVER, B.C. V6B 2Y5
(604) 669-6939

NIELSEN DESIGN CONSULTANTS
1314 FULTON
WEST VANCOUVER, B.C. V7T 1N8
(604) 926-6801

NOVUS BUSINESS ENVIRONMENTS INC.
1108 HOMER STREET
VANCOUVER, B.C. V6B 2X6
(604) 688-2394

PARK ASSOCIATES
1141 WEST 8TH AVENUE
VANCOUVER, B.C. V6H 1C5
(604) 736-7664

**PAVELEK & ASSOCIATES – LANDSCAPE –
INTERIOR ARCHITECTS LTD.**
148 ALEXANDER
VANCOUVER, B.C. V6A 1B5
(604) 687-4566

PRESTON'S INTERIORS LTD.
2574 VINE STREET
VANCOUVER, B.C. V6K 3L1
(604) 733-8345

PURCELL & ASSOCIATES LTD.
1490 HORNBY STREET
VANCOUVER, B.C. V6Z 1X3
(604) 687-8544

R INTERIORS
4 – 1003 WOLFE AVENUE
VANCOUVER, B.C. V6H 1V6
(604) 734-1942

RAMSAY–MATTHEWS DESIGN GROUP
445 MOUNTAIN HWY
VANCOUVER, B.C. V7J 2L1
(604) 986-3331

RICHARDS, VIRGINIA & ASSOCIATES LTD.
1494 HORNBY STREET
VANCOUVER, B.C. V6Z 1X3
(604) 689-1885

RIDGEWOOD STUDIOS & ASSOCIATES LTD.
2199 GRANVILLE
VANCOUVER, B.C. V6H 3E9
(604) 733-9434

ROL FIELDWALKER ARCHITECTS
900 WEST HASTINGS 9TH FLR.
VANCOUVER, B.C. V6C 1W4
(604) 688-8601

SALTER, RICHARD INTERIORS LTD.
863 HAMILTON STREET
VANCOUVER, B.C. V6B 2R7
(604) 688-2284

SASSAFRASS INTERIORS LTD.
3701 WEST 1ST
VANCOUVER, B.C. V6R 1H3
(604) 228-9245

**SEETON SHINKEWSKI
DESIGN GROUP LTD.**
510 – 119 WEST PENDER STREET
VANCOUVER, B.C. V6B 1S4
(604) 685-4301

**SIMON ASSOCIATES
DESIGN GROUP INC.**
1328 SEYMOUR STREET
VANCOUVER, B.C. V6B 3P3
(604) 687-9548

SPIRO GROUP, THE
1 WEST 7TH
VANCOUVER, B.C. V5Y 1L5
(604) 875-9131

STUDIO INTERIORS LTD.
6045 BOULEVARD WEST
VANCOUVER, B.C. V6M 3X2
(604) 266-0010

SYNCOR BUSINESS ENVIRONMENTS LTD.
601 – 889 WEST PENDER STREET
VANCOUVER, B.C. V6C 3B2
(604) 688-0052

TERRA FIRMA DESIGN LTD.
2358 WEST 41ST
VANCOUVER, B.C. V6M 2A4
(604) 266-9718

TOTALPLAN INC.
806 – 750 WEST PENDER
VANCOUVER, B.C. V6C 2T8
(604) 689-7241

UPTOWN DESIGN GROUP INC.
207 – 601 WEST CORDOVA STREET
VANCOUVER, B.C. V6B 1G1
(604) 669-7043

VANCOUVER DESIGN TEAM LTD.
503 – 321 WATER STREET
VANCOUVER, B.C. V6B 1B8
(604) 669-1125

WALKER REINHOLD DESIGN GROUP
310 – 675 WEST HASTINGS STREET
VANCOUVER, B.C. V6B 1N2
(604) 687-8470

WATTS, JOHN L. INTERIORS
1 – 252 EAST 1ST STREET
VANCOUVER, B.C. V7L 1B3
(604) 987-6214

**YOUNGREN, CATHERINE
INTERIOR DESIGNERS INC.**
2110 WEST 12TH AVENUE
VANCOUVER, B.C. V6K 2N2
(604) 734-3231

Victoria

BRISTO, BARBARA INTERIOR DESIGNER
2033 OAK BAY
VICTORIA, B.C. V8R 1E5
(604) 598-9116

DEKORIS INTERIORS LTD.
2880 SEAVIEW ROAD
VICTORIA, B.C. V8N 1L1
(604) 477-2353

DESIGN ASSOCIATES
4699 AMBLEWOOD
VICTORIA, B.C. V8Y 1C4
(604) 658-1389

• **EATON'S CONTRACT INTERIORS**
660 FORT STREET
VICTORIA, B.C. V8W 1G8
(604) 382-7141 **Pg. 52, 108, 143**

EGO INTERIORS
1028 FORT
VICTORIA, B.C. V8V 3K4
(604) 382-3200

INTEREX CONTRACT INTERIORS INC.
3318 OAK STREET
VICTORIA, B.C. V8X 1R1
(604) 384-3033

INTERIORS BY HAROLD E. TWETEN
1608 FORT STREET
VICTORIA, B.C. V8R 1H9
(604) 598-2151

IVEY, S.E. IMPORTS LTD.
911 FORT STREET
VICTORIA, B.C. V8V 3K3
(604) 385-7111

LIESCH INTERIORS LTD.
2020 DOUGLAS STREET
VICTORIA, B.C. V8T 4L1
(604) 384-8321

NORTH PARK DESIGNS LTD.
1619 STORE STREET
VICTORIA, B.C. V8W 3K3
(604) 381-3422

SAGER'S
1802 GOVERNMENT STREET
VICTORIA, B.C. V8T 4N5
(604) 382-3200

▶ ATLANTIC CANADA

FOWLER BAULD & MITCHEL LTD.
1717 BARRINGTON
HALIFAX, NOVA SCOTIA
(902) 429-4100

LEE INTERIORS LTD.
39 DUNDAS
HALIFAX, NOVA SCOTIA
(902) 466-7536

LYNCH, LYNDON ASSOCIATES LTD.
1741 GRAFTON
HALIFAX, NOVA SCOTIA
(902) 422-1476

WEBER HARRINGTON WELD GROUP INC.
5409 RAINNIE DRIVE
HALIFAX, NOVA SCOTIA
(902) 429-5190

▶ QUEBEC

ABCO DESIGNS INC.
5005 JEAN TALON OUEST
MONTREAL, QUEBEC
(514) 731-9479

BRAM GROUPE DESIGN INC.
103 MONTEE DU MOULIN,
LAVAL, QUEBEC H7N 3Y7
(514) 667-1421

**CONSORTIUM DESIGN
INTERNATIONAL INC.**
239, ST-SACREMENT
MONTREAL, QUEBEC
(514) 845-8141

CONTINUUM DESIGN INC.
7881, RUE DECARIE
MONTREAL, QUEBEC
(514) 739-7708

DALLAIRE MICHEL DESIGNERS INC.
2151-A, RUE DE LA MONTAGNE
MONTREAL, QUEBEC
(514) 282-9262

DALLEGRET FRANCOIS ARTORIUM INC.
353, PRINCE ALBERT
MONTREAL, QUEBEC
(514) 486-1444

DESIGN & COMMUNICATION INC.
4465, RUE SHERBROOKE OUEST
MONTREAL, QUEBEC
(514) 932-1428

DUCHARME, BENOIT & ASSOCIES INC.
65, RUE DE LA CASTELNAU OUEST
MONTREAL, QUEBEC
(514) 495-1719

• **G.S.M. DESIGN**
317, PLACE D'YOUVILLE
MONTREAL, QUEBEC H2Y 2B5
(514) 288-4233 **Pg. 54**

JOLY JORISCH ET ASSOCIES
1463, RUE PREFONTAINE
MONTREAL, QUEBEC
(514) 521-2541

LALANDE, PHILIPPE DESIGNERS INC.
370, GUY
MONTREAL, QUEBEC
(514) 932-8582

LAVAL BLUTEAU LEVESQUE
1648-C, RUE SHERBROOKE OUEST
MONTREAL, QUEBEC
(514) 931-9249

LOCAS BERNARD DESIGNERS LTEE
391, ST-JACQUES
MONTREAL, QUEBEC
(514) 284-2288

MORELLI MICHEL DESIGNERS INC.
1463, RUE PREFONTAINE
MONTREAL, QUEBEC
(514) 521-9288

MORIN LESSARD McINNIS & ASSOCIES
1840, RUE SHERBROOKE OUEST
MONTREAL, QUEBEC
(514) 935-5409

MULTIFORME DESIGN INC.
8255, MOUNTAIN SIGHTS
MONTREAL, QUEBEC
(514) 342-6024

• **OVE DESIGN INTERIORS INC.**
356, RUE LE MOYNE
VIEUX-MONTREAL, QUEBEC H2Y 1Y3
(514) 844-8421 **Pg. 70**

NORMAN SLATER INC.
4845, RUE SHERBROOKE OUEST
MONTREAL, QUEBEC
(514) 932-4164

PRODESIGN LTEE
296, ST-PAUL OUEST
MONTREAL, QUEBEC
(514) 844-3349

SERI PLUS
304, RUE NOTRE DAME EST
MONTREAL, QUEBEC H2Y 1C7
(514) 861-2343

SOUCY, RICHARD DESIGN
53 MILTON STREET
MONTREAL, QUEBEC H2X 1V2
(514) 489-4579

UNILIGHT LTD.
4999, ST-CATHERINE OUEST
MONTREAL, QUEBEC
(514) 482-1710

WELGOLAN DESIGN INC.
4846 SHERBROOKE OUEST
MONTREAL, QUEBEC
(514) 483-5073

▶ ONTARIO

ADAMS, LEONARD INC.
65 HIGH PARK AVENUE
TORONTO, ONTARIO M6P 2R7
(416) 769-2814

ADAMSON INDUSTRIAL DESIGN
174 AVENUE ROAD
TORONTO, ONTARIO M5R 2J1
(416) 963-9356

ALMAS, PAUL R. & ASSOCIATES LTD.
492 SPEERS
TORONTO, ONTARIO
(416) 842-1944

ALMDESIGN
74 WALMER
TORONTO, ONTARIO
(416) 923-4944

AMBIANT
76 RICHMOND STREET EAST
TORONTO, ONTARIO
(416) 863-0863

AMBIANT WOODWORKS
980 ALLIANCE ROAD
PICKERING, ONTARIO
(416) 831-3011

ANDOFF MICHAEL WORKSHOP
32 SCOLLARD
TORONTO, ONTARIO
(416) 921-0836

ARATO DESIGNS LTD.
180 DUNCAN MILL
TORONTO, ONTARIO
(416) 445-9480

ARCHITECTURAL DESIGN SYSTEMS
166 NORSEMAN
TORONTO, ONTARIO
(416) 237-0187

• **ARCONAS CORPORATION**
580 ORWELL STREET
MISSISSAUGA, ONTARIO L5A 3V7
(416) 272-0727 **Pg. 168**

A.R.E.A
334 KING STREET EAST
TORONTO, ONTARIO
(416) 367-5850

ARNOTT, JOHN & ASSOCIATES LTD.
7 POLSON
TORONTO, ONTARIO
(416) 461-8149

AZIZ DESIGNS
493 DAVENPORT ROAD
TORONTO, ONTARIO
(416) 921-3809

BANRI & ASSOCIATES
173 MARGUERETTA STREET
TORONTO, ONTARIO M6H 3S4
(416) 535-5933

BURGESS ASSOCIATES
2333 DUNDAS STREET WEST
MISSISSAUGA, ONTARIO
(416) 536-3657

LORIS CALZOLARI
772 RICHMOND STREET WEST
TORONTO, ONTARIO
(416) 360-7151

• **D. CHENIER ASSOCIATES LTD.**
236 AVENUE ROAD
TORONTO, ONTARIO M5R 2J4
(416) 964-1545 **Pg. 46**

COLLIER FURNITURE LTD.
1377 LAWRENCE AVENUE EAST
TORONTO, ONTARIO M3A 3M4
(416) 449-7655

CONCEPT B
388 CARLAW AVENUE
TORONTO, ONTARIO M4M 2T4
(416) 462-1700

CRAFTWOOD PRODUCTS
191 FINCHDENE SQUARE
SCARBOROUGH, ONTARIO M1X 1B9
(416) 297-1100

DALLAS
7370 WOODBINE AVENUE, UNIT 4
MARKHAM, ONTARIO L3R 1A7
(416) 477-6296

• **DESIGN COOPERATIVE, THE**
135 TECUMSETH STREET
TORONTO, ONTARIO M6J 2H2
(416) 947-1684 **Pg. 158**

• **DESIGNWERKE**
366 KING STREET EAST
TORONTO, ONTARIO M5A 1K9
(416) 362-6000 **Pg. 156**

DICKSON JAMIE DESIGN INC.
77 MOWAT AVENUE
TORONTO, ONTARIO
(416) 536-2973

• **FORUM & FUNCTION**
749 QUEEN STREET WEST
TORONTO, ONTARIO M6J 1G1
(416) 364-7251 **Pg. 160**

FORTUNE, MICHAEL
278A GLADSTONE AVENUE
TORONTO, ONTARIO M6J 3L6
(416) 532-4607

BRIAN FOSTER LTD.
1560 BAYVIEW AVENUE
TORONTO, ONTARIO
(416) 487-2330

GROUP FOUR
25-5 CONNELL COURT
TORONTO, ONTARIO M8Z 1E8
(416) 251-1128

• **HARRIS, STEPHEN DESIGNS**
35 BOOTH AVENUE
TORONTO, ONTARIO M4M 2M3
(416) 466-5892 **Pg. 161**

HATCH, MICHAEL DESIGNS LTD.
46 ELLERBECK
TORONTO, ONTARIO
(416) 465-9406

HATHAWAY DESIGN GROUP
99 CHARLES STREET EAST
TORONTO, ONTARIO
(416) 925-4158

• **KEILHAUER INDUSTRIES LTD.**
946 WARDEN AVENUE
TORONTO, ONTARIO M1L 4C9
(416) 759-5665 **Pg. 191**

KINETICS FURNITURE
110 CARRIER DRIVE
REXDALE, ONTARIO M9W 5R1
(416) 675-4300

• **KURTZ MANN DESIGN**
390 DUPONT STREET
TORONTO, ONTARIO M5R 1V9
(416) 927-0353 **Pg. 154**

KUYPERS NORTON LTD.
76 RICHMOND STREET EAST
TORONTO, ONTARIO
(416) 362-7737

LESER DESIGN INC.
499 ADELAIDE STREET WEST
TORONTO, ONTARIO
(416) 360- 7432

L'IMAGE
418 EGLINTON AVENUE WEST
TORONTO, ONTARIO M5N 1A2
(416) 488-2268

MACHIKO DESIGNS
608 MARKHAM STREET
TORONTO, ONTARIO M6G 2L8
(416) 588-1760

HERMAN MILLER CANADA, INC.
2360 ARGENTIA ROAD
MISSISSAUGA, ONTARIO L5N 4G9
(416) 858-7955

MULLER, KEITH LTD.
56 THE ESPLANADE
TORONTO, ONTARIO M5E 1A7
(416) 362-6446

THOMAS L. LAMB
31 MARIETTA STREET
OXBRIDGE, ONTARIO L0C 1K0
(416) 852-6859

NICHOLLS & GILL LIMITED
479 RICHMOND STREET
LONDON, ONTARIO N6A 3E4
(519) 672-6001

• **NIENKAMPER**
415 FINCHDENE SQUARE
TORONTO, ONTARIO M1X 1B7
(416) 298-5700 **Pg. 196**

PANACHE DESIGN LIMITED
361 KING STREET EAST
TORONTO, ONTARIO M5A 1L1
(416) 369-0084

• **PETERAN, GORDON**
248 DUPONT STREET
TORONTO, ONTARIO M5R 1V7
(416) 925-5342 **Pg. 161**

PICCALUGA, FRANCESCO & ALDO
615 YONGE STREET
TORONTO, ONTARIO M4Y 2T4
(416) 923-9582

• **PIEROBON, PETER**
35 BOOTH AVENUE
TORONTO, ONTARIO M4M 2M3
(416) 466-5892 **Pg. 161**

• **PRESTON**
500 UNIVERSITY AVENUE, 10TH FLOOR
TORONTO, ONTARIO M5G 1V7
(416) 598-3540 **Pg. 72, 148**

• **PRISMATIQUE DESIGNS LTD.**
265 DAVENPORT ROAD
TORONTO, ONTARIO M5R 1J9
(416) 961-7333 **Pg. 197**

RADUN DESIGN PLANNING LTD.
287 MACPHERSON
TORONTO, ONTARIO
(416) 968-6767

ROBBIE ARCHITECTS PLANNERS
3 ROWANWOOD AVENUE
TORONTO, ONTARIO
(416) 961-5444

SOHEIL MOSUN LTD.
1862 KIPLING AVENUE
REXDALE, ONTARIO M9W 4J1
(416) 243-1600

• **SNYDER FURNITURE LTD.**
87 COLVILLE ROAD
TORONTO, ONTARIO M6M 2Y6
(416) 247-6285 **Pg. 202**

STRATA
191½ KING STREET EAST
TORONTO, ONTARIO M5A 1J5
(416) 366-5915

STUDIO INNOVA INC.
8 CLARENCE SQUARE
TORONTO, ONTARIO M5V 1H1
(416) 595-5991

• **STUDIO STORE, THE**
353 EASTERN AVENUE
TORONTO, ONTARIO M4M 1B7
(416) 461-2086 **Pg. 204**

STEWART, MICHAEL
77 SOUTH DRIVE
TORONTO, ONTARIO
(416) 923-0827

• **SUNARHAUSERMAN**
1 SUNSHINE AVENUE
WATERLOO, ONTARIO N2J 4K5
(519) 886-2000 **Pg. 208**

THURSTON DESIGN CORPORATION
864 CARLAW AVENUE
TORONTO, ONTARIO M4K 3L4
(416) 466-5244

• **WHITELEY, WM. LIMITED**
214 LAIRD DRIVE
TORONTO, ONTARIO M4G 3W4
(416) 429-7503 **Pg. 214**

▶ W E S T E R N   C A N A D A

J. BUDD & ASSOCIATES LTD.
1440 9TH STREET NW
CALGARY, ALBERTA T2M 3L2
(403) 284-3699

DESIGN SYSTEMS
1330 CHURCH
WINNIPEG, MANITOBA
(204) 632-0149

DESIN INC.
490 NIAGARA STREET
WINNIPEG, MANITOBA R3N 0V5
(204) 477-0619

ENVIRONMENTAL SPACE PLANNING LTD.
300-290 VAUGHAN
WINNIPEG, MANITOBA
(204) 944-9272

HOSALUK, MICHAEL
RR NO. 2
SASKATOON, SASKATCHEWAN S7K 3J5
(306) 382-2380

KONAD, KELLY & ASSOCIATES
32 MOHAWK
ST-BONIFACE, MANITOBA
(204) 257-3794

MITCHELL, MARK & ASSOCIATES INC.
245 BELL
WINNIPEG, MANITOBA
(204) 477-0481

ZAIDMAN, PAUL DESIGNS LTD.
1647 ST. JAMES STREET
ST. JAS., MANITOBA
(204) 775-4455

▶ B R I T I S H   C O L U M B I A

ATELIER DESIGN CONSULTANTS LTD.
202 – 1089 W BROADWAY
VANCOUVER, B.C.
(604) 738-7250

B.C. RESEARCH
3650 WESBROOK MALL
VANCOUVER, B.C.
(604) 224-4331

BRADFORD DESIGN & ASSOCIATES
13270 – 87B AVENUE
SURREY, B.C.
(604) 594-5787

CITY INTERIORS LTD.
595 BURRARD
VANCOUVER, B.C. V7X 1K8
(604) 661-5010

DESIGN ART
205-1089 W. BROADWAY
VANCOUVER, B.C.
(604) 733-5518

PURCELL, C. & ASSOCIATES LTD.
1490 HORNBY STREET
VANCOUVER, B.C.
(604) 687-8544

GEPPERT W.A. & ASSOCIATES INC.
1015 BURRARD
VANCOUVER, B.C.
(604) 684-3722

• **GROUP 5 DESIGN ASSOCIATES LTD.**
1305 W. GEORGIA STREET
VANCOUVER, B.C. V6E 3K6
(604) 681-8155 **Pg. 55**

HOPPING KOVACH GRINNELL
DESIGN CONSULTANTS LTD.
81 WEST CORDOVA STREET
VANCOUVER, B.C. V6B 1C8
(604) 684-6438

LEAR INDUSTRIAL DESIGN
A-1535 WEST 3RD STREET
VANCOUVER, B.C.
(604) 732-6581

LIONEL HOLT ASSOCIATES
337 EAST, 10TH STREET
N. VANCOUVER, B.C.
(604) 980-2361

RAMSAY – MATTEWS DESIGN GROUP
445 MOUNTAIN
N. VANCOUVER, B.C.
(604) 986-3331

ROGERS INTER DESIGNS INC.
1164 HAMILTON
VANCOUVER, B.C.
(604) 687-4462

VANCOUVER DESIGN TEAM LTD.
503-321 WATER STREET
VANCOUVER, B.C. V6B 1B8
(604) 669-1125

▶ QUEBEC

AMENAGEMENT EXPOSITIONS TCD INC.
605, RUE DESLAURIERS
MONTREAL, QUEBEC
(514) 335-0820

ARCHEX LTEE
2630, RUE SABOURIN
MONTREAL, QUEBEC
(514) 334-1012

AU PINCEAU D'ARLEQUIN INC.
760, RUE ST-FELIX
MONTREAL, QUEBEC
(514) 878-9166

CONTINUUM DESIGN INC.
7881, DECARIE
MONTREAL, QUEBEC
(514) 739-7708

DANESCO DEWINTER DESIGN INC.
7200 TRANSCANADA HWY.
MONTREAL, QUEBEC H4T 1A3
(514) 735-5757

DELCO COMMERCIAL CONCEPTS INC.
1850, BEAULAC
MONTREAL, QUEBEC
(514) 335-3000

EXPO 4 INC.
2300, VICTORIA
LACHINE, QUEBEC
(514) 637-4625

EXPO GRAPHICS AND DISPLAYS
65, RUE ADRIEN ROBERTS
HULL, QUEBEC J8Y 3S3
(819) 770-5167

PROPS ETALAGE INC.
1591, RUE CLARK
MONTREAL, QUEBEC H2X 2R4
(514) 843-8871

▶ ONTARIO

**ADAMSON INDUSTRIAL DESIGN
ASSOCIATES INC.**
174 AVENUE ROAD
TORONTO, ONTARIO M5R 2J1
(416) 963-9356

ALPHAFORM EXHIBITS & DESIGN INC.
76 RICHMOND STREET EAST
TORONTO, ONTARIO M5C 1P1
(416) 366-9403

B.C.C. GROUP
166 NORSEMAN STREET
TORONTO, ONTARIO M8Z 2R4
(416) 237-0071

• **BGM COLOUR LABORATORIES LTD.**
497 KING STREET EAST
TORONTO, ONTARIO M5A 1L9
(416) 947-1325 **Pg. 267**

BLACKSHAW DISPLAY INC.
52 HAYDEN
TORONTO, ONTARIO
(416) 922-8182

C.D.A. INDUSTRIES
1430 BIRCHMOUNT
SCARBOROUGH, ONTARIO M1P 2E8
(416) 752-2301

C.E.S. EXHIBITS INC.
9 HANNA AVENUE
TORONTO, ONTARIO M6K 1W8
(416) 530-4411

CANADIAN DESIGN CONSULTANTS
697 CRAWFORD
TORONTO, ONTARIO
(416) 536-2806

CLICK SYSTEMS
7270 TORBRAM
MALTON, ONTARIO
(416) 677-0541

CURR DESIGN CORPORATION
464 KING STREET EAST
TORONTO, ONTARIO
(416) 366-2234

DANN DUNN DESIGNS INC.
3240A YONGE STREET
TORONTO, ONTARIO M4N 2L4
(416) 483-0629

DESIGN ALTERNATIVES
25 LLOYD MANOR
ISLINGTON, ONTARIO
(416) 231-9310

EXHIBITIONARCHITECTURE
71 McCAUL
TORONTO, ONTARIO
(416) 591-6302

EXHIBITS ROAD INTERNATIONAL
55 FIELDWAY
TORONTO, ONTARIO M8Z 3L4
(416) 231-2818

EXPOSYSTEMS CANADA LTD.
2161 MIDLAND AVENUE
SCARBOROUGH, ONTARIO M1P 4T3
(416) 291-2932

FIFTY-ONE DESIGN
101 AMBER
MARKHAM, ONTARIO
(416) 475-7795

GERON ASSOCIATES LTD.
20 PROGRESS AVENUE
SCARBOROUGH, ONTARIO M1P 2Y4
(416) 293-2441

GORING ASSOCIATES INC.
77 MOWAT AVENUE
TORONTO, ONTARIO
(416) 536-3509

HOLMAN DESIGN INC.
21 KERN ROAD
DON MILLS, ONTARIO M3B 1S9
(416) 441-1877

KEPAC CANADA
288 JUDSON
TORONTO, ONTARIO M8Z 5T6
(416) 252-3145

KUYPERS NORTON LTD.
76 RICHMOND STREET EAST
TORONTO, ONTARIO
(416) 362-7737

**McMANUS & ASSOCIATES
DESIGN CONSULTANTS LTD.**
275 SPADINA ROAD
TORONTO, ONTARIO M5R 2B3
(416) 922-7661

OCTANORM CANADA LTD.
214-A NORTH QUEEN STREET
ETOBICOKE, ONTARIO M9C 4Y1
(416) 621-9120

PIDDI DESIGN ASSOCIATES LTD.
1 BEAVERDALE ROAD
TORONTO, ONTARIO
(416) 259-3768

SEARS & RUSSELL CONSULTANTS
145 DAVENPORT ROAD
TORONTO, ONTARIO M5R 1J1
(416) 926-8242

SEVEN CONTINENTS ENTERPRISES INC.
350 WALLACE AVENUE
TORONTO, ONTARIO
(416) 535-5101

SMYTH-FISHER LTD.
1596 BONHILL ROAD
MISSISSAUGA, ONTARIO L5T 1C8
(416) 677-0026

• **STUDIO STORE, THE**
353 EASTERN AVENUE
TORONTO, ONTARIO M4M 1B7
(416) 461-2086 **Pg. 204**

**TAYLOR
MANUFACTURING INDUSTRIES INC.**
78 ADVANCE ROAD
TORONTO, ONTARIO M8Z 2T9
(416) 232-1671

WORDEN-WATSON LTD.
12 PROGRESS AVENUE
SCARBOROUGH, ONTARIO M1P 2Y4
(416) 291-3432

▶ MANITOBA

ECLIPSE-3 LTD.
300-66 KING
WINNIPEG, MANITOBA
(204) 943-7557

HORIZON DISPLAYS INC.
303 NAIRN
WINNIPEG, MANITOBA
(204) 667-7962

LOWE MARTIN PORTER LTD.
444 DUFFERIN
WINNIPEG, MANITOBA
(204) 775-8441

TETRAD DESIGN GROUP INC.
1691 ST. MATTHEWS
ST. JAS, MANITOBA
(204) 775-8441

▶ ALBERTA

ADDENDA STUDIOS LTD.
4414 97TH STREET
EDMONTON, ALBERTA
(403) 438-1156

BRANN, WERNER DESIGNS LTD.
643 MARYVALE NE
CALGARY, ALBERTA
(403) 273-4174

BY DESIGN LTD.
200-10361 82ND AVENUE
EDMONTON, ALBERTA
(403) 439-5015

• **CAMPBELL, STEPHEN DESIGN LTD.**
2ND FLOOR, 224 11TH AVENUE SW
CALGARY, ALBERTA T2R 0C3
(403) 262-7416 **Pg. 86**

DANTRADE INTERNATIONAL LTD.
10708 181ST STREET
EDMONTON, ALBERTA
(403) 483-6395

DISPLAY DESIGN SYSTEMS LTD.
10608 172ND STREET
EDMONTON, ALBERTA
(403) 483-6355

DURA COM IMAGES LTD.
10710 176TH STREET
EDMONTON, ALBERTA
(403) 484-2291

I. TANK & ASSOCIATES DESIGN LTD.
405–10357 109TH STREET
EDMONTON, ALBERTA
(403) 423-0434

XIBITA LTD.
200–10361 82ND AVENUE
EDMONTON, ALBERTA
(403) 439-5015

▶ B R I T I S H C O L U M B I A

ALDRICH PEARS ASSOCIATES
1573 EAST PENDER
VANCOUVER B.C.
(604) 253-1125

**D.D. DISPLAY & DESIGN
ASSOCIATES CO. LTD.**
1139 WEST 14TH
NORTH VANCOUVER, B.C.
(604) 987-3816

DHARMA DESIGN & CONSULTATION LTD.
504–134 ABBOTT
VANCOUVER, B.C.
(604) 687-7701

EXCLUSIVE DISPLAYS LTD.
302 WEST 2ND
VANCOUVER, B.C.
(604) 879-6936

EXPOSYSTEMS LTD. CANADA
955 HOMER STREET
VANCOUVER, B.C. V6B 2W6
(604) 681-9102

**HOPPING KOVACH GRINNELL
DESIGN CONSULTANTS LTD.**
81 WEST CORDOVA STREET
VANCOUVER, B.C. V6B 1C8
(604) 684-6438

VANCOUVER DESIGN TEAM LTD.
503 – 321 WATER STREET
VANCOUVER, B.C.
(604) 669-1125

ABITARE DESIGN INC.
51 FRONT STREET EAST
TORONTO, ONTARIO M5E 1B3
(416) 363-1667

• ABSTRACTA SYSTEMS INC.
30 MALLEY ROAD
SCARBOROUGH, ONTARIO M1L 2E3
(416) 751-2717   **Pg. 165**

ADAMS, JANE CUSTOM ACCESSORIES
1390 SHERBROOKE STREET WEST
MONTREAL, QUEBEC H3G 1J9
(514) 845-7592

• ALEXANDER'S FINE FURNITURE
717 KIPLING AVENUE
ETOBICOKE, ONTARIO M8Z 5G4
(416) 252-9347   **Pg. 166**

AMBIANT SYSTEMS LTD.
76 RICHMOND STREET EAST
TORONTO, ONTARIO M5C 1P1
(416) 863-0863

AREA
334 KING STREET EAST
TORONTO, ONTARIO M5A 1K8
(416) 367-5850

ARTISTIC GLASS CO. LTD.
2108 DUNDAS STREET WEST
TORONTO, ONTARIO M6R 1W9
(416) 531-4881

ASHTON'S
267 QUEEN STREET EAST
TORONTO, ONTARIO M5A 1S6
(416) 366-6846

• AU COURANT
354 DAVENPORT ROAD
TORONTO, ONTARIO M5R 1K6
(416) 922-5611   **Pg. 218**

• BONAVENTURE
FURNITURE INDUSTRIES LTD.
894 BLOOMFIELD
MONTREAL, QUEBEC H2V 3S7
(514) 270-7311   **Pg. 170**

BUSINESS ACCESSORIES INC.
415 DUNDAS STREET
CAMBRIDGE, ONTARIO N1R 5Y2
(519) 622-2222

• CODD AND COMPANY
344 DUPONT STREET
TORONTO, ONTARIO M5R 1V9
(416) 923-0066   **Pg. 176**

• CONTEMPORA DESIGNS INT'L INC.
887 YONGE STREET
TORONTO, ONTARIO M4W 2H2
(416) 964-9295   **Pg. 178**

• DACOTA INC.
175 TORYORK DRIVE
WESTON, ONTARIO M9L 1X9
(416) 747-6282   **Pg. 180**

DESIGNERS I
1226 BISHOP STREET
MONTREAL, QUEBEC H3G 2E3
(514) 871-3931

DOOR STORE, THE
118 SHERBOURNE STREET
TORONTO, ONTARIO M5A 2R2
(416) 863-1590

EILEY, JOAN & ASSOCIATES LTD.
326 DAVENPORT ROAD
TORONTO, ONTARIO M5R 1K6
(416) 968-0778

FINNISH DESIGN IMPORTS LTD.
92C SCOLLARD STREET
TORONTO, ONTARIO M5R 1G2
(416) 961-9858

• GINGER'S BATHROOMS
945 EGLINTON AVENUE EAST
TORONTO, ONTARIO M4G 4B5
(416) 429-3444   **Pg. 246**

HERITAGE INTERIORS
224 DAVENPORT ROAD
TORONTO, ONTARIO M5R 1J6
(416) 922-6448

HERMAN MILLER CANADA, INC.
2360 ARGENTIA ROAD
MISSISSAUGA, ONTARIO L5N 4G9
(416) 858-7955

HEWI CANADA LIMITED
170 ESNA PARK DRIVE
MARKHAM, ONTARIO L3R 1E3
(416) 477-5990

ITALINTERIORS LTD.
359 KING STREET EAST
TORONTO, ONTARIO M5A 1L1
(416) 366-9540

JOHNSON, CRAIG & ASSOCIATES INC.
462 WELLINGTON STREET WEST
TORONTO, ONTARIO M5B 1E3
(416) 597-0733

L'IMAGE DESIGN
418 EGLINTON AVENUE WEST
TORONTO, ONTARIO M5N 1A2
(416) 488-3268

• MARBLE TREND
2050 STEELES AVENUE WEST
CONCORD, ONTARIO L4K 2V1
(416) 738-0400   **Pg. 239**

• MARCUS, H.D. ENTERPRISES INC.
294 BERKELEY STREET
TORONTO, ONTARIO M5A 2X5
(416) 967-7617   **Pg. 276**

MILNE & ASSOCIATES INC.
49 SPADINA AVENUE
TORONTO, ONTARIO M5V 2J1
(416) 591-9114

MOSUN, SOHEIL
1872 KIPLING AVENUE
REXDALE, ONTARIO M9W 4J1
(416) 243-1600

• NIENKAMPER
300 KING STREET EAST
TORONTO, ONTARIO M5A 1K4
(416) 362-3434   **Pg. 196**

NORMAN CARRIERE AGENCIES INC.
478 QUEEN STREET EAST
TORONTO, ONTARIO M5A 1T7
(416) 363-1152

OLAN DESIGNS
700 BAY STREET
TORONTO, ONTARIO M5G 1Z6
(416) 979-2600

• PRIMAVERA
INTERIOR ACCESSORIES LTD.
300 KING STREET EAST
TORONTO, ONTARIO M5A 1K4
(416) 368-3455   **Pg. 223**

QUINTESSENCE DESIGNS
1657 BAYVIEW AVENUE
TORONTO, ONTARIO M4G 3C1
(416) 482-1252

SHAW-PEZZO & ASSOCIATES INC.
146 DUPONT
TORONTO, ONTARIO M5R 1V2
(416) 961-8213

• SHELAGH'S OF CANADA
354 DAVENPORT ROAD
TORONTO, ONTARIO M5R 1K6
(416) 924-7331   **Pg. 200**

SUMMERHILL HARDWARE LTD.
24 BIRCH AVENUE
TORONTO, ONTARIO M4V 1C8
(416) 962-0471

SUPREME ALUMINUM INDUSTRIES LTD.
3600 DANFORTH AVENUE
SCARBOROUGH, ONTARIO M1N 2E6
(416) 691-2141

SWITZER, W. & ASSOCIATES LTD.
291 EAST 2ND AVENUE
VANCOUVER, B.C. V5T 1B8
(604) 872-7611

• TENDEX SILKO INC.
264 THE ESPLANADE
TORONTO, ONTARIO M5A 4J6
(416) 361-1555   **Pg. 211**

• TRIEDE DESIGN INC.
460 McGILL STREET
MONTREAL, QUEBEC H2Y 2H2
(514) 288-0063   **Pg. 212**

WHITE, ALBERT & CO. LTD.
82 SPADINA AVENUE
TORONTO, ONTARIO M5V 2J4
(416) 363-2171

• WHITELEY, WM. LTD.
214 LAIRD DRIVE
TORONTO, ONTARIO M4G 3W4
(416) 429-7503   **Pg. 214**

WYLIE, GLENN J. & ASSOCIATES LTD.
81 KELFIELD STREET, UNITS 5 & 6
REXDALE, ONTARIO M9W 5A3
(416) 243-7770

► QUEBEC

BANYO CANADA LTD.
5500 FULLUM STREET
MONTREAL, QUEBEC H3G 2H3
(514) 274-3646

CERATEC INC.
414, ST-SACREMENT
QUEBEC, QUEBEC G1N 3Y3
(418) 681-0101

CORANCO CORP. LTD.
2409–46TH AVENUE
LACHINE, QUEBEC H8T 3C9
(514) 636-4067

CRANE CANADA LTD.
5800 COTE DE LIESSE ROAD
MONTREAL, QUEBEC H4T 1B4
(514) 735-3592

DESIGN FOCUS INC.
1000 RUE DE LA MONTAGNE
MONTREAL, QUEBEC H3G 1Y7
(514) 866-1893

► ONTARIO

AMERICAN STANDARD
80 WARD STREET
TORONTO, ONTARIO M6H 4A7
(416) 536-1078

APSCO PRODUCTS LTD.
4075 GORDON BAKER ROAD
AGINCOURT, ONTARIO M1W 2P4
(416) 499-5600

AQUALINE PRODUCTS LTD.
1677 AIMCO BLVD.
MISSISSAUGA, ONTARIO L4H 1H7
(416) 625-9301

ARTWIN PRODUCTS LTD.
1249 ADVANCE ROAD
BURLINGTON, ONTARIO L7M 1G7
(416) 335-1474

C & M PRODUCTS LTD.
189 BULLOCK DRIVE
MARKHAM, ONTARIO L3P 1W4
(416) 294-9570

CANADIAN GYPSUM CO. LTD.
790 BAY STREET
TORONTO, ONTARIO M5W 1K8
(416) 495-8800

CARPANO INTERIORS
80 HANLAN ROAD
WOODBRIDGE, ONTARIO L4L 3P6
(416) 851-5552

CERAMIC DECOR ONTARIO LTD.
4544 DUFFERIN STREET
DOWNSVIEW, ONTARIO M3H 5R9
(416) 665-8787

EMCO LIMITED
1108 DUNDAS STREET EAST, BOX 5330
LONDON, ONTARIO N6A 4N7
(519) 451-1250

• **GINGER'S BATHROOMS**
945 EGLINTON AVENUE EAST
TORONTO, ONTARIO M4G 4B5
(416) 429-3444 **Pg. 246**

KIRSCH OF CANADA LTD.
100 NORWICH AVENUE
WOODSTOCK, ONTARIO N4S 7Z1
(519) 537-5531

• **SUNCITY TRADING CO. LTD./
KOHLER CENTRE**
1979 LESLIE STREET
DON MILLS, ONTARIO M3B 2M3
(416) 449-3171 **Pg. 247**

K I T C H E N S

► QUEBEC

DOR-VAL MFG. LTD.
2760, BOUL. LAURENTIAN
ST-LAURENT, QUEBEC H4K 2E1
(514) 336-7780

**STANDARD DESK
DIV. JOYCE BUSINESS FURNITURE**
1000 ST. MARTIN BLVD.
LAVAL, QUEBEC H7S 1M7
(514) 663-3030

MULTIFORM KITCHENS LTD.
5525 UPPER LACHINE
MONTREAL, QUEBEC H4A 2A5
(514) 483-1800

► ONTARIO

ABBEY LANE KITCHEN
2042 AVENUE ROAD
TORONTO, ONTARIO M5M 4A6
(416) 481-9327

ALAR FURNITURE INC.
707 CLAYSON ROAD
WESTON, ONTARIO M9M 2H4
(416) 743-1925

BECKERMAN CUSTOM KITCHENS LTD.
44 OTONABEE DRIVE
KITCHENER, ONTARIO N2C 1L6
(519) 893-6280

CARPANO INTERIORS
80 HANLAN ROAD
WOODBRIDGE, ONTARIO L4L 3P6
(416) 851-5552

CASSIDY'S LTD.
95 EASTSIDE DRIVE
TORONTO, ONTARIO M9L 5N2
(416) 239-3171

**INTERHOME
INTERNATIONAL FURNITURE**
8400 WOODBINE AVENUE
UNIONVILLE, ONTARIO
(416) 475-0705

HANOVER KITCHENS TORONTO LTD.
2725 YONGE STREET
TORONTO, ONTARIO M4N 2H8
(416) 485-7615

JOHN HAUSER IRON WORKS LTD.
148 BEDFORD ROAD
KITCHENER, ONTARIO N2G 3W9
(519) 744-1138

KNAPE & VOGT CANADA LTD.
340 CARLINGVIEW DRIVE
REXDALE, ONTARIO M9W 5G5
(416) 675-3451

LAURENTIDE KITCHENS
945 EGLINTON AVENUE EAST
TORONTO, ONTARIO M4G 4B5
(416) 429-4900

MUSTERRING INTERNATIONAL LTD.
3105 ORLANDO DRIVE
MISSISSAUGA, ONTARIO L4V 1C5
(416) 677-6445

NEW WORLD KITCHENS
366 ADELAIDE STREET EAST
TORONTO, ONTARIO M5A 3X9
(416) 869-0300

NIMA KITCHENS
2060 STEELES AVENUE WEST
CONCORD, ONTARIO L4K 1A1
(416) 667-8910

PARIS KITCHENS
95 DOLOMITE DRIVE
DOWNSVIEW, ONTARIO M3J 2N1
(416) 661-0630

POGGENPOHL KITCHEN STUDIO
5200 DIXIE ROAD
MISSISSAUGA, ONTARIO L4W 1E4
(416) 625-8811

• **ROBINSON GROUP, THE**
263 DAVENPORT ROAD
TORONTO, ONTARIO M5R 1J9
(416) 923-1333 **Pg. 141**

SNAIDERO CANADA LTD.
481 HANLAN ROAD
WOODBRIDGE, ONTARIO L4L 3T1
(416) 851-7777

▶ QUEBEC

ARMSTRONG CORK INDUSTRIES LTD.
6911 DECARIE
MONTREAL, QUEBEC H3W 3E5
(514) 739-2796

ITALITE INC.
9855 MEILEUR STREET
MONTREAL, QUEBEC H3L 3J6
(514) 382-2793

LIGHTOLIER CANADA LTD.
3015 LOUIS A. AMOS
LACHINE, QUEBEC H8N 1H8
(514) 636-0670

MASONITE CANADA LTD.
418 GOLF AVENUE
GATINEAU, QUEBEC J8R 6K2
(819) 633-5331

TAYLOR EVANS LTD.
4645, RUE DES GRANDES PRAIRIES
MONTREAL, QUEBEC H1R 1A5
(514) 325-7700

VAL ABEL TEXTILES LTD.
55 MT. ROYAL AVENUE WEST
MONTREAL, QUEBEC H2T 2S6
(514) 842-9503

VENAIR DISTRIBUTING INC.
7950 ALFRED STREET
ANJOU, QUEBEC H1J 1J1
(514) 354-2230

▶ ONTARIO

ARMSTRONG WORLD INDUSTRIES
2233 ARGENTIA ROAD
MISSISSAUGA, ONTARIO L5N 2X7
(416) 826-4551

BALMER ARCHITECTURAL ART
69 PAPE AVENUE
TORONTO, ONTARIO M4M 2V5
(416) 466-6306

BIRSAY MESH LTD
2520 RENA ROAD
MISSISSAUGA, ONTARIO L4T 3C9
(416) 677-8985

CDA INDUSTRIES INC.
1430 BIRCHMOUNT ROAD
SCARBOROUGH, ONTARIO M1P 2E8
(416) 752-2301

C & M PRODUCTS LTD.
189 BULLOCK DRIVE
MARKHAM, ONTARIO L3P 1W4
(416) 294-9570

CANADIAN GYPSUM CO. LTD.
790 BAY STREET
TORONTO, ONTARIO M5W 1K8
(416) 595-8800

CANADIAN JOHNS-MANVILLE
295 THE WEST MALL
TORONTO, ONTARIO
(416) 626-5200

CANADIAN PITTSBURGH IND.
50 ST. CLAIR AVENUE WEST
TORONTO, ONTARIO M4V 1M8
(416) 924-8701

CANFOR LTD.
44 MEDULLA AVENUE
TORONTO, ONTARIO M8Z 5P9
(416) 236-1851

CREATIVE CEILING DESIGN
404-406 ORMONT DRIVE
TORONTO, ONTARIO M9G 1N9
(416) 748-1462

• **DAMPA**
2050 ELLESMERE ROAD
SCARBOROUGH, ONTARIO M1H 3A9
(416) 438-9640 **Pg. 244**

DONN CANADA LTD.
735 4TH LINE
OAKVILLE, ONTARIO
(419) 920-0270

FIBERGLASS CANADA INC.
3080 YONGE STREET
TORONTO, ONTARIO M4N 3N1
(416) 482-2836

FORMS & SURFACES
49 SPADINA AVENUE
TORONTO, ONTARIO M5V 2J1
(416) 591-9114

• **HUNTER DOUGLAS**
7535 BATH ROAD
MISSISSAUGA, ONTARIO L4T 4C1
(416) 678-1133 **Pg. 243**

HALO OF CANADA LIGHTING INC.
5130 CREEKBANK ROAD
MISSISSAUGA, ONTARIO L4W 2G2
(416) 625-2511

MILNE & ASSOC. INC.
49 SPADINA AVENUE
TORONTO, ONTARIO M5V 2J1
(416) 591-9114

ONTARIO CORK CO. LTD.
36 ASHWARREN ROAD
TORONTO, ONTARIO M3J 1Z5
(416) 630-9702

• **RAAK LIGHTING OF CANADA LTD.**
147 CHURCH STREET
TORONTO, ONTARIO M5B 1Y4
(416) 863-1990 **Pg. 219**

REVEL LUMINAIRES INC.
381 RICHMOND STREET EAST
TORONTO, ONTARIO M5A 1P6
(416) 364-6500

ROHM & HAAS CAN. INC.
2 MANSE ROAD
WEST HILL, ONTARIO M1E 3T9
(416) 284-4711

SOUND SOLUTIONS
6235 TOMKEN ROAD
MISSISSAUGA, ONTARIO L5T 1K2
(416) 678-6363

WESTROC INDUSTRIES LTD.
2650 LAKESHORE ROAD WEST
MISSISSAUGA, ONTARIO L5J 1K4
(416) 823-9881

D R A P E R I E S

▶ ATLANTIC CANADA

**ATLANTIC VENETIAN BLINDS
AND DRAPERIES LTD.**
22 WADDELL AVENUE
DARTMOUTH, NOVA SCOTIA B3B 1K3
(902) 463-2263

H.G. ROGERS LTD.
87 GERMAIN STREET
SAINT JOHN, N.B. E2L 4S3
(506) 657-8350

▶ QUEBEC

AVANT-GARDE FABRICS LTD.
7955 ALFRED
ANJOU, QUEBEC H1J 1J3
1-(800) 361-8886

CLAIRE FABRICS INC.
5445 IBERVILLE STREET
MONTREAL, QUEBEC H2G 2B2
(514) 260-1227

COMMONWEALTH CURTAIN CO.
1100 PORT ROYAL STREET
MONTREAL, QUEBEC H2C 2B4
(514) 384-8920

**CONNAISSANCE FABRICS &
WALLCOVERING LTD.**
1632 SHERBROOKE STREET WEST
MONTREAL, QUEBEC H3H 2L4
(514) 931-2437

WALTER DEPPING INC.
3157, BOUL. ROBERT
MONTREAL, QUEBEC H1Z 1X9
(514) 728-3609

J.T. DILLON DECOR
555 CHABAUD
MONTREAL, QUEBEC H2N 2H8
(514) 384-7440

HAFNER FABRICS OF CANADA LTD.
1405 PEEL STREET
MONTREAL, QUEBEC H3A 1S5
(514) 842-8172

LAURA ASHLEY SHOPS LTD.
2110 CRESCENT STREET
MONTREAL, QUEBEC H3G 2B8
(514) 284-9225

ROSEDALE DRAPERIES INC.
1100 PORT ROYAL EAST
MONTREAL, QUEBEC H2C 2B4
(514) 384-8290

SALETEX FABRICS LTD.
4716 THIMENS BLVD.
ST-LAURENT, QUEBEC H4R 2B2
(514) 334-7533

SCANGIFT LTD.
10245 COTE DE LIESSE
DORVAL, QUEBEC H9P 1A3
(514) 631-6703

TELIO & CIE
1390 SHERBROOKE STREET WEST
MONTREAL, QUEBEC H3G 1J9
(514) 842-9116

VAL ABEL TEXTILES LTD.
55 MT. ROYAL AVENUE WEST
MONTREAL, QUEBEC H2T 2S6
(514) 842-9503

VISION TEXTILES INC.
100 PORT ROYAL EAST
MONTREAL, QUEBEC H3L 1H7
(514) 381-5941

▶ ONTARIO

ANTHONY FOSTER & SONS
297 CARLINGVIEW DRIVE
REXDALE, ONTARIO M9W 5G4
(416) 675-7000

APPEL LIMITED
321 DAVENPORT ROAD
TORONTO, ONTARIO M5R 1K5
(416) 922-3935

ARJAY TEXTILES LIMITED
221 ADVANCE BLVD.
BRAMPTON, ONTARIO L6T 4J2
(416) 454-0444

BAUMANN FABRICS LTD.
302 KING STREET EAST
TORONTO, ONTARIO M5A 1K6
(416) 869-1221

W.H. BILBROUGH & CO. LTD.
326 DAVENPORT ROAD
TORONTO, ONTARIO M5R 1K6
(416) 960-1611

BONGAERTS TEXTILES LTD.
112 ST. CLAIR AVENUE WEST
TORONTO, ONTARIO M4V 2Y3
(416) 964-9363

H. BROWN SILK CO. LTD.
530 ADELAIDE STREET WEST
TORONTO, ONTARIO M5V 1T5
(416) 364-2377

• **JEFF BROWN FINE FABRICS LTD.**
1785 ARGENTIA ROAD
MISSISSAUGA, ONTARIO L5N 3A2
(416) 821-3666 **Pg. 220**

BRUNSCHWIG & FILS
320 DAVENPORT ROAD
TORONTO, ONTARIO M5R 1K6
(416) 968-0699

CARLTON MANUFACTURING INC.
8 DARBY WAY
THORNHILL, ONTARIO L3T 5V1
(416) 886-1050

CAYA FABRICS LTD.
P.O. BOX 304, 130 WEBER STREET WEST
KITCHENER, ONTARIO N2G 3Z2
(519) 743-0623

COMMERCIAL DRAPERIES LTD.
3180A LAKESHORE BLVD. WEST
TORONTO, ONTARIO M8V 1L7
(416) 251-6568

CRESCENT FABRICS LTD.
50 DON PARK ROAD
MARKHAM, ONTARIO L3R 1J3
(416) 475-0192

CROWN WALLPAPER CO.
88 RONSON DRIVE
REXDALE, ONTARIO M9W 1B9
(416) 245-2900

DRAPERY CONTRACT SERVICES
334 LAUDER AVENUE
TORONTO, ONTARIO M6E 3H8
(416) 651-5757

D.C.S. DRAPERY LTD.
DRAPERY CONTRACT SERVICES
579 RICHMOND STREET WEST
TORONTO, ONTARIO M5V 1Y4
(416) 368-4855

FABRICS INTERNATIONAL
1090 AEROWOOD DRIVE
MISSISSAUGA, ONTARIO L4W 1Y5
(416) 624-5104

FINNISH DESIGN IMPORTS LTD.
92C SCOLLARD STREET
TORONTO, ONTARIO M5R 1G2
(416) 961-9858

GREFF FABRICS INC.
170 BEDFORD ROAD
TORONTO, ONTARIO M5R 2K9
(416) 960-8222

• **HABERT ASSOCIATES LIMITED**
321 DAVENPORT ROAD
TORONTO, ONTARIO M5R 1K5
(416) 960-5323 **Pg. 221**

JOANNE FABRICS CO. LTD.
1090 AEROWOOD DRIVE
MISSISSAUGA, ONTARIO L4W 1Y5
(416) 624-5104

JOHNSON, CRAIG & ASSOCIATES
462 WELLINGTON STREET WEST
TORONTO, ONTARIO M5V 1E3
(416) 597-0733

KAREN BULOW LTD.
14 DUNCAN STREET
TORONTO, ONTARIO M5H 3G8
(416) 977-2004

KOBE FABRICS LTD.
5380 SOUTH SERVICE RD., P.O. BOX 939
BURLINGTON, ONTARIO L7R 3Y7
(416) 639-2730

• **LAURII TEXTILES**
354 DAVENPORT ROAD
TORONTO, ONTARIO M5R 1K6
(416) 922-5514 **Pg. 222**

LIONS WALLCOVERINGS & FABRICS INC.
265 DAVENPORT ROAD
TORONTO, ONTARIO M5R 1K5
(416) 924-7779

MACUSHLA AGENCY
368 KING STREET EAST
TORONTO, ONTARIO M5A 1K9
(416) 947-9155

MODERN WINDOW SHADES LTD.
267 DAVENPORT ROAD
TORONTO, ONTARIO M5R 1J9
(416) 927-0292

ONTARIO WALLCOVERINGS
462 FRONT STREET WEST
TORONTO, ONTARIO M5V 1B6
(416) 593-4519

PANACHE DESIGN LIMITED
361 KING STREET EAST
TORONTO, ONTARIO M5A 1L1
(416) 369-0084

PRIDE OF PARIS FABRICS LTD.
WEST RIVER STREET, BOX 130
PARIS, ONTARIO N3L 3E9
(519) 443-6351

• **PRIMAVERA**
INTERIOR ACCESSORIES LTD.
300 KING STREET EAST
TORONTO, ONTARIO M5A 1K4
(416) 368-3456 **Pg. 223**

ROBBIE TEXTILES
487 CHAMPAGNE DRIVE
DOWNSVIEW, ONTARIO M3J 2C6
(416) 630-2493

• **SAMO TEXTILES LTD.**
67 ST. REGIS CRESCENT NORTH
DOWNSVIEW, ONTARIO M3J 1Y9
(416) 636-7273 **Pg. 224**

• **SAMO INTERNATIONAL**
320 DAVENPORT ROAD
TORONTO, ONTARIO M5R 1K6
(416) 920-3020 **Pg. 224**

SANDERSON, A. & SONS LTD.
320 DAVENPORT ROAD
TORONTO, ONTARIO M5R 1K6
(416) 323-1168

SEVEN CONTINENTS ENTERPRISES LTD.
350 WALLACE AVENUE
TORONTO, ONTARIO M6P 3P2
(416) 535-5101

SEWING ROOM, THE
170 BEDFORD ROAD
TORONTO, ONTARIO M5R 2K9
(416) 961-5536

SUREWAY TRADING ENTERPRISES
111 PETER STREET
TORONTO, ONTARIO M5V 2H1
(416) 596-1887

TANDEM FABRICS INC.
129 DOLPH STREET WEST
CAMBRIDGE, ONTARIO N3H 2B9
(519) 653-5781

TELIO & CIE
113 DUPONT STREET
TORONTO, ONTARIO M5R 1V4
(416) 968-2020

UNIFAB LTD.
250 WYECROFT ROAD
OAKVILLE, ONTARIO L6K 3T7
(416) 844-7433

VICRTEX, L.E. CARPENTER CO.
1200 AEROWOOD DRIVE
MISSISSAUGA, ONTARIO L4W 2S7
(416) 624-4614

• **WALTER L. BROWN LTD.**
17 VICKERS ROAD
TORONTO, ONTARIO M9B 1C2
(416) 231-4499 **Pg. 226**

E. WOELLER FABRICS LTD.
38 FRANCIS STREET SOUTH, P.O. BOX 666
KITCHENER, ONTARIO N2G 4B8
(519) 578-7880

WOOL BUREAU CANADA LTD.
33 YONGE STREET
TORONTO, ONTARIO M5E 1G4
(416) 485-9491

▶ W E S T E R N C A N A D A

CRAWFORD DAWSON AGENCY
520 CORYDON AVENUE
WINNIPEG, MANITOBA R3L 0P1
(204) 453-4832

DAIMART DRAPERY CONTRACTORS
2023B–33RD AVENUE SW
CALGARY, ALBERTA T2T 1Z5
(403) 249-5581

▶ B R I T I S H C O L U M B I A

SWITZER, W. & ASSOC. LTD.
291 EAST 2ND AVENUE
VANCOUVER, B.C. V5T 1B6
(604) 872-7611

U P H O L S T E R Y

▶ Q U E B E C

AVANT-GARDE FABRICS LTD.
7955 ALFRED
ANJOU, QUEBEC H1J 1J3
1-(800) 361-8886

CONNAISSANCE FABRICS &
WALLCOVERINGS LTD
1632 SHERBROOKE STREET WEST
MONTREAL, QUEBEC H2H 2L4
(514) 931-2437

HAFNER FABRICS OF CANADA LTD.
1405 PEEL STREET
MONTREAL, QUEBEC H3A 1S5
(514) 842-8172

NOVAX WALLCOVERINGS
740 PLACE TRANS CANADA
LONGUEUIL, QUEBEC J4G 1P1
(514) 651-7120

TELIO & CIE
1390 SHERBROOKE STREET WEST
MONTREAL, QUEBEC H3G 1J9
(514) 842-9116

VAL ABEL TEXTILES LTD.
55 MT. ROYAL AVENUE WEST
MONTREAL, QUEBEC H2T 2S6
(514) 842-9503

▶ O N T A R I O

ARJAY TEXTILES LIMITED
221 ADVANCE BLVD.
BRAMPTON, ONTARIO L6T 4J2
(416) 454-0444

APPEL LIMITED
321 DAVENPORT ROAD
TORONTO, ONTARIO M5R 1K5
(416) 922-3935

BAUHAUS DESIGNS LTD.
895 FENMAR DRIVE
WESTON, ONTARIO M9L 1C8
(416) 742-5185

W.H. BILBROUGH & CO. LTD.
326 DAVENPORT ROAD
TORONTO, ONTARIO M5R 1K6
(416) 960-1611

BONGAERTS TEXTILES LTD.
112 ST. CLAIR AVENUE WEST
TORONTO, ONTARIO M4V 2Y3
(416) 964-9363

• **JEFF BROWN FINE FABRICS LTD.**
1785 ARGENTIA ROAD
MISSISSAUGA, ONTARIO L5N 3A2
(416) 821-3666 **Pg. 220**

H. BROWN SILK CO. LTD.
530 ADELAIDE STREET WEST
TORONTO, ONTARIO M5V 1T5
(416) 364-2377

BRUNSCHWIG & FILS
320 DAVENPORT ROAD
TORONTO, ONTARIO M3R 1K6
(416) 968-0699

CAYA FABRICS LTD.
P.O. BOX 304, 130 WEBER STREET WEST
KITCHENER, ONTARIO N2G 3Z2
(519) 743-0623

CONTEMPO CONTRACT SALES
190 HWY. NO. 7 WEST, UNIT 32-33
BRAMPTON, ONTARIO L6V 1A1
(416) 459-1227

CRESCENT FABRICS LTD.
50 DON PARK ROAD
MARKHAM, ONTARIO L3R 1J3
(416) 475-0192

CROWN WALLPAPER CO.
88 RONSON DRIVE
REXDALE, ONTARIO M9W 1B9
(416) 245-2900

D.C.S. DRAPERY LTD.
DRAPERY CONTRACT SERVICES
334 LAUDER AVENUE
TORONTO, ONTARIO M6E 3H8
(416) 651-5757

DELUXE UPHOLSTERY INTERIORS
34 DONCASTER AVENUE
THORNHILL, ONTARIO L3T 4S1
(416) 881-0439

EGAN LAING LTD.
1067 WESTPORT CRESCENT
MISSISSAUGA, ONTARIO L5T 1E8
(416) 678-9131

FABRICS INTERNATIONAL
1090 AEROWOOD DRIVE
MISSISSAUGA, ONTARIO L4W 1Y5
(416) 624-5104

FINNISH DESIGN IMPORTS LTD.
92C SCOLLARD STREET
TORONTO, ONTARIO M5R 1G2
(416) 961-9858

GENERAL FABRICS
100 CLAREMONT STREET
TORONTO, ONTARIO M6J 3R2
(416) 368-7684

GREEFF FABRICS INC.
170 BEDFORD ROAD
TORONTO, ONTARIO M5R 2K9
(416) 960-8222

• HABERT ASSOCIATES LIMITED
321 DAVENPORT ROAD
TORONTO, ONTARIO M5R 1K5
(416) 960-5323 **Pg. 221**

INTERIORS INTERNATIONAL LTD.
180 NORELCO DRIVE
WESTON, ONTARIO M9L 1S4
(416) 745-4000

JOANNE FABRICS CO. LTD.
1090 AEROWOOD DRIVE
MISSISSAUGA, ONTARIO L4W 1Y5
(416) 624-5104

JOHNSON, CRAIG & ASSOCIATES INC.
462 WELLINGTON STREET WEST
TORONTO, ONTARIO M5V 1B3
(416) 597-0733

KAREN BULLOW LTD.
14 DUNCAN STREET
TORONTO, ONTARIO M5H 3G8
(416) 977-2004

KOBE FABRICS LTD.
5380 SOUTH SERVICE RD., P.O. BOX 939
BURLINGTON, ONTARIO L7R 3Y7
(416) 639-2730

• LAURII TEXTILES
354 DAVENPORT ROAD
TORONTO, ONTARIO M5R 1K6
(416) 922-5514 **Pg. 222**

LIONS WALLCOVERINGS & FABRICS INC.
265 DAVENPORT ROAD
TORONTO, ONTARIO M5R 1K5
(416) 924-7779

MAJESTIC FURNITURE &
UPHOLSTERY CO. LTD.
1255 EGLINTON AVENUE EAST
MISSISSAUGA, ONTARIO L4W 1K7
(416) 625-2020

MORBERN INC.
80 BOUNDARY ROAD
CORNWALL, ONTARIO K6H 5V3
(613) 932-8811

ONTARIO WALLCOVERINGS
462 FRONT STREET WEST
TORONTO, ONTARIO M5V 1B6
(416) 593-4519

PRIDE OF PARIS FABRICS LTD.
WEST RIVER STREET, BOX 130
PARIS, ONTARIO N3L 3E9
(519) 443-6351

• PRIMAVERA
INTERIOR ACCESSORIES LTD.
300 KING STREET EAST
TORONTO, ONTARIO M5A 1K4
(416) 368-3456 **Pg. 223**

ROBBIE TEXTILES
487 CHAMPAGNE DRIVE
DOWNSVIEW, ONTARIO M3J 2C6
(416) 630-2493

RODA WALLCOVERINGS LTD.
80 TYCOS DRIVE
TORONTO, ONTARIO M6B 1V9
(416) 782-1168

• SAMO TEXTILES LIMITED
67 ST. REGIS CRESCENT NORTH
DOWNSVIEW, ONTARIO M3J 1Y9
(416) 628-7171 **Pg. 224**

• SAMO INTERNATIONAL
320 DAVENPORT ROAD
TORONTO, ONTARIO M5R 1K6
(416) 920-3020 **Pg. 224**

SANDERSON, A. & SONS LTD.
320 DAVENPORT ROAD
TORONTO, ONTARIO M5R 1K6
(416) 323-1168

SPINNEYBECK ENTERPRISES LTD.
RR NO. 4
STOUFFVILLE, ONTARIO L0H 1L0
(416) 888-1987

TANDEM FABRICS INC.
129 DOLPH STREET SOUTH
CAMBRIDGE, ONTARIO N3H 2B9
(519) 653-5781

TELIO & CIE
113 DUPONT STREET
TORONTO, ONTARIO M5R 1V4
(416) 968-2020

UNIFAB LTD.
250 WYECROFT ROAD
OAKVILLE, ONTARIO L6K 3T7
(416) 844-7433

VICRTEX, L.E. CARPENTER CO.
1200 AEROWOOD DRIVE
MISSISSAUGA, ONTARIO L4W 2S7
(416) 624-4614

• WALTER L. BROWN LTD.
17 VICKERS ROAD
TORONTO, ONTARIO M9B 1C2
(416) 231-4499 **Pg. 226**

E. WOELLER FABRICS LTD.
38 FRANCIS STREET SOUTH, P.O. BOX 666
KITCHENER, ONTARIO N2G 4B8
(519) 578-7880

▶ W E S T E R N   C A N A D A

J. ENNIS FABRICS
12163–68TH STREET
EDMONTON, ALBERTA T5B 1P9
(403) 474-5414

▶ B R I T I S H   C O L U M B I A

W.SWITZER & ASSOCIATES LTD.
291 EAST 2ND AVENUE
VANCOUVER, B.C. V5T 1B6
(604) 872-7611

CARPETS & RUGS

▶ A T L A N T I C C A N A D A

H.G. ROGERS LTD.
87 GERMAIN STREET
SAINT JOHN, N.B. E2L 4S3
(506) 657-8350

▶ Q U E B E C

ARMSTRONG CORK INDUSTRIES LTD.
6911, BOUL. DECARIE
MONTREAL, QUEBEC H3W 3E5
(514) 739-2796

CARNIVAL RUGS LTD.
5151 SAVANE STREET
MONTREAL, QUEBEC H4P 1V1
(514) 735-1198

CELANESE CANADA INC.
800 DORCHESTER WEST
MONTREAL, QUEBEC H3C 3K8
(514) 871-5511

CENTURY CARPET DISTRIBUTORS INC.
350 McCAFFREY STREET
ST. LAURENT, QUEBEC H4T 1N1
(514) 735-1356

DUROLAM LTD.
P.O. BOX 400
ST. JOVITE, QUEBEC J0T 2H0
(819) 425-2708

• **HEUGA CANADA LTD.**
P.O. BOX 1353, D MART, PL. BONAVENTURE
MONTREAL, QUEBEC H5A 1H2
(514) 878-2785 **Pg. 233**

PEERLESS CARPET CORPORATION
P.O. BOX 944, PLACE BONAVENTURE
MONTREAL, QUEBEC H5A 1E8
(514) 878-6800

PEETERS CARPETS
100 ALEXIS NIHON BLVD.
ST-LAURENT, QUEBEC H3C 3Z3
(514) 747-7531

• **TANGI COLLECTION/
TECH-STYLE RUG G.A. INC.**
85, RUE ST-PAUL OUEST
MONTREAL, QUEBEC H2Y 3V4
(514) 842-9272 **Pg. 235**

TAPIS LIPMAN CARPET
9450 L'ACADIE BOUL.
MONTREAL, QUEBEC H4N 1L7
(514) 381-7279

▶ O N T A R I O

ANGLO ORIENTAL LTD.
68 PRINCE ANDREW PLACE
DON MILLS, ONTARIO M3C 2H4
(416) 445-8111

APPEL LIMITED
321 DAVENPORT ROAD
TORONTO, ONTARIO M5R 1K5
(416) 922-3935

ATLAS RUG CO. LTD.
1014-16 BATHURST STREET
TORONTO, ONTARIO
(416) 534-4300

• **BASF FIBERS INC.**
QUEEN'S QUAY TERMINAL, SUITE 410
207 QUEEN'S QUAY WEST, P.O. BOX 111
TORONTO, ONTARIO M5J 1A7
(416) 862-7762 **Pg. 228**

BARRYMORE CARPET INC.
190 LIBERTY STREET
TORONTO, ONTARIO M6K 1G1
(416) 537-1201

W.H. BILBROUGH & CO. LTD.
326 DAVENPORT ROAD
TORONTO, ONTARIO M5R 1K6
(416) 960-1611

• **WALTER L. BROWN LTD.**
17 VICKERS ROAD
TORONTO, ONTARIO M9B 1C2
(416) 231-4499 **Pg. 226**

**BURLINGTON CARPET MILLS
CANADA LTD.**
45 GLIDDEN ROAD
BRAMALEA, ONTARIO L6T 2H9
(416) 457-6600

CLASSIC INTERIOR DESIGNS LTD.
477 ELIZABETH STREET
BURLINGTON, ONTARIO L7R 2M3
(416) 823-2105

CONSTELLATION CARPETS
3688 NASHUA DRIVE
MISSISSAUGA, ONTARIO L4V 1M5
(416) 677-5623

CORONET CARPETS INC.
4000 NASHUA DRIVE
MALTON, ONTARIO L4V 1P8
(416) 678-9595

CROSSLEY KARASTAN CARPETS LTD.
40 CONSTELLATION COURT
REXDALE, ONTARIO M9W 1K2
(416) 675-3030

• **DE JOURNO, THOMAS E. &
ASSOCIATES**
115 DUPONT STREET
TORONTO, ONTARIO M5R 1V4
(416) 967-0154 **Pg. 230**

**DESIGNER CLASSICS CARPET
MANUFACTURING LTD.**
405 PHILLIP STREET
WATERLOO, ONTARIO N2L 3X2
(519) 886-2320

DOMINION RUG INC.
3420 YONGE STREET
TORONTO, ONTARIO M4N 2M9
(416) 485-9488

• **DU PONT OF CANADA INC.**
P.O. BOX 26, TORONTO DOMINION CENTRE
TORONTO, ONTARIO M5K 1B6
(416) 362-3555 **Pg. 229**

ELTE CARPETS LTD.
45 EASTERN AVENUE
TORONTO, ONTARIO M5A 3X8
(416) 365-0600

FABRICUSHION LTD.
259 STEELCASE ROAD
MARKHAM, ONTARIO L5R 2P6
(416) 475-0800

• **FRANCO-BELGIAN CO. LTD.**
115 DUPONT STREET
TORONTO, ONTARIO M5R 1V4
(416) 967-0115 **Pg. 231**

GILT EDGE CARPETS LTD.
42 CONSTELLATION COURT
REXDALE, ONTARIO M9W 1K1
(416) 675-6442

GREEFF FABRICS INC.
170 BEDFORD ROAD
TORONTO, ONTARIO M5R 2K9
(416) 960-8222

• **H. & I. CARPET CORPORATION**
162 BEDFORD ROAD
TORONTO, ONTARIO M5R 2K9
(416) 961-6891 **Pg. 232**

HARDING CARPETS
85 MORRELL STREET
BRANTFORD, ONTARIO N3T 4J6
(519) 746-5241

• **INTERFACE FLOORING SYSTEMS
CANADA**
P.O. BOX 1182 LAIRD DRIVE
BELLEVILLE, ONTARIO K8N 5E8
(613) 966-8090 **Pg. 234**

KOBE FABRICS LTD.
5380 SOUTH SERVICE ROAD, P.O. BOX 939
BURLINGTON, ONTARIO L7R 3Y7
1-800-263-6640

KRAUS CARPET MILLS LTD.
565 CONESTOGA ROAD
WATERLOO, ONTARIO N2L 4E1
(519) 884-2310

KUTNER KREMER LTD.
1460 WHITEHORSE ROAD
DOWNSVIEW, ONTARIO M3J 3A7
(416) 636-4700

3M CANADA LTD.
P.O. BOX 5757
LONDON, ONTARIO N6A 4T1
(519) 451-2500

MILLIKEN INDUSTRIES OF CANADA LTD.
P.O. BOX 530, 70 DUNDAS STREET WEST
DESERONTO, ONTARIO K0K 1X0
(613) 396-3421

O'NEIL, MARY & ASSOC.
166 SECOND STREET
OTTAWA, ONTARIO
(613) 235-6634

OSHAWA GLASS FIBRE PRODUCTS
341 DURHAM STREET
OSHAWA, ONTARIO
(416) 579-1433

OZITE CORP. OF CANADA LTD.
95 BARBER GREEN ROAD
DON MILLS, ONTARIO M3C 2A2
(416) 441-4030

PAGE FLOORING ENTERPRISES INC.
50 PRODUCTION DRIVE
SCARBOROUGH, ONTARIO M1H 2X8
(416) 438-6750

PERFECTION RUG CO. LTD.
113 DUPONT STREET
TORONTO, ONTARIO M5R 1V4
(416) 920-5900

• **PRIMAVERA
INTERIOR ACCESSORIES LTD.**
300 KING STREET EAST
TORONTO, ONTARIO M5A 1K4
(416) 368-3456 **Pg. 223**

REEVES BROS. CANADA LTD.
415 EVANS AVENUE
TORONTO, ONTARIO M8W 2T2
(416) 259-8451

SANDS, GORDON T. LTD.
40 TORBAY ROAD
MARKHAM, ONTARIO L3R 1G6
(416) 495-6380

STRATTON CARPET INDUSTRIES LTD.
835 BROCK ROAD SOUTH
PICKERING, ONTARIO L1W 3J2
(416) 831-1112

• **TANGI COLLECTION/
FRANCO-BELGIAN CO. LTD.**
115 DUPONT STREET
TORONTO, ONTARIO M5R 1V4
(416) 967-0115 **Pg. 235**

TAPIS D'ORIENT
1440 BATHURST STREET
TORONTO, ONTARIO
(416) 651-8223

TEMPLETON, P.L. ANTIQUE CARPETS LTD.
198½ DAVENPORT ROAD
TORONTO, ONTARIO M5R 1J2
(416) 923-2147

TISSAGE CANADIEN INC., LE
1376 RAINBOW CRESCENT
GLOUCESTER, ONTARIO K1J 8E2
(613) 744-0159

WILDER, DENNIS ENTERPRISES LTD.
26 JUBILEE COURT
BRAMPTON, ONTARIO L6S 2H2
(416) 791-5633

WOOL BUREAU CANADA LTD.
33 YONGE STREET
TORONTO, ONTARIO M5E 1G4
(416) 485-9491

WYANT & CO. LTD.
2040 ELLESMERE ROAD
SCARBOROUGH, ONTARIO M1H 3A8
(416) 438-6140

▶ WESTERN CANADA

CHRISTOPHER CARPETS
12520 ST. ALBERT TRAIL
EDMONTON, ALBERTA T5L 4H4
(403) 452-9011

▶ BRITISH COLUMBIA

CLIFFORD E. WILSON LTD.
1416 W 8TH AVENUE
VANCOUVER, B.C. V6H 1E1
(604) 736-8631

TILES

▶ QUEBEC

AMERICAN BILTRITE (CANADA) LTD.
200 BANK STREET
SHERBROOKE, QUEBEC J1H 4K3
(819) 556-6660

AMTICO FLOORING
P.O. BOX 310
SHERBROOKE, QUEBEC J1H 5J1
(819) 556-6660

CERATEC INC.
414 ST-SACREMENT
QUEBEC, QUEBEC G1N 3Y3
(418) 681-0101

DOMCO INDUSTRIES LTD.
1001 YAMASKA EAST
FARMHAM, QUEBEC J2N 2R4
(514) 866-5461

ENTERPRISES TUILES MONGIAT
10972 ESPLANADE
MONTREAL, QUEBEC H3L 2Y6
(514) 331-4761

MONDO RUBBER CANADA LTD.
2655 FRANCIS HUGHES
LAVAL, QUEBEC H7L 3S8
(514) 663-6260

RAMCA LTD.
1085, VAN HORNE AVENUE
MONTREAL, QUEBEC H2V 1J6
(514) 270-9192

▶ ONTARIO

CENTRAL SUPPLY CO.
53 APEX ROAD
TORONTO, ONTARIO M6A 2V6
(416) 785-5151

CONNOLLY CONTRACTORS LTD.
140 ASHWARREN ROAD
DOWNSVIEW, ONTARIO M3J 1Z8
(416) 638-5500

COUNTRY TILES
321 DAVENPORT ROAD
TORONTO, ONTARIO M5R 1K5
(416) 922-9214

CROSS-CAN AGENCIES INC.
238 GALAXY BLVD.
REXDALE, ONTARIO M9W 5R8
(416) 675-7565

FERLEO IMPORT EXPORT CO. LTD.
6650 FINCH AVENUE WEST
TORONTO, ONTARIO M9W 5Y6
(416) 675-0075

• **MARBLE TREND LTD.**
2050 STEELES AVENUE WEST
CONCORD, ONTARIO L4K 2V1
(416) 738-0400 **Pg. 239**

MILNE & ASSOC. LTD.
49 SPADINA AVENUE
TORONTO, ONTARIO M5V 2J1
(416) 591-9114

PAGE FLOORING ENTERPRISES INC.
50 PRODUCTION DRIVE
SCARBOROUGH, ONTARIO M1H 2X8
(416) 438-6750

PHOENIX FLOOR & WALL PRODUCTS
111 WESTMORE DRIVE
REXDALE, ONTARIO M9W 3Y6
(416) 745-4200

RAMCA TILE ONTARIO LTD.
1185 CALEDONIA ROAD
TORONTO, ONTARIO M6A 2X2
(416) 781-5521

SPINNEYBECK ENTERPRISES LTD.
RR NO. 4
STOUFVILLE, ONTARIO L0H 1L0
(416) 888-1987

T.M.T. MARBLE SUPPLY LTD.
900 KEELE STREET
TORONTO, ONTARIO M6N 3E7
(416) 653-6111

THAMES VALLEY BRICK & TILE
14 DORCHESTER AVENUE
TORONTO, ONTARIO M8Z 4W3
(416) 252-5811

TIVOLI MARBLE & CERAMIC INC.
4801 KEELE STREET
DOWNSVIEW, ONTARIO M3J 3A4
(416) 667-0010

▶ WESTERN CANADA

CERAMATILE LTD.
383 CHENTON AVENUE
WINNIPEG, MANITOBA R3G 0O3H
(204) 339-0217

▶ BRITISH COLUMBIA

C & S CERAMIC TILE DISTRIBUTORS
2720 INGLETON AVENUE
BURNABY, B.C. V5C 5X4
(604) 435-4431

C O R P O R A T E

▶ A T L A N T I C C A N A D A

H.G. ROGERS LTD.
87 GERMAIN STREET
SAINT JOHN, N.B. E2L 4S3
(506) 657-8350

SEAMAN-CROSS LTD.
46 WRIGHT AVENUE
DARTMOUTH, NOVA SCOTIA B3B 1G6
(902) 469-8190

▶ Q U E B E C

AARKASH CHAIR CO. OF CANADA LTD.
1350 TELLIER STREET
LAVAL, QUEBEC H7C 2H2
(514) 661-1271

• **ALLSTEEL CANADA LTD.**
3500 COTE-VERTU ROAD
MONTREAL, QUEBEC H4R 1R1
(514) 334-0150 **Pg. 167**

ALPHA VICO CANADA LTD.
1035 MAGENTA BLVD. EAST
FARNHAM, QUEBEC J2N 1B9
(514) 293-5354

ANGLE INTERNATIONAL
296 ST-PAUL OUEST
MONTREAL, QUEBEC H2Y 2A3
(514) 284-2619

ARMSTRONG CORK INDUSTRIES LTD.
6911, BOUL. DECARIE
MONTREAL, QUEBEC H3W 3E5
(514) 739-2796

ARTOPEX INC.
2121 BERLIER
LAVAL, QUEBEC H7L 3M9
(514) 332-4420

BAUHAUS DESIGNS LTD.
85, RUE ST-PAUL OUEST
MONTREAL, QUEBEC H2Y 3V4
(514) 844-8812

• **BILTRITE NIGHTINGALE INC.**
10251, BOUL. RAY LAWSON
MONTREAL, QUEBEC H1J 1L7
(514) 352-7770 **Pg. 169**

• **BONAVENTURE
FURNITURE INDUSTRIES LTD.**
894 BLOOMFIELD
MONTREAL, QUEBEC H2V 3S6
(514) 270-7311 **Pg. 170**

BURO DECOR
7700 TRANSCANADA HWY.
MONTREAL, QUEBEC H4T 1A5
(514) 731-3385

• **CHATEAU D'AUJOURD'HUI , LE**
1828, LE CORBUSIER BLVD.
LAVAL, QUEBEC H7S 2K1
(514) 382-4710 **Pg. 174**

DECABOIS INC.
234 ST-URBAIN
GRANBY, QUEBEC J2G 7T4
(514) 378-7976

DOR-VAL MFG. LTD.
2760, BOUL. LAURENTIAN
ST-LAURENT, QUEBEC H4K 2E1
(514) 336-7780

ERGOFORM INC.
685 MELOCHE AVENUE
DORVAL, QUEBEC H9P 2S4
(514) 636-6682

• **FRASER CONTRACT FURNITURE INC.**
5525, COTE DE LIESSE
MONTREAL, QUEBEC H4P 1A1
(514) 748-7306 **Pg. 182**

• **HAWORTH OFFICE SYSTEMS, LTD.**
2000 McGILL COLLEGE AVENUE, 5TH FLR.
MONTREAL, QUEBEC H3A 3H3
(514) 842-2622 **Pg. 188**

**HENDERSON
DIV. LES MEUBLES RADISSON LTEE.**
199 AVENUE UPPER EDISON
ST-LAMBERT, QUEBEC J4R 2R3
(514) 671-7221

INTERNATIONAL UPHOLSTERY
5005 BUCHAN STREET
MONTREAL, QUEBEC H4P 1S4
(514) 735-1501

ISHI-MOBART
7490 JEAN VALETS AVENUE
MONTREAL, QUEBEC H1E 3A1
(514) 648-7477

KNOLL OFFICE, INC.
2755 SABOURIN STREET
ST-LAURENT, QUEBEC H4S 1M9
(514) 336-2848

NOVELLA
646 GIFFARD
LONGUEUIL, QUEBEC J4G 1T8
(514) 651-9133

PRECISION MFG. INC.
2200 – 52ND AVENUE
LACHINE, QUEBEC H8T 2Y6
(514) 631-2120

PROMOSTYLE INTERNATIONAL INC.
6969 TRANS CANADA HWY.
ST-LAURENT, QUEBEC H4T 1V8
(514) 336-3646

PROULX FURNITURE
10367, ARMAND LAVERGNE
MONTREAL NORD, QUEBEC H1H 3N8
(514) 322-8010

• **STANDARD DESK
DIV. JOYCE FURNITURE INC.**
1000 ST. MARTIN BLVD. WEST
LAVAL, QUEBEC H7S 1M7
(514) 663-3030 **Pg. 201**

• **TELLA SYSTEMS**
161 STERLING AVENUE
LA SALLE, QUEBEC H8R 3P3
(514) 364-0511 **Pg. 210**

• **TRIEDE DESIGN INC.**
460 McGILL STREET
MONTREAL, QUEBEC H2Y 2H2
(514) 288-0063 **Pg. 212**

XCEPTION DESIGN LTD.
2875 INDUSTRIAL BLVD.
LAVAL, QUEBEC H7L 3Y8
(514) 668-0710

YMAC FURNITURE AGENCIES
6969 TRANS CANADA HWY.
ST. LAURENT, QUEBEC H4T 1V8
(514) 334-4733

▶ O N T A R I O

• **AID 2000**
101 FRESHWAY DRIVE, UNIT 66D
CONCORD, ONTARIO L9K 1R9
(416) 661-6433 **Pg. 164**

AREA
334 KING STREET EAST
TORONTO, ONTARIO M5A 1K8
(416) 367-5850

ABITARE DESIGN INC.
51 FRONT STREET EAST
TORONTO, ONTARIO M5E 1B3
(416) 363-1667

• **ALEXANDER'S FINE FURNITURE**
717 KIPLING AVENUE
TORONTO, ONTARIO M8Z 5G4
(416) 252-9347 **Pg. 166**

• **ALLSTEEL CANADA**
207 QUEEN'S QUAY WEST
TORONTO, ONTARIO M5J 1A7
(416) 367-5880 **Pg. 167**

AMBIANT SYSTEMS LTD.
76 RICHMOND STREET EAST
TORONTO, ONTARIO M5C 1P1
(416) 863-0863

• **ARCONAS CORPORATION**
580 ORWELL STREET
MISSISSAUGA, ONTARIO L5A 3V7
(416) 272-0727 **Pg. 168**

ART SHOPPE
2131 YONGE STREET
TORONTO, ONTARIO M4S 2A6
(416) 487-3211

**ATWOOD'S
EXECUTIVE OFFICE INTERIORS**
110 BLOOR STREET WEST
TORONTO, ONTARIO M5S 2W7
(416) 968-0820

BBF OFFICE INTERIORS
4362 CHESSWOOD DRIVE
DOWNSVIEW, ONTARIO M3J 2B9
(416) 636-9311

BAUHAUS DESIGNS LTD.
40 DENISON ROAD EAST
TORONTO, ONTARIO M9N 3T7
(416) 244-2592

- **BILTRITE NIGHTINGALE INC.**
  200 ADELAIDE STREET WEST
  TORONTO, ONTARIO M5H 1W7
  (416) 593-2501 **Pg. 169**

- **BONAVENTURE
  FURNITURE INDUSTRIES LIMITED**
  146 DUPONT STREET
  TORONTO, ONTARIO M5R 1V2
  (416) 961-5900 **Pg. 170**

- **BRUNSWICK MANUFACTURING CO. LTD.**
  21 RESEARCH ROAD
  TORONTO, ONTARIO M4G 2G7
  (416) 421-5858 **Pg. 171**

  BURGESS BUSINESS INTERIORS LTD.
  316 DALHOUSIE STREET
  OTTAWA, ONTARIO K1N 7E7
  (613) 233-2636

  BURO DECOR
  3 CHURCH STREET
  TORONTO, ONTARIO M5E 1M2
  (416) 860-1400

  BUSINESS ACCESSORIES INC.
  415 DUNDAS STREET
  CAMBRIDGE, ONTARIO N1R 5Y2
  (519) 622-2222

  CAPITAL OFFICE INTERIORS
  17 AURIGA DRIVE
  NEPEAN, ONTARIO K2E 7T9
  (613) 723-2000

- **CARDELL DESIGN INC.**
  85 BOWES ROAD
  CONCORD, ONTARIO L4K 1H5
  (416) 738-1035 **Pg. 172**

  CHARVOZ CANADA
  151 TELSON ROAD
  MARKHAM, ONTARIO L3R 1E7
  (416) 449-4101

- **CODD AND COMPANY**
  344 DUPONT STREET
  TORONTO, ONTARIO M5R 1V9
  (416) 923-0066 **Pg. 176**

  CORPORATE BUSINESS INTERIORS
  562 EGLINTON AVENUE EAST
  TORONTO, ONTARIO M4P 1B9
  (416) 485-5111

  COLLIER FURNITURE LTD.
  1377 LAWRENCE AVENUE EAST
  DON MILLS, ONTARIO M3A 3M4
  (416) 449-7655

- **CON·SPEC**
  146 LAIRD DRIVE
  TORONTO, ONTARIO M4G 3V7
  (416) 429-5206 **Pg. 177**

  CRAFTWOOD PRODUCTS
  191 FINCHDENE SQUARE
  SCARBOROUGH, ONTARIO M1X 1B9
  (416) 297-1100

  CREATIVE CUSTOM FURNISHINGS INC.
  134 OAKDALE ROAD
  DOWNSVIEW, ONTARIO M3N 1V9
  (416) 742-7450

  CROYDON FURNITURE SYSTEMS INC.
  1 HESPELER ROAD
  CAMBRIDGE, ONTARIO N1R 5V4
  (519) 621-6300

- **CURTIS PRODUCTS LTD.**
  495 BALL STREET
  COBOURG, ONTARIO K9A 4P9
  (416) 372-2184 **Pg. 179**

- **DACOTA INC.**
  175 TORYORK DRIVE
  WESTON, ONTARIO M9L 1X9
  (416) 747-6282 **Pg. 180**

  DAVID HUMPHREY INC.
  411 RICHMOND STREET EAST
  TORONTO, ONTARIO M5A 3S5
  (416) 364-3887

  DESIGN CASE INTERNATIONAL LTD.
  1080 FEWSTER DRIVE NO. 8
  MISSISSAUGA, ONTARIO L4W 2T2
  (416) 624-7285

  DESIGN FORUM
  260 RICHMOND STREET WEST
  TORONTO, ONTARIO M5V 1W5
  (416) 977-0987

- **EATONS CONTRACT INTERIORS**
  2130 LAWRENCE AVENUE EAST
  SCARBOROUGH, ONTARIO M1R 3A6
  (416) 752-4900 **Pg. 143**

  FAIR LINE PRODUCTS LTD.
  55 WOODLAWN AVENUE
  MISSISSAUGA, ONTARIO L5G 3K7
  (416) 274-3616

  FINNISH DESIGN IMPORTS LTD.
  92C SCOLLARD STREET
  TORONTO, ONTARIO M5R 1G2
  (416) 961-9858

- **FURNISHINGS FOR BUSINESS INC./
  INTEFAC INC.**
  5420 TIMBERLEA BLVD.
  MISSISSAUGA, ONTARIO L4W 2T7
  (416) 624-6700 **Pg. 145**

  GEMINI FURNITURE SALES LTD.
  29–1 CONNELL COURT
  TORONTO, ONTARIO M8Z 5T7
  (416) 252-4656

  GLOBAL UPHOLSTERY CO. LTD.
  560 SUPERTEST ROAD
  DOWNSVIEW, ONTARIO M3J 2M6
  (416) 661-3660

  GROUP FOUR FURNITURE INC.
  25–5 CONNELL COURT
  TORONTO, ONTARIO M8Z 1E8
  (416) 251-1128

- **GUILDHALL CABINET SHOPS LTD.**
  11 JUTLAND ROAD
  TORONTO, ONTARIO M8Z 2G6
  (416) 255-3425 **Pg. 184**

- **HARTER FURNITURE**
  536 IMPERIAL ROAD
  GUELPH, ONTARIO N1H 6L5
  (519) 824-2850 **Pg. 186**

- **HAWORTH OFFICE SYSTEMS, LTD.**
  33 YONGE STREET, SUITE 270
  TORONTO, ONTARIO M5E 1G4
  (416) 363-0702 **Pg. 188**

  HAUSERMAN LTD.
  125 BETHRIDGE ROAD
  REXDALE, ONTARIO M9W 1N4
  (416) 743-3211

  HERITAGE INTERIORS
  244 DAVENPORT ROAD
  TORONTO, ONTARIO M5R 1J7
  (416) 922-6448

  HERMAN MILLER CANADA, INC.
  2360 ARGENTIA ROAD
  MISSISSAUGA, ONTARIO L5N 4G9
  (416) 858-7955

  BRIAN G. HOLMES LTD.
  81 McPHERSON STREET
  MARKHAM, ONTARIO L3R 3L3
  (416) 475-0166

- **HOLMES & BRAKEL LTD.**
  830 BROCK ROAD SOUTH
  PICKERING, ONTARIO L1W 1Z8
  (416) 683-6222 **Pg. 144**

- **INTARC LIMITED**
  3300 YONGE STREET
  TORONTO, ONTARIO M4N 2L6
  (416) 482-1804 **Pg. 187**

  INTERIORS INTERNATIONAL LTD.
  180 NORELCO DRIVE
  WESTON, ONTARIO M9L 1S4
  (416) 745-4000

  INTERIORS PLUS
  50 GALAXY BLVD.
  REXDALE, ONTARIO M9W 4Y5
  (416) 675-7993

  INTERNA FURNITURE DESIGN LTD.
  76 SIGNET DRIVE
  WESTON, ONTARIO M9L 1T2
  (416) 741-4211

  IRWIN SEATING CANADA LTD.
  21 BELMONT STREET
  TORONTO, ONTARIO M5R 1P9
  (416) 929-3371

  ITALINTERIORS LIMITED
  359 KING STREET EAST
  TORONTO, ONTARIO M5A 1L1
  (416) 366-9540

- **JEFFREY-CRAIG LTD.**
  763 WARDEN AVENUE, UNIT 2A
  SCARBOROUGH, ONTARIO M1L 4B7
  (416) 757-4154 **Pg. 190**

  KARL GUTMANN INC.
  P.O. BOX 1569
  CORNWALL, ONTARIO K6H 5V6
  (613) 932-0108

- **KEILHAUER INDUSTRIES LTD.**
  946 WARDEN AVENUE
  TORONTO, ONTARIO M1L 4C9
  (416) 759-5665 **Pg. 191**

KINETICS FURNITURE
110 CARRIER DRIVE
REXDALE, ONTARIO M9W 5R1
(416) 675-4300

KNOLL OFFICE, INC.
160 PEARS AVENUE
TORONTO, ONTARIO M5R 1T2
(416) 960-9819

• **KRUG FURNITURE INC.**
421 MANITOU DRIVE, P.O. BOX 9035
KITCHENER, ONTARIO N2G 4J3
(519) 893-1100 **Pg. 192**

LMJ EXECUTIVE FURNISHING LTD.
254 GARYRAY DRIVE
WESTON, ONTARIO M9L 1P1
(416) 746-1410

LEIF JACOBSEN LTD
130 YORKLAND BLVD
WILLOWDALE, ONTARIO M2J 1R5
(416) 491-3333

L'IMAGE DESIGN
418 EGLINTON AVENUE WEST
TORONTO, ONTARIO M5N 1A2
(416) 488-3268

• **LOOMIS & TOLES CO. LTD.**
214 ADELAIDE STREET WEST
TORONTO, ONTARIO M5H 1W7
(416) 977-8877 **Pg. 193**

MAYHEW AND PETERSON INC.
64 PRINCE ANDREW PLACE
DON MILLS, ONTARIO M3C 2S2
(416) 444-7315

METALSMITHS CO. LTD.
431 ALDEN ROAD
MARKHAM, ONTARIO L3R 3R4
(416) 475-3380

NKR ENVIRONMENTS LTD.
1045 MATHESON BLVD.
MISSISSAUGA, ONTARIO L4W 3P1
(416) 624-1657

• **SVEND NIELSEN**
280 SIGNET DRIVE
WESTON, ONTARIO M9L 1V2
(416) 749-0131 **Pg. 195**

• **NIENKAMPER**
300 KING STREET EAST
TORONTO, ONTARIO M5A 1K4
(416) 362-3434 **Pg. 196**

NORMAN CARRIERE AGENCIES INC.
478 QUEEN STREET EAST
TORONTO, ONTARIO M5A 1T7
(416) 363-1152

OFFICE SPECIALTY
322 KING STREET WEST
TORONTO, ONTARIO M5V 1J2
(416) 977-6007

O'NEAL, MARY & ASSOCIATES
166 SECOND STREET
OTTAWA, ONTARIO
(613) 235-6634

OTTAWA BUSINESS INTERIORS
183 COLONNADE ROAD
OTTAWA, ONTARIO K2E 7J4
(613) 226-4090

• **POI BUSINESS INTERIOR**
120 VALLEYWOOD DRIVE
MARKHAM, ONTARIO L3R 6A7
(416) 479-1123 **Pg. 146**

• **PRESTON**
500 UNIVERSITY AVENUE, 10TH FLR
TORONTO, ONTARIO M5G 1V7
(416) 598-3540 **Pg. 148**

• **PRESTON**
310 SOMERSET STREET WEST
OTTAWA, ONTARIO K2P 0J9
(613) 232-7175 **Pg. 148**

• **PRIMAVERA**
INTERIOR ACCESSORIES LTD.
300 KING STREET EAST
TORONTO, ONTARIO M5A 1K4
(416) 368-3456 **Pg. 223**

• **PRISMATIQUE DESIGNS LTD.**
265 DAVENPORT ROAD
TORONTO, ONTARIO M5R 1J9
(416) 961-7333 **Pg. 197**

RRL DESIGNS LTD.
3414 FONTENAY COURT
OTTAWA, ONTARIO K1V 7S9
(613) 521-9130

RAM PARTITION, DIV. INDAL LTD.
125 OAKDALE ROAD
DOWNSVIEW, ONTARIO M3N 1W2
(416) 745-2244

• **REFF INCORPORATED**
1000 ARROW ROAD
WESTON, ONTARIO M9M 2Y7
(416) 741-5453 **Pg. 198**

ROCHNOR FURNITURE LTD.
80 HANLAN ROAD
WOODBRIDGE, ONTARIO L4L 3R7
(416) 851-1567

RUSCANA FURNITURE LTD.
3544 NASHUA DRIVE
MISSISSAUGA, ONTARIO L4V 1L2
(416) 673-2850

• **SALIX SYSTEMS LTD.**
1220 ELLESMERE ROAD
SCARBOROUGH, ONTARIO M1P 2X5
(416) 292-0090 **Pg. 149**

SHAT IMPORT AGENCIES
P.O. BOX 202, STATION M
TORONTO, ONTARIO M6S 4T3
(416) 769-0812

SHAW-PEZZO & ASSOCIATES INC.
146 DUPONT STREET
TORONTO, ONTARIO M5R 1V2
(416) 961-8213

SIMMONS LTD
6900 AIRPORT ROAD
MISSISSAUGA, ONTARIO L4V 1E8
(416) 671-1033

• **SIMSONS**
COMMERCIAL INTERIORS & DESIGN
49 GERVAIS DRIVE
DON MILLS, ONTARIO M3C 1Y9
(416) 449-0110 **Pg. 150**

• **SNYDER FURNITURE LTD.**
87 COLVILLE ROAD
TORONTO, ONTARIO M6M 2Y6
(416) 247-6285 **Pg. 202**

• **STEELCASE CANADA LTD.**
P.O. BOX 9
DON MILLS, ONTARIO M3C 2R7
1-800-268-1121 **Pg. 205**

• **STOW & DAVIS**
P.O. BOX 9
DON MILLS, ONTARIO M3C 2R7
1-800-268-1121 **Pg. 207**

STORWAL INTERNATIONAL INC.
156 FRONT STREET WEST
TORONTO, ONTARIO M5J 2L6
(416) 598-0716

• **SUNAR HAUSERMAN**
1 SUNSHINE AVENUE
WATERLOO, ONTARIO N2J 4K5
(519) 886-2000 **Pg. 208**

• **TEKNION FURNITURE SYSTEMS INC.**
607 CANARCTIC DRIVE
DOWNSVIEW, ONTARIO M3J 2P9
(416) 661-3370 **Pg. 206**

• **TENDEX SILKO INC.**
264 THE ESPLANADE
TORONTO, ONTARIO M5A 4J6
(416) 361-1515 **Pg. 211**

• **TELLA SYSTEMS INC.**
124 BERMONDSEY ROAD
TORONTO, ONTARIO M5A 1X5
(416) 752-7750 **Pg. 210**

• **TODAY'S BUSINESS PRODUCTS**
393 NUGGET AVENUE
SCARBOROUGH, ONTARIO M1S 4G3
(416) 292-5155 **Pg. 151**

• **TRIEDE DESIGN INC.**
254 KING STREET EAST
TORONTO, ONTARIO M5A 1K3
(416) 367-0667 **Pg. 212**

• **ULTIMATE SOURCE GROUP, THE**
855 HARRINGTON COURT
BURLINGTON, ONTARIO L7N 3P3
(416) 639-7474 **Pg. 152**

WILLIAMS BUSINESS INTERIORS
2465 CAWTHRA ROAD
MISSISSAUGA, ONTARIO L5A 3P2
(416) 277-1463

ZEST FURNITURE INDUSTRIES LTD.
75 BROWN'S LINE
TORONTO, ONTARIO M8W 3S5
(416) 255-2324

• **ZIGGURAT CONCEPT INC.**
251 KING STREET EAST
TORONTO, ONTARIO M5A 1K2
(416) 362-5900 **Pg. 215**

▶ W E S T E R N C A N A D A

ACCUCRAFT OFFICE PRODUCTS LTD.
10940-120 STREET
EDMONTON, ALBERTA T5H 3P7
(403) 452-5796

ACME BEDDING & FURNITURE CO.
450 SHEPPARD STREET
WINNIPEG, MANITOBA R2X 2P8
(204) 633-9840

ACME CHROME FURNITURE LTD.
10 HUTCHINGS STREET
WINNIPEG, MANITOBA R2X 2R4
(204) 633-8432

ARTMET PRODUCTS LTD.
15935 114TH AVENUE
EDMONTON, ALBERTA T5M 2Z3
(403) 452-7522

GREGORY CARTWRIGHT
812 WALL STREET
WINNIPEG, MANITOBA R3G 2T8
(204) 786-8601

KNOLL OFFICE, INC
700 4TH AVENUE, SW, SUITE 1070
CALGARY, ALBERTA T2P 3J4
(403) 269-7873

SMED MANUFACTURING INC.
7303 30TH STREET SE
CALGARY, ALBERTA T2C 1N6
(403) 279-2575

WESCAB INDUSTRIES LTD.
8910 YELLOWHEAD TRAIL
EDMONTON, ALBERTA T5B 1G2
(403) 474-6461

WESTNOFA OF CANADA LTD.
691 GOLSPIE STREET
WINNIPEG, MANITOBA R2K 2V3
(204) 677-7106

▶ B R I T I S H C O L U M B I A

DANICA IMPORTS LTD.
22 EAST 2ND AVENUE
VANCOUVER, B.C. V5T 1B1
(604) 872-0277

INFORM INTERIORS INC.
97 WATER STREET
VANCOUVER, B.C. V6B 1A1
(604) 682-3868

**SCALI DURANTE
FURNITURE MANUFACTURERS LTD.**
5371 REGENT
BURNABY, B.C.
(604) 291-7551

W. SWITZER & ASSOCIATES LTD.
291 EAST 2ND AVENUE
VANCOUVER, B.C. V5T 1B6
(604) 872-7611

C O M M E R C I A L

I N S T I T U T I O N A L

▶ A T L A N T I C C A N A D A

ATLANTIC STORES FIXTURES LTD.
105 HENRI DUNANT STREET
MONCTON, N.B. E1C 9J1
(506) 855-5530

DOMINION CHAIR CO.
MAPLE AVENUE
BASS RIVER, NOVA SCOTIA B0M 1B0
(902) 353-2883

▶ Q U E B E C

**AARKASH CHAIR
CO. OF CANADA LTD.**
1350 TELLIER STREET
LAVAL, QUEBEC H7C 2H2
(514) 661-1271

• **ALLSTEEL CANADA LTD.**
3500 COTE-VERTU ROAD
MONTREAL, QUEBEC H4R 1R1
(514) 334-0150 **Pg. 167**

ALPHA VICO CANADA LTD.
1035 MAGENTA BLVD. EAST
FARNHAM, QUEBEC J2N 1B9
(514) 293-5354

ANGLE INTERNATIONAL
296 RUE ST-PAUL OUEST
MONTREAL, QUEBEC H2Y 2A3
(514) 284-2619

• **ARTEMIDE LTD.**
2408, RUE DE LA PROVINCE
LONGUEUIL, QUEBEC J4G 1G1
(514) 679-3717 **Pg. 217**

ARTOPEX INC.
2121 BERLIER
LAVAL, QUEBEC H7L 3M9
(514) 332-4420

BAUHAUS DESIGNS LTD.
85, RUE ST-PAUL OUEST
MONTREAL, QUEBEC H2Y 3V4
(514) 844-8812

• **BONAVENTURE
FURNITURE INDUSTRIES LTD.**
894 BLOOMFIELD
MONTREAL, QUEBEC H2V 3S6
(514) 270-7311 **Pg. 170**

CAMO FURNITURE INC.
3155 HOWARD
ST. HUBERT, QUEBEC J3Y 4Z5
(514) 676-8469

DOR-VAL MFG. LTD.
2760, BOUL. LAURENTIAN
ST-LAURENT, QUEBEC H4K 2E1
(514) 336-7780

**HENDERSON
DIV. LES MEUBLES RADISSON LTEE.**
199 AVENUE UPPER EDISON
ST-LAMBERT, QUEBEC J4R 2R3
(514) 671-7221

ISHI-MOBART
7490 JEAN VALETS AVENUE
MONTREAL, QUEBEC H1E 3A1
(514) 648-7477

INTERNATIONAL UPHOLSTERY
5005 BUCHAN STREET
MONTREAL, QUEBEC H4P 1S4
(514) 735-1501

LEACO FURNITURE LTD.
4960 BOURG STREET
ST. LAURENT, QUEBEC H4T 1J2
(514) 731-7501

MEUBLES SITA INC., LES
8421 ALFRED BOSSEAU
MONTREAL, QUEBEC H1E 3H5
(514) 648-1115

NOVELLA
646, RUE GIFFARD
LONGUEUIL, QUEBEC J4G 1T8
(514) 651-9133

PRECISION MFG. INC.
2200-52ND AVENUE
LACHINE, QUEBEC H8T 2Y6
(514) 631-2120

PROULX FURNITURE
10367 ARMAND LAVERGNE
MONTREAL, QUEBEC H1H 3N8
(514) 322-8010

SYME & ASSOCIATES INC.
2062 TRANS CANADA HWY.
DORVAL, QUEBEC H9P 2N4
(514) 685-1865

• **TRIEDE DESIGN INC.**
460 McGILL STREET
MONTREAL, QUEBEC H2Y 2H2
(514) 288-0063 **Pg. 212**

YU-GO FURNITURE CO.
331 ST. MARC STREET
LOUISEVILLE, QUEBEC J5Y 2G2
(819) 228-5546

▶ O N T A R I O

ABITARE DESIGN INC.
51 FRONT STREET EAST
TORONTO, ONTARIO M5E 1B3
(416) 363-1667

• **ABSTRACTA SYSTEMS INC.**
30 MALLEY ROAD
SCARBOROUGH, ONTARIO M1L 2E3
(416) 751-2717 **Pg. 165**

ALAR FURNITURE INC.
707 CLAYSON ROAD
WESTON, ONTARIO M9M 2H4
(416) 743-1925

ALBERT WHITE & CO. LTD.
82 SPADINA AVENUE
TORONTO, ONTARIO M5V 2J4
(416) 363-2171

ALLSTEEL CANADA LTD.
207 QUEEN'S QUAY WEST
TORONTO, ONTARIO M5J 1A7
(416) 367-5880 **Pg. 167**

AMBIANT SYSTEMS LTD.
76 RICHMOND STREET EAST
TORONTO, ONTARIO M5C 1P1
(416) 863-0863

AMERICAN FIXTURE CO. LTD.
370 MAIN STREET EAST
HAMILTON, ONTARIO L8N 1J6
(416) 522-1257

ARCONAS CORPORATION
580 ORWELL STREET
MISSISSAUGA, ONTARIO L5A 3V7
(416) 272-0727 **Pg. 168**

ARTEMIDE CANADA LTD.
354 DAVENPORT ROAD
TORONTO, ONTARIO M5R 1K5
(416) 964-6234 **Pg. 217**

AVENGER DESIGNS
1121 INVICTA DRIVE, NO. 2
OAKVILLE, ONTARIO L6J 5C1
(416) 845-3338

BAUHAUS DESIGNS LTD.
40 DENISON ROAD EAST
TORONTO, ONTARIO M9N 3T7
(416) 244-2592

BEAUTILINE SYSTEMS LTD.
420 EDDYSTONE AVENUE
DOWNSVIEW, ONTARIO M3N 1H7
(416) 742-5360

BRODA ENTERPRISES INC.
72 VICTORIA STREET SOUTH
KITCHENER, ONTARIO N2G 2A9
(416) 578-9630

CANDESCO 1978 INTERIORS
81 BENTLEY STREET
MARKHAM, ONTARIO L3R 3L1
(416) 475-5553

CARPANO INTERIORS
80 HANLAN ROAD
WOODBRIDGE, ONTARIO L4L 3P6
(416) 851-5552

CASSIDY'S LTD.
95 EASTSIDE DRIVE
TORONTO, ONTARIO M9L 5N2
(416) 239-3171

CENTRAC INDUSTRIES LTD.
2650 ST. CLAIR AVENUE WEST
TORONTO, ONTARIO M6N 1M2
(416) 763-4551 **Pg. 173**

CODD AND COMPANY
344 DUPONT STREET
TORONTO, ONTARIO M5R 1V9
(416) 923-0066 **Pg. 176**

COLLIER FURNITURE LTD.
1377 LAWRENCE AVENUE EAST
DON MILLS, ONTARIO M3A 3M4
(416) 449-7655

CONTEMPORA DESIGNS INT'L INC.
887 YONGE STREET
TORONTO, ONTARIO M4W 2H2
(416) 964-9295 **Pg. 178**

CRAFTWOOD PRODUCTS
191 FINCHDENE SQUARE
SCARBOROUGH, ONTARIO M1X 1B9
(416) 297-1100

CREATIVE CUSTOM FURNISHINGS INC.
134 OAKDALE ROAD
DOWNSVIEW, ONTARIO M3N 1V9
(416) 742-7450

CURTIS PRODUCTS LTD.
495 BALL STREET
COBOURG, ONTARIO K9A 4P9
(416) 372-2184 **Pg. 179**

DAVID HUMPHREY INC.
411 RICHMOND STREET EAST
TORONTO, ONTARIO M5A 3S5
(416) 364-3887

DESIGN BASICS FURNITURE LTD.
409 QUEEN STREET
OTTAWA, ONTARIO K1R 5A6
(613) 235-7177

DESIGN FORUM
260 RICHMOND STREET WEST
TORONTO, ONTARIO M5V 1W5
(416) 977-0987

DUBARRY FURNITURE LTD.
23 CONNELL COURT
TORONTO, ONTARIO M8Z 1E8
(416) 251-2295

THE EMPORIUM
12 BIRCH AVENUE
TORONTO, ONTARIO M5V 1C8
(416) 923-0485

EPOCA INTERIORS
28 ATLANTIC AVENUE
TORONTO, ONTARIO M6K 1X8
(416) 530-4140 **Pg. 181**

FAIR LINE PRODUCTS LTD.
551 WOODLAWN AVENUE
MISSISSAUGA, ONTARIO L5G 3K7
(416) 274-3616

FREEMAN MFG. LTD.
477 ELLESMERE ROAD
SCARBOROUGH, ONTARIO M1R 4E5
(416) 751-9633

GLOBALCARE
325 LIMESTONE CRESCENT
DOWNSVIEW, ONTARIO M3J 2R1
(416) 736-8700 **Pg. 183**

GLOBAL UPHOLSTERY CO. LTD.
560 SUPERTEST ROAD
DOWNSVIEW, ONTARIO M3J 2M6
(416) 661-3660

GROUP FOUR FURNITURE INC.
25–5 CONNELL COURT
TORONTO, ONTARIO M8Z 1E8
(416) 251-1128

GUILDHALL CABINET SHOPS LTD.
11 JUTLAND ROAD
TORONTO, ONTARIO M8Z 2G6
(416) 255-3425 **Pg. 184**

HARTER FURNITURE LTD.
536 IMPERIAL ROAD
GUELPH, ONTARIO N1H 6L5
(519) 824-2850 **Pg. 186**

JOHN HAUSER IRON WORKS LTD.
148 BEDFORD ROAD
KITCHENER, ONTARIO N2G 3W9
(519) 744-1138

HEIDT METAL PRODUCTS
290 MARSLAND DRIVE, P.O. BOX 8
WATERLOO, ONTARIO N2J 3Z6
(519) 884-4030

HERMAN MILLER CANADA, INC.
2360 ARGENTIA ROAD
MISSISSAUGA, ONTARIO L5N 4G9
(416) 858-7955

HOLMAN DESIGN
21 KERN ROAD
DON MILLS, ONTARIO M3B 1S9
(416) 441-1877

**INTERHOME
INTERNATIONAL FURNITURE**
8400 WOODBINE AVENUE
UNIONVILLE, ONTARIO
(416) 475-0705

INTERIORS PLUS
50 GALAXY BLVD.
REXDALE, ONTARIO M9W 4Y5
(416) 675-7993

INTERNATIONAL CONTRACT FURNITURE
90 NOLAN COURT, UNIT 21
MARKHAM, ONTARIO L3P 9Z0
(416) 477-0575

ITALINTERIORS LIMITED
359 KING STREET EAST
TORONTO, ONTARIO M5A 1L1
(416) 366-9540

JEFFREY-CRAIG LTD.
763 WARDEN AVENUE
SCARBOROUGH, ONTARIO M1L 4B7
(416) 757-4154 **Pg. 190**

KEILHAUER INDUSTRIES LTD.
946 WARDEN AVENUE
TORONTO, ONTARIO M1L 4C9
(416) 759-5665 **Pg. 191**

KINETICS FURNITURE
110 CARRIER DRIVE
REXDALE, ONTARIO M9W 5R1
(416) 675-4300

KNAPE & VOGT CANADA LTD.
340 CARLINGVIEW DRIVE
REXDALE, ONTARIO M9W 5G5
(416) 675-3451

• **KRUG FURNITURE INC.**
421 MANITOU DRIVE, P.O. BOX 9035
KITCHENER, ONTARIO N2G 4J3
(519) 893-1100 **Pg. 192**

LMJ EXECUTIVE FURNISHING LTD.
254 GARYRAY DRIVE
WESTON, ONTARIO M9L 1P1
(416) 746-1410

L'IMAGE DESIGN
418 EGLINTON AVENUE WEST
TORONTO, ONTARIO M5N 1A2
(416) 488-3268

• **LOUIS INTERIORS INC.**
2539 YONGE STREET
TORONTO, ONTARIO M4P 2H9
(416) 488-8844 **Pg. 194**

LUNDIA LTD.
209 MINETS POINT ROAD
BARRIE, ONTARIO L4N 4C2
(705) 737-5222

McFADDEN HARDWOODS LTD.
2650 RUNA ROAD
MISSISSAUGA, ONTARIO L4T 3C8
(416) 677-4272

MILNE & ASSOC. INC.
49 SPADINA AVENUE
TORONTO, ONTARIO M5V 2J1
(416) 591-9114

NICHOLLS & GILL LIMITED
479 RICHMOND STREET
LONDON, ONTARIO N6A 3E4
(519) 672-6001

• **SVEND NIELSEN LTD.**
280 SIGNET DRIVE
WESTON, ONTARIO M9L 1V2
(416) 749-0131 **Pg. 195**

• **NIENKAMPER**
300 KING STREET EAST
TORONTO, ONTARIO M5A 1K4
(416) 362-3434 **Pg. 196**

NORMAN CARRIERE AGENCIES INC.
478 QUEEN STREET EAST
TORONTO, ONTARIO M5A 1T7
(416) 363-1152

OFFICE SPECIALTY
322 KING STREET WEST
TORONTO, ONTARIO M5V 1J2
(416) 977-6007

• **PRISMATIQUE DESIGNS LTD.**
265 DAVENPORT ROAD
TORONTO, ONTARIO M5R 1J9
(416) 961-7333 **Pg. 197**

RUSCANA FURNITURE LTD.
3544 NASHUA DRIVE
MISSISSAUGA, ONTARIO L4V 1L2
(416) 673-2850

SCHAT IMPORT AGENCIES
P.O. BOX 202, STATION M
TORONTO, ONTARIO M6S 4T3
(416) 769-0812

SHAW-PEZZO & ASSOCIATES INC.
146 DUPONT ROAD
TORONTO, ONTARIO M5R 1V2
(416) 961-8213

SHEPHERD PRODUCTS LTD.
37 ESNA PARK DRIVE
MARKHAM, ONTARIO L3R 1C9
(416) 475-6454

• **SNYDER FURNITURE LTD.**
87 COLVILLE ROAD
TORONTO, ONTARIO M6M 2Y6
(416) 247-6285 **Pg. 202**

STUDIO PLASTICS
329 DEERHIDE CRESCENT
TORONTO, ONTARIO M9M 2Z2
(416) 741-2119

• **TENDEX SILKO INC.**
264 THE ESPLANADE
TORONTO, ONTARIO M5A 4J6
(416) 361-1555 **Pg. 211**

THAMES VALLEY ANTIQUES
260 SPADINA AVENUE
TORONTO, ONTARIO M5T 2E4
(416) 596-8898

• **TRIEDE DESIGN INC.**
254 KING STREET EAST
TORONTO, ONTARIO M5A 1K3
(416) 367-0667 **Pg. 212**

WESTEEL-ROSCO LTD.
1 ATLANTIC AVENUE
TORONTO, ONTARIO M6K 1X7
(416) 537-4411

WINDSOR HOUSE COLLECTION
1311 ALNESS STREET
CONCORD, ONTARIO L4K 1E8
(416) 665-9300

J.A WILSON DISPLAY LTD.
1645 AIMCO BLVD.
MISSISSAUGA, ONTARIO L4W 1H8
(416) 625-9200

• **WOODRITES LTD.**
940 QUEEN STREET WEST
TORONTO, ONTARIO M6J 1G8
(416) 532-9621 **Pg. 261**

WYLIE, GLEN J. & ASSOCIATES LTD.
81 KELFIELD STREET
REXDALE, ONTARIO M9W 5A3
(416) 243-7770

ZEST FURNITURE INDUSTRIES LTD.
75 BROWN'S LINE
TORONTO, ONTARIO M8W 3S5
(416) 255-2324

• **ZIGGURAT CONCEPT INC.**
251 KING STREET EAST
TORONTO, ONTARIO M5A 1K2
(416) 362-5900 **Pg. 215**

▶ W E S T E R N   C A N A D A

ACME CHROME FURNITURE LTD.
10 HUTCHINGS STREET
WINNIPEG, MANITOBA R2X 2R4
(204) 633-8432

WESTNOFA OF CANADA LTD.
691 GOLSPIE STREET
WINNIPEG, MANITOBA R2K 2V3
(204) 677-7106

▶ B R I T I S H   C O L U M B I A

INFORM INTERIORS INC.
97 WATER STREET
VANCOUVER, B.C. V6B 1A1
(604) 682-3868

LEE IMPORTERS LTD.
21 WATER STREET, 3RD FLOOR
VANCOUVER, B.C. V6B 1A1
(604) 681-5371

**SCALI DURANTE
FURNITURE MANUFACTURERS LTD.**
5371 REGENT
BURNABY, B.C.
(604) 291-7551

W. SWITZER & ASSOCIATES LTD.
291 EAST 2ND AVENUE
VANCOUVER, B.C. V5T 1B6
(604) 872-7611

R E S I D E N T I A L

▶ Q U E B E C

**AARKASH CHAIR
CO. OF CANADA LTD.**
1350 TELLIER STREET
LAVAL, QUEBEC H7C 2H2
(514) 661-1271

ALPHA VICO CAN. LTD.
1035 MAGENTA BLVD. EAST
MONTREAL, QUEBEC J2N 1B9
(514) 293-5354

ARMSTRONG CORK INDUSTRIES LTD.
6911, BOUL. DECARIE
MONTREAL, QUEBEC H3H 3E5
(514) 739-2796

• **ARTEMIDE LTD.**
2408, RUE DE LA PROVINCE
LONGUEUIL, QUEBEC J4G 1G1
(514) 679-3717   **Pg. 217**

BAUHAUS DESIGNS LTD.
85, RUE ST-PAUL OUEST
MONTREAL, QUEBEC H2Y 3V4
(514) 844-8812

• **BONAVENTURE
FURNITURE INDUSTRIES LTD.**
894 BLOOMFIELD
MONTREAL, QUEBEC H2V 3S6
(514) 270-7311   **Pg. 170**

CAMO FURNITURE INC.
3155 HOWARD
ST-HUBERT, QUEBEC J3Y 4Z5
(514) 676-8469

• **CHATEAU D'AUJOURD'HUI , LE**
1828, LE CORBUSIER BLVD.
LAVAL, QUEBEC H7S 2K1
(514) 382-4710   **Pg. 174**

DOR-VAL MFG. LTD.
2760, BOUL. LAURENTIAN
ST-LAURENT, QUEBEC H4K 2E1
(514) 336-7780

EL RAN FURNITURE LTD.
8315 PLACE LORRAINE
VILLE D'ANJOU, QUEBEC H1J 1E5
(514) 354-1220

INTERNATIONAL UPHOLSTERY
5005 BUCHAN STREET
MONTREAL, QUEBEC H4P 1A1
(514) 735-1501

MAISON CORBEIL
5692-5700, RUE JEAN TALON EST
MONTREAL, QUEBEC H1S 1M2
(514) 254-9951

MEUBLES SITA INC., LES
8421 ALFRED BROSSEAU
MONTREAL, QUEBEC H1E 3H5
(514) 648-1115

NOVELLA
646, RUE GIFFARD
LONGUEUIL, QUEBEC J4G 1T8
(514) 651-9133

PROULX FURNITURE
10367 ARMAND LAVERGNE
MONTREAL NORD, QUEBEC H1H 3N8
(514) 322-8010

RATTAN INDUSTRIES INC.
9566 BOIVIN STREET
LASALLE, QUEBEC H8R 2E7
(514) 366-6363

• **TRIEDE DESIGN INC.**
460 McGILL STREET
MONTREAL, QUEBEC H2Y 2H2
(514) 288-0063   **Pg. 212**

YMAC FURNITURE AGENCIES
6969 TRANS CANADA HWY.
ST-LAURENT, QUEBEC H4T 1V8
(514) 334-4733

YU-GO FURNITURE CO.
331 ST. MARC STREET
LOUISEVILLE, QUEBEC J5Y 2G2
(819) 228-5546

▶ O N T A R I O

AREA
334 KING STREET EAST
TORONTO, ONTARIO M5A 1K8
(416) 367-5850

ABITARE DESIGN INC.
51 FRONT STREET EAST
TORONTO, ONTARIO M5E 1B3
(416) 363-1667

ADAMS, LEONARD INC.
65 HIGH PARK AVENUE, APT. 1008
TORONTO, ONTARIO M6P 2B7
(416) 769-2814

• **ALEXANDER'S FINE FURNITURE**
717 KIPLING AVENUE
TORONTO, ONTARIO M8Z 5G4
(416) 252-9347   **Pg. 166**

AMBIANT SYSTEMS LTD.
76 RICHMOND STREET EAST
TORONTO, ONTARIO M5C 1P1
(416) 863-0863

ART SHOPPE
2131 YONGE STREET
TORONTO, ONTARIO M4S 2A6
(416) 487-3211

• **ARTEMIDE CANADA LTD.**
354 DAVENPORT ROAD
TORONTO, ONTARIO M5R 1K5
(416) 964-6234   **Pg. 217**

**ATWOOD'S,
AN ETHAN ALLEN GALLERY**
2161 DUNDAS STREET WEST
TORONTO, ONTARIO L5K 1R2
(416) 828-2264

**ATWOOD'S,
AN ETHAN ALLEN GALLERY**
8134 YONGE STREET
THORNHILL, ONTARIO L4J 1W4
(416) 889-7761

BARRYMORE FURNITURE CO.
1137 KING STREET WEST
TORONTO, ONTARIO M6K 1E2
(416) 532-2891

BAUHAUS DESIGNS LTD.
895 FENMAR DRIVE
WESTON, ONTARIO M9L 1C8
(416) 742-5185

• **BONAVENTURE
FURNITURE INDUSTRIES LIMITED**
146 DUPONT STREET
TORONTO, ONTARIO M5R 1V2
(416) 961-5900   **Pg. 170**

• **BRUNSWICK MANUFACTURING CO. LTD.**
21 RESEARCH ROAD
TORONTO, ONTARIO M4G 2G7
(416) 421-5858   **Pg. 171**

CANTU INTERIORS
2562 EGLINTON AVENUE WEST
TORONTO, ONTARIO M6M 1T4
(416) 653-3353

• **CODD AND COMPANY**
344 DUPONT STREET
TORONTO, ONTARIO M5R 1V9
(416) 923-0066   **Pg. 176**

COLLIER FURNITURE LTD.
1377 LAWRENCE AVENUE EAST
DON MILLS, ONTARIO M3A 3M4
(416) 449-7655

CONCEPT B
388 CARLAW AVENUE
TORONTO, ONTARIO M4M 2T4
(416) 462-1700

• **CONTEMPORA DESIGNS INT'L INC.**
887 YONGE STREET
TORONTO, ONTARIO M4W 2H2
(416) 964-9295   **Pg. 178**

CRAFTWOOD PRODUCTS
191 FINCHDENE SQUARE
SCARBOROUGH, ONTARIO M1X 1B9
(416) 297-1100

CREATIVE CUSTOM FURNISHINGS INC.
134 OAKDALE ROAD
DOWNSVIEW, ONTARIO M3N 1V9
(416) 742-7450

• **DESIGN COOPERATIVE, THE**
135 TECUMSETH STREET
TORONTO, ONTARIO M6J 2H2
(416) 947-1684   **Pg. 158**

DUBARRY FURNITURE LTD.
23 CONNELL COURT
TORONTO, ONTARIO M8Z 1E8
(416) 251-2295

• **EPOCA INTERIORS**
28 ATLANTIC AVENUE
TORONTO, ONTARIO M6K 1X8
(416) 530-4140   **Pg. 181**

FINNISH DESIGN IMPORTS LTD.
92C SCOLLARD STREET
TORONTO, ONTARIO M5R 1G2
(416) 961-9858

GROUP FOUR FURNITURE INC.
25-5 CONNELL COURT
TORONTO, ONTARIO M8Z 1E8
(416) 251-1128

• **GUILDHALL CABINET SHOPS LTD.**
11 JUTLAND ROAD
TORONTO, ONTARIO M8Z 2G6
(416) 255-3425   **Pg. 184**

- **HABERT ASSOCIATES LTD.**
321 DAVENPORT ROAD
TORONTO, ONTARIO M5R 1K5
(416) 960-5323 **Pg. 221**

HEIDT METAL PRODUCTS
290 MARSLAND DRIVE, P.O. BOX 8
WATERLOO, ONTARIO N2J 3Z6
(519) 884-4030

HENTSCHEL BAETZ LTD.
500 WEBER STREET NORTH
WATERLOO, ONTARIO N2L 4E9
(519) 884-2511

HERITAGE INTERIORS
244 DAVENPORT ROAD
TORONTO, ONTARIO M5R 1J7
(416) 922-6448

- **INTARC LIMITED**
3300 YONGE STREET
TORONTO, ONTARIO M4N 2L6
(416) 482-1804 **Pg. 187**

INTERNA FURNITURE DESIGN LTD.
76 SIGNET DRIVE
WESTON, ONTARIO M9L 1T2
(416) 741-4211

ITALINTERIORS LIMITED
359 KING STREET EAST
TORONTO, ONTARIO M5A 1L1
(416) 366-9540

- **JEFFREY-CRAIG LTD.**
763 WARDEN AVENUE
SCARBOROUGH, ONTARIO M1L 4B7
(416) 757-4154 **Pg. 190**

KAUFMAN OF COLLINGWOOD
190 BALSAM STREET
COLLINGWOOD, ONTARIO L9Y 3Y6
(705) 445-6000

- **LOUIS INTERIORS INC.**
2539 YONGE STREET
TORONTO, ONTARIO M4P 2H9
(416) 488-8844 **Pg. 194**

- **KEILHAUER INDUSTRIES LTD.**
946 WARDEN AVENUE
TORONTO, ONTARIO M1L 4C9
(416) 759-5665 **Pg. 191**

- **KRUG FURNITURE INC.**
421 MANITOU DRIVE, P.O. BOX 9035
KITCHENER, ONTARIO N2G 4J3
(519) 893-1100 **Pg. 192**

- **KURTZ MANN DESIGN**
390 DUPONT STREET, SUITE 203
TORONTO, ONTARIO M5R 1V9
(416) 927-0353 **Pg. 154**

L'IMAGE DESIGN
418 EGLINTON AVENUE WEST
TORONTO, ONTARIO M5N 1A2
(416) 488-3268

- **MARCUS, H.D. ENTERPRISES INC.**
294 BERKELEY STREET
TORONTO, ONTARIO M5A 2X5
(416) 967-7617 **Pg. 276**

NICHOLLS & GILL LIMITED
479 RICHMOND STREET
LONDON, ONTARIO N6A 3E4
(519) 672-6001

- **NIENKAMPER**
300 KING STREET EAST
TORONTO, ONTARIO M5A 1K4
(416) 362-3434 **Pg. 196**

NOXON METAL SMITHS LIMITED
431 ALDEN ROAD
UNIONVILLE, ONTARIO L3R 3R4
(416) 475-3380

PRESTON MFG. LTD.
185 KING STREET
CAMBRIDGE, ONTARIO N3H 4S1
(519) 653-7143

- **PRIMAVERA
INTERIOR ACCESSORIES LTD.**
300 KING STREET EAST
TORONTO, ONTARIO M5A 1K4
(416) 368-3456 **Pg. 223**

- **PRISMATIQUE DESIGNS LTD.**
265 DAVENPORT ROAD
TORONTO, ONTARIO M5R 1J9
(416) 961-7333 **Pg. 197**

RENAISSANCE INC.
146 DUPONT STREET
TORONTO, ONTARIO M5R 1V2
(416) 927-0126

RIDPATH'S LIMITED
906 YONGE STREET
TORONTO, ONTARIO M4W 2J2
(416) 920-4441

ROCHNOR FURNITURE LTD.
80 HANLAN ROAD
WOODBRIDGE, ONTARIO L4L 3R7
(416) 851-1567

RUSCANA FURNITURE LTD.
3544 NASHUA DRIVE
MISSISSAUGA, ONTARIO L4V 1L2
(416) 673-2850

SCHAT IMPORT AGENCIES
P.O. BOX 202, STATION M
TORONTO, ONTARIO M6S 4T3
(416) 769-0912

**SEBASTIAN DEL LORENZIS
CUSTOM FURNITURE LTD.**
505 HESPELER ROAD
CAMBRIDGE, ONTARIO N1R 6J2
(519) 623-0210

SHAW-PEZZO & ASSOCIATES INC.
146 DUPONT ROAD
TORONTO, ONTARIO M5R 1V2
(416) 961-8213

- **SHELAGH'S OF CANADA LTD.**
354 DAVENPORT ROAD
TORONTO, ONTARIO M5R 1K6
(416) 924-7331 **Pg. 200**

SKLAR FURNITURE LTD.
617 VICTORIA STREET EAST
WHITBY, ONTARIO L1N 5S7
(416) 668-3315

SIMMONS LTD.
6900 AIRPORT ROAD
MISSISSAUGA, ONTARIO L4V 1E8
(416) 671-1033

- **SNYDER FURNITURE LTD.**
87 COLVILLE ROAD
TORONTO, ONTARIO M6M 2Y6
(416) 247-6285 **Pg. 202**

- **STUDIO STORE, THE**
353 EASTERN AVENUE, SUITE 206
TORONTO, ONTARIO M4M 1B7
(416) 461-2086 **Pg. 204**

- **SUNARHAUSERMAN**
1 SUNSHINE AVENUE
WATERLOO, ONTARIO N2J 4K5
(519) 886-2000 **Pg. 208**

- **TENDEX SILKO**
264 THE ESPLANADE
TORONTO, ONTARIO M5A 4J6
(416) 361-1555 **Pg. 211**

THAMES VALLEY ANTIQUES
260 SPADINA AVENUE
TORONTO, ONTARIO M5T 2E4
(416) 596-8898

- **TRIEDE DESIGN INC.**
254 KING STREET EAST
TORONTO, ONTARIO M5A 1K3
(416) 367-6667 **Pg. 212**

VAN LEEUWEN BOOMKAMP LTD.
430 HAZELDEAN ROAD
KANATA, ONTARIO K2L 1T9
(613) 836-1400

WINDSOR HOUSE COLLECTION
1311 ALNESS STREET
CONCORD, ONTARIO L4K 1E8
(416) 665-9300

- **ZIGGURAT CONCEPT INC.**
251 KING STREET EAST
TORONTO, ONTARIO M5A 1K2
(416) 362-5900 **Pg. 215**

▶ W E S T E R N   C A N A D A

ACME BEDING & FURNITURE CO.
450 SHEPARD STREET
WINNIPEG, MANITOBA R2X 2P2
(204) 633-9840

▶ B R I T I S H   C O L U M B I A

DANICA IMPORTS LTD.
22 EAST 2ND AVENUE
VANCOUVER, B.C. V5T 1B1
(604) 872-0277

W. SWITZER & ASSOCIATES LTD.
291 EAST 2ND AVENUE
VANCOUVER, B.C. V5T 1B6
(604) 872-7611

LEATHER

ABITARE DESIGN INC.
51 FRONT STREET EAST
TORONTO, ONTARIO M5E 1B3
(416) 363-1667

• **ARCONAS CORPORATION**
580 ORWELL STREET
MISSISSAUGA, ONTARIO L5A 3V7
(416) 272-0727 **Pg. 168**

ART SHOPPE
2131 YONGE STREET
TORONTO, ONTARIO M4S 2A6
(416) 487-3211

• **BONAVENTURE
FURNITURE INDUSTRIES INC.**
894 BLOOMFIELD
MONTREAL, QUEBEC H2V 3S6
(514) 270-7311 **Pg. 170**

• **CHATEAU D'AUJOURD'HUI, LE**
1828, LE CORBUSIER BLVD.
LAVAL, QUEBEC H7S 2K1
(514) 382-4710 **Pg. 174**

COLLIER FURNITURE LTD.
1377 LAVRENCE AVENUE EAST
DON MILLS, ONTARIO M3A 3M4
(416) 449-7655

• **CONTEMPORA DESIGNS
INTERNATIONAL INC.**
887 YONGE STREET
TORONTO, ONTARIO M4W 2H2
(416) 964-9295 **Pg. 178**

• **FRASER CONTRACT FURNITURE INC.**
5525 COTE DE LIESSE
MONTREAL, QUEBEC H4P 1A1
(514) 748-7306 **Pg. 182**

• **HARTER FURNITURE LTD.**
536 IMPERIAL ROAD
GUELPH, ONTARIO N1H 6L5
(519) 824-2850 **Pg. 186**

HERMAN MILLER CANADA, INC.
2360 ARGENTIA ROAD
MISSISSAUGA, ONTARIO L5N 4G9
(416) 858-7955

• **INTARC LTD.**
3300 YONGE STREET
TORONTO, ONTARIO M4N 2L6
(416) 482-1804 **Pg. 187**

ITALINTERIORS LIMITED
359 KING STREET EAST
TORONTO, ONTARIO M5A 1L1
(416) 366-9540

• **KEILHAUER INDUSTRIES LTD.**
946 WARDEN AVENUE
TORONTO, ONTARIO M1L 4C9
(416) 759-5665 **Pg. 191**

L'IMAGE DESIGN
418 EGLINTON AVENUE WEST
TORONTO, ONTARIO M5N 1A2
(416) 488-3268

MAISON CORBEIL
5692-5700, RUE JEAN TALON EST
MONTREAL, QUEBEC H1S 1M2
(514) 254-9951

• **NIENKAMPER**
300 KING STREET EAST
TORONTO, ONTARIO M5A 1K4
(416) 362-3434 **Pg. 196**

ROCHNOR FURNITURE LTD.
80 HANLAN ROAD
WOODBRIDGE, ONTARIO L4L 3R7
(416) 851-1567

• **SAMO TEXTILES LTD.**
67 ST. REGIS CRESCENT NORTH
DOWNSVIEW, ONTARIO M3J 1Y9
(416) 636-7273 **Pg. 224**

• **SNYDER FURNITURE LTD.**
87 COLVILLE ROAD
TORONTO, ONTARIO M6M 2Y6
(416) 247-6285 **Pg. 202**

SPINNEYBECK
RR NO. 4
STOUFFVILLE, ONTARIO L0H 1L0
(416) 888-1987

• **SUNARHAUSERMAN**
1 SUNSHINE AVENUE
WATERLOO, ONTARIO N2J 4K5
(519) 886-2000 **Pg. 208**

• **TENDEX SILKO**
264 THE ESPLANADE
TORONTO, ONTARIO M5A 4J6
(416) 361-1555 **Pg. 211**

• **ZIGGURAT CONCEPT INC.**
251 KING STREET EAST
TORONTO, ONTARIO M5A 1K2
(416) 362-5900 **Pg. 215**

METAL

ABITARE DESIGN INC.
51 FRONT STREET EAST
TORONTO, ONTARIO M5E 1B3
(416) 363-1667

• **ABSTRACTA SYSTEMS INC.**
30 MALLEY ROAD
SCARBOROUGH, ONTARIO M1L 2E3
(416) 751-2717 **Pg. 165**

• **ALLSTEEL CANADA LTD.**
3500 COTE VERTU ROAD
MONTREAL, QUEBEC H4R 1R1
(514) 334-0150 **Pg. 167**

ARTOPEX INC.
2121 BERLIER
LAVAL, QUEBEC H7L 3M9
(514) 332-4420

• **ARTEMIDE LIMITED**
2408 DE LA PROVINCE
LONGUEUIL, QUEBEC J4G 1G1
(514) 679-3717 **Pg. 217**

BUSINESS ACCESSORIES INC.
415 DUNDAS STREET
CAMBRIDGE, ONTARIO M4W 2H2
(416) 964-9295 **Pg. 178**

ITALINTERIORS LIMITED
359 KING STREET EAST
TORONTO, ONTARIO M5A 1L1
(416) 366-9540

L'IMAGE DESIGN
418 EGLINTON AVENUE WEST
TORONTO, ONTARIO M5N 1A2
(416) 488-3268

METALSMITHS CO. LTD.
431 ALDEN ROAD, STE. 16
MARKHAM, ONTARIO L3R 3R4
(416) 475-3380

OFFICE SPECIALTY
322 KING STREET WEST
TORONTO, ONTARIO M5V 1J2
(416) 366-9640

STORWAL INTERNATIONAL INC.
156 FRONT STREET WEST
TORONTO, ONTARIO M5J 2L6
(416) 598-0716

• **TENDEX SILKO INC.**
264 THE ESPLANADE
TORONTO, ONTARIO M5A 4J6
(416) 361-1555 **Pg. 211**

• **TRIEDE DESIGN INC.**
460 McGILL
MONTREAL, QUEBEC H2Y 2H2
(514) 288-0063 **Pg. 212**

▶ A T L A N T I C   C A N A D A

LIGHTOLIER CANADA INC.
174 AMARANTH CRESCENT
DARTMOUTH, NOVA SCOTIA B2W 4B9
(902) 434-4520

H.G. ROGERS LTD.
87 GERMAIN STREET
SAINT JOHN, N.B. E2L 4S3
(506) 657-8350

▶ Q U E B E C

• **ACTUEL 5 IMPORT DESIGN**
550 SHERBROOKE WEST
MONTREAL, QUEBEC H3A 1B9
(514) 842-1139   **Pg. 216**

• **ALLSTEEL CANADA LTD.**
3500 COTE VERTU ROAD
MONTREAL, QUEBEC H4R 1R1
(514) 334-0150   **Pg. 167**

ANGLE INTERNATIONAL
296, ST. PAUL STREET
MONTREAL, QUEBEC H2Y 2A3
(514) 284-2619

APPELLO SALES & MARKETING INC.
13 LAKESIDE ROAD
KNOWLTON, QUEBEC J0E 1V0
(514) 534-3334

• **ARTEMIDE LTD.**
2408 DE LA PROVINCE
LONGUEUIL, QUEBEC J4G 1G1
(514) 679-3717   **Pg. 217**

• **BONAVENTURE
FURNITURE INDUSTRIES LTD.**
894 BLOOMFIELD
MONTREAL, QUEBEC H2V 3S7
(514) 270-7311   **Pg. 170**

• **CHATEAU D'AUJOURD'HUI, LE**
1828, LE CORBUSIER BLVD.
LAVAL, QUEBEC H7S 2K1
(514) 382-4710   **Pg. 174**

DANESCO OF CANADA LTD.
7200 TRANS CANADA HWY
MONTREAL, QUEBEC H4T 1A3
(514) 735-5757

DESIGN FOCUS INC.
1000, RUE DE LA MONTAGNE
MONTREAL, QUEBEC H3G 1Y7
(514) 866-1893

DESIGNER'S I
1226 BISHOP STREET
MONTREAL, QUEBEC H3G 2E3
(514) 871-3931

LA GALERIE DE NEON
5042 ST-LAURENT
MONTREAL, QUEBEC H2T 1R7
(514) 276-6984

IMPORTATIONS VOLT, LES
283 LAURIER OUEST
MONTREAL, QUEBEC H2V 2K1
(514) 279-8478

INTALITE INC.
9855 MEILEUR STREET
MONTREAL, QUEBEC H3L 3J6
(514) 382-2793

JOHNSON-LAZARE (CANADA) LTD.
7310 MT. SIGHTS AVENUE
MONTREAL, QUEBEC H4P 2A6
(514) 731-3763

LIGHTOLIER CANADA LTD.
3015 LOUIS A. AMOS
LACHINE, QUEBEC H8T 1C4
(514) 636-0670

**L'IMAGE, A DIVISION OF
CLEVEMONT INDUSTRIES LTD.**
8155 LARRY STREET
VILLE D'ANJOU, QUEBEC H1J 2L5
(514) 353-8762

LUCI LIGHTING LTD.
646 GIFFARD STREET
LONGUEUIL, QUEBEC J4G 1T8
(514) 651-9192

LUMEC INC.
618, BOUL. CURE BOIVIN
BOISBRIAND, QUEBEC J7G 2A7
(514) 430-7040

LUMICAN INC.
BOX 266
KNOWLTON, QUEBEC J0E 1V0
(514) 243-6854

LUTREX
204 LAURIER OUEST
MONTREAL, QUEBEC H2T 2N8
(514) 270-5133

LUXO LAMP LTD.
P.O. BOX 460
STE-THERESE, QUEBEC J7E 4J9
(514) 435-1971

NOVELLA
646 GIFFARD STREET
LONGUEUIL, QUEBEC J4G 1T8
(514) 651-9133

PRECISION MFG. INC.
2200 – 52ND AVENUE
LACHINE, QUEBEC H8T 2Y6
(514) 631-2120

SCANGIFT LTD.
10245 COTE DE LIESSE
DORVAL, QUEBEC H9P 1A3
(514) 631-6703

S. THAU INC.
4537 DROLET STREET
MONTREAL, QUEBEC H2T 2G3
(514) 845-1186

• **TRIEDE DESIGN INC.**
460 McGILL COLLEGE STREET
MONTREAL, QUEBEC H2Y 2H2
(514) 288-0063 **Pg. 212**

VENAIR DISTRIBUTING INC.
7950 ALFRED STREET
ANJOU, QUEBEC H1J 1J1
(514) 354-2230

▶ O N T A R I O

ABITARE DESIGN INC.
51 FRONT STREET EAST
TORONTO, ONTARIO M5E 1B3
(416) 363-1667

• **ALLSTEEL CANADA LTD.**
207 QUEEN'S QUAY WEST
TORONTO, ONTARIO M5J 1A7
(416) 367-5880 **Pg. 167**

• **ARTEMIDE LTD.**
354 DAVENPORT ROAD
TORONTO, ONTARIO M5R 1K5
(416) 964-6234 **Pg. 217**

ARTISTIC GLASS CO. LTD.
2108 DUNDAS STREET WEST
TORONTO, ONTARIO M6R 1W9
(416) 531-0481

• **AU COURANT**
354 DAVENPORT ROAD
TORONTO, ONTARIO M5R 1K6
(416) 922-5611 **Pg. 218**

AUSTIN PRODUCTIONS (CANADA) LTD.
1148 BELLAMY ROAD NORTH
SCARBOROUGH, ONTARIO M1H 1H2
(416) 438-6446

C & M PRODUCTS LTD.
189 BULLOCK DRIVE
MARKHAM, ONTARIO L3P 1W4
(416) 294-9570

CANADIAN GENERAL ELECTRIC
25 KING STREET WEST
TORONTO, ONTARIO M5L 1J2
(416) 862-5500

• **CODD & COMPANY**
344 DUPONT STREET
TORONTO, ONTARIO M5R 1V9
(416) 923-0066 **Pg. 176**

• **CONTEMPORA DESIGNS INTL. INC.**
887 YONGE STREET
TORONTO, ONTARIO M4N 3N6
(416) 964-9295 **Pg. 178**

CRAFTWOOD PRODUCTS
191 FINCHDENE SQUARE
SCARBOROUGH, ONTARIO M1X 1B9
(416) 297-1100

DALY, ALAN R. LTD.
9 DAVIES AVENUE
TORONTO, ONTARIO M4M 2A6
(416) 461-0717

DANBEL INDUSTRIES LTD.
222 ISLINGTON AVENUE
ETOBICOKE, ONTARIO M8V 3W7
(416) 252-9434

DANISH FURNITURE INDUSTRIES CO. LTD.
425 COMSTOCK ROAD
SCARBOROUGH, ONTARIO M1L 2H4
(416) 751-0798

DANISH IMPORT CO.
20 SCARLETT ROAD
TORONTO, ONTARIO M5N 4K1
(416) 769-3381

DAVID HUMPHREY INC.
411 RICHMOND STREET EAST
TORONTO, ONTARIO M5A 3S5
(416) 364-3887

DESIGN FORUM
260 RICHMOND STREET WEST
TORONTO, ONTARIO M5V 1W5
(416) 977-0987

DESIGN LIGHTING LTD.
75 DONCASTER AVENUE
THORNHILL, ONTARIO L3T 1L6
(416) 889-8320

ENGELITE LIGHTING
777 RICHMOND STREET WEST
TORONTO, ONTARIO M6J 1C8
(416) 366-2843

• **FURNISHINGS FOR BUSINESS /
INTEFAC INC.**
5420 TIMBERLEA BLVD.
MISSISSAUGA, ONTARIO L4W 2T7
(416) 624-6700 **Pg. 145**

GALAXY LIGHTING
110 JARDIN DRIVE, UNIT 4
CONCORD, ONTARIO L4K 2T7
(416) 669-6990

THE GLASS MENAGERIE
1520 TRINITY DRIVE
MISSISSAUGA, ONTARIO L5T 1L6
(416) 678-1030

THE GLASS STUDIO
118 SHERBOURNE STREET
TORONTO, ONTARIO M5A 2R2
(416) 863-1598

HALO OF CANADA LIGHTING INC.
5130 CREEKBANK ROAD
MISSISSAUGA, ONTARIO L4W 2G2
(416) 625-2511

JOHN HAUSER IRON WORKS LTD.
148 BEDFORD ROAD
KITCHENER, ONTARIO N2G 3W9
(519) 744-1138

• **HAWORTH OFFICE SYSTEMS, LTD.**
33 YONGE STREET, SUITE 270
TORONTO, ONTARIO M5E 1G4
(416) 363-0702 **Pg. 188**

• **INTARC LTD.**
3300 YONGE STREET
TORONTO, ONTARIO M4N 2L6
(416) 482-1804 **Pg. 187**

INTEGRATED A.V. & LIGHTING
132 BERKELEY STREET
TORONTO, ONTARIO M4H 1J9
(416) 361-0958

ITALINTERIORS LIMITED
359 KING STREET EAST
TORONTO, ONTARIO M5A 1L1
(416) 366-9540

**L'IMAGE, A DIVISION OF
CLEVEMONT INDUSTRIES LTD.**
120 ORFUS ROAD
NORTH YORK, ONTARIO M6A 1L9
(416) 783-4245

L'IMAGE DESIGN
418 EGLINTON AVENUE WEST
TORONTO, ONTARIO M5N 1A2
(416) 488-3268

JOHNSON, CRAIG & ASSOCIATES INC.
462 WELLINGTON STREET WEST
TORONTO, ONTARIO M5V 1B3
(416) 597-0733

LIGHTING PERCEPTIONS INC.
90 NOLAN COURT, SUITE 23
MARKHAM, ONTARIO L3R 4L9
(416) 495-9023

LIGHTOLIER CANADA INC.
488 COLONNADE ROAD
NEPEAN, ONTARIO K2K 7S6
(613) 224-0330

• **LOOMIS & TOLES CO. LTD.**
214 ADELAIDE STREET WEST
TORONTO, ONTARIO M5H 1W7
(416) 977-8877 **Pg. 193**

MILNE & ASSOCIATES
49 SPADINA AVENUE
TORONTO, ONTARIO M5V 2J1
(416) 591-9114

NKR ENVIRONMENTS LTD.
1045 MATHESON BLVD.
MISSISSAUGA, ONTARIO L4W 3P1
(416) 624-1657

• **NIENKAMPER**
300 KING STREET EAST
TORONTO, ONTARIO M5A 1K4
(416) 298-5700 **Pg. 196**

NORMAN CARRIERE AGENCIES INC.
478 QUEEN STREET EAST
TORONTO, ONTARIO M5A 1T7
(416) 363-1152

PHASE THREE AUDIO & LIGHTING
358 QUEEN STREET EAST
TORONTO, ONTARIO M5A 1T1
(416) 865-1161

PHILIPS ELECTRONICS LTD.
601 MILNER AVENUE
SCARBOROUGH, ONTARIO M1B 1M8
(416) 691-7372

• **PRIMAVERA
INTERIOR ACCESSORIES LTD.**
300 KING STREET EAST
TORONTO, ONTARIO M5A 1K4
(416) 368-3456 **Pg. 223**

• **PRISMATIQUE DESIGNS LTD.**
265 DAVENPORT STREET
TORONTO, ONTARIO M5R 1J9
(416) 961-7333 **Pg. 197**

QUINTESSENCE DESIGNS
1657 BAYVIEW AVENUE
TORONTO, ONTARIO M4G 3C1
(416) 482-1252

• **RAAK LIGHTING OF CANADA LTD.**
147 CHURCH STREET
TORONTO, ONTARIO M5B 1Y4
(416) 863-1990 **Pg. 219**

RENAISSANCE GLASS LTD.
5230 DUNDAS STREET WEST
ISLINGTON, ONTARIO M9B 1A9
(416) 232-1740

REGENCY LIGHTING INC.
6900 AIRPORT ROAD
MISSISSAUGA, ONTARIO L4V 1E8
(416) 781-6502

REVEL LUMINAIRES INC.
381 RICHMOND STREET EAST
TORONTO, ONTARIO M5A 1P6
(416) 364-6500

SESCOLITE LIGHTING
1461 CASTLEFIELD AVENUE
TORONTO, ONTARIO M6M 1Y4
(416) 651-6570

SHAW – PEZZO & ASSOCIATES INC.
146 DUPONT STREET
TORONTO, ONTARIO M5R 1V2
(416) 961-8213

• **SHELAGH'S OF CANADA LTD.**
354 DAVENPORT ROAD
TORONTO, ONTARIO M5R 1K6
(416) 924-7331 **Pg. 200**

SINGER LIGHTING
201 CARLAW AVENUE
TORONTO, ONTARIO M4M 2S3
(416) 461-0291

SOHEIL MOSUN LTD.
1862 KIPLING AVENUE
REXDALE, ONTARIO M9W 4J1
(416) 243-1600

• **STEELCASE CANADA LTD.**
P.O. BOX 9
DON MILLS, ONTARIO M3C 2R7
1-800-268-1121 **Pg. 205**

• **SUNARHAUSERMAN**
1 SUNSHINE AVENUE
WATERLOO, ONTARIO N2J 4K5
(416) 364-9384 **Pg. 208**

SUNBURST ELECTRIC
1331 CRESTLAWN DRIVE, UNIT F
MISSISSAUGA, ONTARIO L4W 2P9
(416) 625-2206

• **TENDEX SILKO**
264 THE ESPLANADE
TORONTO, ONTARIO M5A 4J6
(416) 361-1555 **Pg. 211**

• **TRIEDE DESIGN INC.**
254 KING STREET EAST
TORONTO, ONTARIO M5A 1K3
(416) 367-0667 **Pg. 212**

• **ZIGGURAT CONCEPT INC.**
251 KING STREET EAST
TORONTO, ONTARIO M5A 1K2
(416) 362-5900 **Pg. 215**

► WESTERN CANADA

ASSALY INTERIOR ASSOC.
10024 JASPER AVENUE
EDMONTON, ALBERTA T5J 1R9
(403) 421-8866

NON-NEON MAGIC
P.O. BOX 3136
WINNIPEG, MANITOBA R3C 4E6
(204) 452-8606

PARK THE POTTER
327 MORLEY AVENUE
WINNIPEG, MANITOBA R3L 0Y4
(204) 475-0019

► BRITISH COLUMBIA

INFORM INTERIORS INC.
97 WATER STREET
VANCOUVER, B.C. V6B 1A1
(604) 682-3668

LANE INDUSTRIES LTD.
5558 LANE
BURNABY, B.C.
(604) 437-4454

LEE IMPORTERS LTD.
21 STREET, 3RD FLOOR
VANCOUVER, B.C. V6B 1A1
(604) 681-5371

LIGHTINGLAND
551 WEST BROADWAY
VANCOUVER, B.C.
(604) 879-6377

LIGHTOLIER CANADA INC.
157 – 10551 SHELLBRIDGE WAY
RICHMOND, B.C.
(604) 273-7732

MAXILITE MANUFACTURING LTD.
3008 SPRING
PORT MOODY, B.C.
(604) 461-4747

NORBURN LIGHTING CENTER
4600 EAST HASTINGS
BURNABY, B.C.
(604) 299-0666

W. SWITZER & ASSOCIATES LTD.
291 EAST 2ND AVENUE
VANCOUVER, B.C. V5T 1B6
(604) 872-7611

▶ QUEBEC

• **ALLSTEEL CANADA LTD.**
3500 COTE VERTU
MONTREAL, QUEBEC H4R 1R1
(514) 334-0150 **Pg. 167**

APPELLO SALES & MARKETING INC.
103 LAKESIDE ROAD
KNOWLTON, QUEBEC J0E 1V0
(514) 534-3334

ARTOPEX INC.
2121 BERLIER
LAVAL, QUEBEC H7L 3M9
(514) 332-4420

• **BNI**
10251, BOUL. RAY LAWSON
MONTREAL, QUEBEC H1J 1L7
(514) 352-7770 **Pg. 169**

• **HAWORTH OFFICE SYSTEMS, LTD.**
2000 McGILL COLLEGE AVENUE
MONTREAL, QUEBEC H3A 3H3
(514) 842-2622 **Pg. 188**

KNOLL OFFICE, INC.
2755 SABOURIN STREET
LT-LAURENT, QUEBEC H4S 1M9
(514) 336-2848

MASONITE CANADA LTD.
418 GOLF AVENUE
GATINEAU, QUEBEC J8R 6K2
(819) 633-5331

PRECISION MFG. INC.
2200 – 52ND AVENUE
LACHINE, QUEBEC H8T 2Y6
(514) 631-2120

• **TELLA SYSTEMS**
161 STERLING AVENUE
LA SALLE, QUEBEC H8R 3P3
(514) 364-0511 **Pg. 210**

▶ ONTARIO

• **ABSTRACTA SYSTEMS INC.**
30 MALLEY ROAD
SCARBOROUGH, ONTARIO M1L 2E3
(416) 751-2717 **Pg. 165**

• **ALLSTEEL CANADA LTD.**
207 QUEEN'S QUAY WEST
TORONTO, ONTARIO M5J 1A7
(416) 367-5880 **Pg. 167**

• **BNI**
200 ADELAIDE STREET WEST
TORONTO, ONTARIO M5H 1W7
(416) 977-7614 **Pg. 169**

**COLE BUSINESS FURNITURE
DIV. OF JOYCE FURNITURE INC.**
1865 BIRCHMOUNT ROAD
SCARBOROUGH, ONTARIO M1P 2J5
(416) 293-8221

FORMS & SURFACES
49 SPADINA AVENUE
TORONTO, ONTARIO M5V 2J1
(416) 591-9114

FAB-LAM LTD.
420 TAPSCOTT ROAD
SCARBOROUGH, ONTARIO M1B 1Y4
(416) 292-6062

• **GILLANDERS**
33 ATOMIC AVENUE
ETOBICOKE, ONTARIO M8Z 5K8
(416) 259-5446 **Pg. 255**

GLOBAL UPHOLSTERY CO. LTD.
560 SUPERTEST ROAD
DOWNSVIEW, ONTARIO M3J 2M6
(416) 661-3660

• **HARTER FURNITURE**
P.O. BOX 636
GUELPH, ONTARIO N1H 6L5
(519) 824-2850 **Pg. 186**

HAUSERMAN LTD.
125 BETHRIDGE ROAD
REXDALE, ONTARIO M9W 1N4
(416) 743-3211

• **HAWORTH OFFICE SYSTEMS, LTD.**
33 YONGE STREET, SUITE 270
TORONTO, ONTARIO M5E 1G4
(416) 363-0702 **Pg. 188**

HERMAN MILLER CANADA, INC.
2360 ARGENTIA ROAD
MISSISSAUGA, ONTARIO L5N 4G9
(416) 858-7955

• **DAMPA**
2050 ELLESMERE ROAD
SCARBOROUGH, ONTARIO M1H 3A9
(416) 438-9640 **Pg. 244**

**INTERHOME
INTERNATIONAL FURNITURE**
8400 WOODBINE AVENUE
UNIONVILLE, ONTARIO
(416) 475-0705

INTERIORS INTERNATIONAL LTD.
180 NORELCO DRIVE
WESTON, ONTARIO M9L 1S4
(416) 745-4000

KAUFMAN OF COLLINGWOOD
190 BALSAM STREET
COLLINGWOOD, ONTARIO L9Y 3Y6
(416) 445-6000

KNOLL OFFICE, INC.
160 PEARS AVENUE
TORONTO, ONTARIO M5R 1T2
(416) 960-9819

• **OCTOPUS PRODUCTS LTD.**
200 GEARY AVENUE
TORONTO, ONTARIO M6H 2B9
(416) 531-5051 **Pg. 237**

RAM PARTITION, DIV. INDAL LTD.
125 OAKDALE ROAD
DOWNSVIEW, ONTARIO M3N 1W2
(416) 745-2244

• **REFF INCORPORATED**
1000 ARROW ROAD
WESTON, ONTARIO M9M 2Y7
(416) 741-5453 **Pg. 198**

SCHAT IMPORT AGENCIES
P.O. BOX 202, STATION M
TORONTO, ONTARIO M6S 4T3
(416) 769-0812

SOUND SOLUTIONS
6235 TOMKEN ROAD
MISSISSAUGA, ONTARIO L5T 1K2
(416) 678-6363

• **STEELCASE CANADA LTD.**
P.O. BOX 9
DON MILLS, ONTARIO M3C 2R7
1-800-268-1121 **Pg. 205**

STRETCHWALL + CANADA
2215 MIDLAND AVENUE
SCARBOROUGH, ONTARIO M1P 3E7
(416) 297-8672

• **SUNARHAUSERMAN**
1 SUNSHINE AVENUE
WATERLOO, ONTARIO N2J 4K5
(519) 886-2000 **Pg. 208**

• **TELLA SYSTEMS INC.**
124 BERMONDSEY ROAD
TORONTO, ONTARIO M5A 1X5
(416) 752-7750 **Pg. 210**

• **TEKNION FURNITURE SYSTEMS INC.**
607 CANARCTIC DRIVE
DOWNSVIEW, ONTARIO M3J 2P9
(416) 661-3370 **Pg. 206**

WESTROC INDUSTRIES LTD.
2650 LAKESHORE HWY.
MISSISSAUGA, ONTARIO L5J 1K4
(416) 823-9881

• **WM. WHITELEY LTD.**
214 LAIRD DRIVE
TORONTO, ONTARIO M4G 3W4
(416) 429-7503 **Pg. 214**

▶ WESTERN CANADA

ARTMET PRODUCTS LTD.
15935 114TH AVENUE
EDMONTON, ALBERTA T5M 2Z3
(403) 452-7522

KNOLL OFFICE, INC.
700 4TH AVENUE SW, SUITE 1070
CALGARY, ALBERTA T2P 3J4
(403) 269-7873

SMED MANUFACTURING INC.
7303 – 30TH STREET SE
CALGARY, ALBERTA T2C 1N6
(403) 247-6285

ARTISTS IN STAINED GLASS
510 FRONT STREET WEST
TORONTO, ONTARIO M5U 1B8
(416) 368-6307

BEAUMARK MIRROR PRODUCTS
1490 BIRCHMOUNT ROAD
SCARBOROUGH, ONTARIO M1P 2E3
(416) 752-8772

CAMBRIAN GLASS
176 NOLIN STREET
SUDBURY, ONTARIO P3C 2U3
(705) 674-7571

CLASSIC CRYSTAL LTD.
50 DRUMLIN CIRCLE
CONCORD, ONTARIO L4K 2T9
(416) 738-2073

CRISTAL SCULPTURE INC.
1668 MIDLAND AVENUE
SCARBOROUGH, ONTARIO M1P 3C2
(416) 752-5233

• **E.J.B. GLASSWORKS**
8731 GENERAL CURRIE ROAD
RICHMOND, B.C. V6Y 1M2
(604) 270-6032 **Pg. 240**

GELLMAN, MIMI – GLASS DESIGNER
517 WELLINGTON STREET WEST
TORONTO, ONTARIO M5V 1G1
(416) 593-8494

LALIQUE DESIGNERS INC.
73 ALNESS STREET
DOWNSVIEW, ONTARIO M3J 2H2
(416) 665-0434

• **STAINED GLASS OVERLAY**
491 EGLINTON AVENUE WEST
TORONTO, ONTARIO M5N 1A8
(416) 440-0140 **Pg. 242**

• **VAST INTERIORS**
96 BOWES ROAD
CONCORD, ONTARIO L4K 1J7
(416) 738-1170 **Pg. 241**

TEXTILES/
WALLPAPER

▶ QUEBEC

APPELLO SALES & MARKETING INC.
103 LAKESIDE ROAD
KNOWLTON, QUEBEC J0E 1V0
(514) 534-3334

CONNAISSANCE FABRICS &
WALLCOVERINGS LTD.
1632 SHERBROOKE STREET WEST
MONTREAL, QUEBEC H3H 2L4
(514) 931-2437

J.T. DILLON DECOR
555 CHABANEL
MONTREAL, QUEBEC H2N 2H8
(514) 384-7440

EGAN-LAING INC.
204, PLACE D'YOUVILLE
MONTREAL, QUEBEC H2Y 2B4
(514) 288-6122

MASONITE CANADA LTD.
418 GOLF AVENUE
GATINEAU, QUEBEC J8R 6K2
(819) 633-5331

NOVAX WALLCOVERINGS
740 PLACE TRANS-CANADA
LONGUEUIL, QUEBEC J4G 1P1
(514) 651-7120

SICO INC.
740 PLACE TRANS-CANADA
LONGUEUIL, QUEBEC J4G 1P1
(514) 651-0273

TELIO & CIE.
1390, RUE SHERBROOKE OUEST
MONTREAL, QUEBEC H3G 1J9
(514) 842-9116

VAL ABEL TEXTILES LTD.
55 MT. ROYAL AVENUE WEST
MONTREAL, QUEBEC H2T 2S6
(514) 842-9503

▶ ONTARIO

BARWOOD SALES (ONTARIO) LTD
80 CROCKFORD BLVD.
SCARBOROUGH, ONTARIO M1R 3C3
(416) 751-7811

BAUMANN FABRICS LTD.
302 KING STREET EAST
TORONTO, ONTARIO M5A 1K6
(416) 869-1221

W.H. BILBROUGH & CO. LTD.
326 DAVENPORT ROAD
TORONTO, ONTARIO M5R 1K6
(416) 960-1611

BRUNSCHWIG & FILS
320 DAVENPORT ROAD
TORONTO, ONTARIO M5R 1K6
(416) 968-0699

CANADA PAINT & WALLCOVERINGS
3275 YONGE STREET
TORONTO, ONTARIO M4N 2L8
(416) 487-1589

CANADIAN GENERAL TOWER
457 REYNOLS STREET
OAKVILLE, ONTARIO L6J 5C8
(416) 844-3213

CONNOLLY CONTRACTORS LTD.
140 ASHWARREN ROAD
DOWNSVIEW, ONTARIO M3J 1Z8
(416) 638-5500

CROWN WALLPAPER CO.
88 RONSON DRIVE
REXDALE, ONTARIO M9W 1B9
(416) 245-2900

EGAN LAING LTD.
1067 WESTPORT CRESCENT
MISSISSAUGA, ONTARIO L5T 1E8
(416) 678-9131

FINNISH DESIGN IMPORTS LTD.
92C SCOLLARD STREET
TORONTO, ONTARIO M5R 1G2
(416) 961-9858

B.F. GOODRICH CANADA INC.
409 WEBER STREET NORTH
KITCHENER, ONTARIO N2H 4B1
(519) 742-3641

GREEFF FABRICS INC.
170 BEDFORD ROAD
TORONTO, ONTARIO M5R 2K9
(416) 960-8222

• **HABERT ASSOCIATES LTD.**
321 DAVENPORT ROAD
TORONTO, ONTARIO M5R 1K5
(416) 960-5323 **Pg. 221**

MARTA HAUER STUDIO LTD.
871 BATHURST STREET
TORONTO, ONTARIO M3G 3G2
(416) 533-3355

INTERNATIONAL WALLCOVERINGS
151 EAST DRIVE
BRAMALEA, ONTARIO L6T 1B5
(416) 791-1547

• **JEFF BROWN FINE FABRICS LTD.**
1785 ARGENTIA ROAD
MISSISSAUGA, ONTARIO L5N 3A2
(416) 821-3666 **Pg. 220**

JOHNSON, CRAIG & ASSOCIATES INC.
462 WELLINGTON STREET WEST
TORONTO, ONTARIO M5V 1B3
(416) 597-0733

KOBE FABRICS LTD.
5380 SOUTH SERVICE RD., P.O. BOX 939
BURLINGTON, ONTARIO L7R 3Y7
(416) 639-2730

LACKAWANNA
LEATHER CO. OF CANADA, THE
604 KING STREET WEST
TORONTO, ONTARIO M5V 1M6
(416) 364-0707

• **LAURII TEXTILES**
354 DAVENPORT ROAD
TORONTO, ONTARIO M5R 1K6
(416) 922-5514 **Pg. 222**

LIONS WALLCOVERINGS & FABRICS INC.
321 DAVENPORT ROAD
TORONTO, ONTARIO M5R 1K5
(416) 923-5045

McFADDEN HARDWOODS LTD.
2650 RENA ROAD
MISSISSAUGA, ONTARIO L4T 3C8
(416) 677-4272

METRO WALLCOVERINGS
66 ORFUS ROAD
TORONTO, ONTARIO M6A 1L9
(416) 787-4261

MILNE & ASSOC. INC.
49 SPADINA AVENUE
TORONTO, ONTARIO M5V 2J1
(416) 591-9114

MORBERN INC.
80 BOUNDARY ROAD
CORNWALL, ONTARIO K6H 5V3
(613) 932-8811

ONTARIO WALLCOVERINGS
462 FRONT STREET WEST
TORONTO, ONTARIO M5V 1B6
(416) 593-4519

PANACHE DESIGN
361 KING STREET EAST
TORONTO, ONTARIO M5A 1L1
(416) 369-0084

PRIDE OF PARIS FABRICS LTD.
WEST RIVER STREET, BOX 130
PARIS, ONTARIO N3L 3E9
(519) 443-6351

• **PRIMAVERA**
INTERIOR ACCESSORIES LTD.
300 KING STREET WEST
TORONTO, ONTARIO M5A 1K4
(416) 368-3456 **Pg. 223**

REED DECORATIVE PRODUCTS
1995 CLARKE BLVD.
BRAMALEA, ONTARIO L6T 3Z9
(416) 791-8788

RODA WALLCOVERINGS LTD.
80 TYCOS DRIVE
TORONTO, ONTARIO M6B 1V9
(416) 782-1168

RODGERS WALLCOVERINGS LIMITED
1809 BRITANNIA ROAD EAST
MISSISSAUGA, ONTARIO L4W 1S6
(416) 673-1600

• **SAMO TEXTILES LTD.**
67 ST. REGIS CRESCENT NORTH
DOWNSVIEW, ONTARIO M3J 1Y9
(416) 636-7273 **Pg. 224**

• **SAMO INTERNATIONAL**
320 DAVENPORT ROAD
TORONTO, ONTARIO M5R 1K6
(416) 920-3020 **Pg. 224**

SANDERSON & SON
320 DAVENPORT ROAD
DOWNSVIEW, ONTARIO M5R 1K6
(416) 323-1168

SELECTONE PAINTS LTD.
39 GAIL GROVE
WESTON, ONTARIO M9M 1M5
(416) 742-8881

SEVEN CONTINENTS ENTERPRISES LTD.
350 WALLACE AVENUE
TORONTO, ONTARIO M6P 3P2
(416) 535-5101

SHIRLITE MFG. CO. LTD.
91 WHITNEY PLACE
KITCHENER, ONTARIO N2G 2X8
(519) 578-7878

SPINNEYBECK ENTERPRISES LTD.
RR NO. 4
STOUFFVILLE, ONTARIO L0H 1L0
(416) 888-1987

SUNWORTHY WALLCOVERINGS
195 WALKER DRIVE
BRAMPTON, ONTARIO L6T 3Z9
(416) 791-8788

TELIO & CO.
113 DUPONT STREET
TORONTO, ONTARIO M5R 1V4
(416) 968-2020

VICRTEX, L.E. CARPENTER CO.
1200 AEROWOOD DRIVE, UNITS 5 & 6
MISSISSAUGA, ONTARIO L4W 2S7
(416) 624-4614

IAN WELSH MANUFACTURING CO. LTD.
787 KING STREET WEST
TORONTO, ONTARIO M5V 1N4
(416) 368-1102

• **WALTER L. BROWN LTD.**
17 VICKERS ROAD
TORONTO, ONTARIO M9B 1C2
(416) 231-4499 **Pg. 226**

▶ W E S T E R N C A N A D A

PARK THE POTTER
327 MORLEY AVENUE
WINNIPEG, MANITOBA R3L 0Y4
(204)475-0019

▶ B R I T I S H C O L U M B I A

ARTEK CONTRACTING LTD.
2203 GRANVILLE STREET
VANCOUVER, B.C. V6H 3G1
(604) 736-0271

CROWN WALLPAPER CO.
910 WEST, 6TH STREET
VANCOUVER, B.C.
(604) 736-4541

DAYCOR WEST WALLCOVERINGS
2131 BURRARD STREET
VANCOUVER, B.C.
(604) 731-4174

DESIGN SOURCE INTERNATIONAL LTD.
923 WEST, 8TH STREET
VANCOUVER, B.C.
(604) 733-1714

ODISSEY DESIGN PRODUCTS LTD.
1310 WEST 6TH STREET
VANCOUVER, B.C.
(604) 734-7667

SELECT WALL COVERINGS LTD.
106 EAST, 7TH STREET
VANCOUVER, B.C.
(604) 872-8181

STUDIO INTERIORS
6045 WEST BOULEVARD
VANCOUVER, B.C.
(604) 266-0010

• **WALTER L. BROWN LTD.**
911 HOMER STREET
VANCOUVER, B.C.
(604) 683-2564 **Pg. 226**

TILES

▶ Q U E B E C

APPELLO SALES & MARKETING INC.
103 LAKESIDE ROAD
KNOWLTON, QUEBEC J0E 1V0
(514) 534-3334

CERATEC INC.
414, ST-SACREMENT
QUEBEC, QUEBEC G1N 3Y3
(418) 681-0101

ENTREPRISES TUILES MONGIAT
10972 ESPLANADE
MONTREAL, QUEBEC H3L 2Y6
(514) 331-4761

MASONITE CANADA LTD.
418 GOLF AVENUE
GATINEAU, QUEBEC J8R 6K2
(819) 633-5331

NORTRA DISTRIBUTIONS
5375 DES GRANDES PRAIRIES
ST-LEONARD, QUEBEC H1R 1B1
(514) 326-0062

PROMOSTYLE INTERNATIONAL INC.
6969 TRANS-CANADA HWY., SUITE 121
ST-LAURENT, QUEBEC H4T 1V8
(514) 336-3646

RAMCA TILES LTD.
1085 AVENUE VAN HORNE
MONTREAL, QUEBEC H2V 1J6
(514) 270-9192

SICO INC.
740 PLACE TRANS-CANADA
LONGUEUIL, QUEBEC J4G 1P1
(514) 651-0273

WORLD MOSAIC INC.
9545 ST. LAWRENCE BLVD.
MONTREAL, QUEBEC
(514) 388-1118

▶ O N T A R I O

ACME SLATE & TILE CO. LTD.
21 GOLDEN GATE COURT
SCARBOROUGH, ONTARIO M1P 3A4
(416) 293-3664

ARTISTIC GLASS CO. LTD.
2108 DUNDAS STREET WEST
TORONTO, ONTARIO M6R 1W9
(416) 531-0481

CANADA PAINT & WALLCOVERINGS
3275 YONGE STREET
TORONTO, ONTARIO M4N 2L8
(416) 487-5555

CENTRAL SUPPLY
53 APEX ROAD
TORONTO, ONTARIO M6A 2V6
(416) 785-5165

CHALLIS WALLCOVERING LTD.
420 TAPSCOP ROAD, UNIT 1
SCARBOROUGH, ONTARIO M1B 1Y9
(416) 292-6062

CONNOLLY CONTRACTORS LTD.
140 ASHWARREN ROAD
DOWNSVIEW, ONTARIO M3J 1Z8
(416) 638-5500

CORONADO STONE PRODUCTS
RR NO. 2, 6691 GUELPH LINE
MILTON, ONTARIO L9T 2X6
(416) 335-3521

COUNTRY TILES
321 DAVENPORT ROAD
TORONTO, ONTARIO M5R 1K5
(416) 922-9214

FERLEO IMPORT-EXPORT CO. LTD.
6650 FINCH AVENUE WEST
REXDALE, ONTARIO M9W 5Y6
(416) 675-0075

FORMS & SURFACES
49 SPADINA AVENUE
TORONTO, ONTARIO M5V 2J1
(416) 591-9114

• **MARBLE TREND LTD.**
2050 STEELES AVENUE WEST
CONCORD, ONTARIO L4K 2V1
(416) 738-0400 **Pg. 239**

McFADDEN HARDWOODS LTD.
2650 RENA ROAD
MISSISSAUGA, ONTARIO L4T 3C8
(416) 677-4272

MICHAEL SHEBA CERAMIC DESIGN
140 EVELYN AVENUE
TORONTO, ONTARIO M6P 2Z7
(416) 766-9411

MILNE & ASSOC. INC.
49 SPADINA AVENUE
TORONTO, ONTARIO M5V 2J1
(416) 591-9114

• **OCTOPUS PRODUCTS LTD.**
200 GEARY AVENUE
TORONTO, ONTARIO M6H 2B9
(416) 531-5051 **Pg. 237**

OLYMPIA FLOOR AND WALL TILE CO.
1000 LAWRENCE AVENUE WEST
TORONTO, ONTARIO
(416) 789-4122

ONTARIO CORK CO. LTD.
36 ASHWARREN ROAD
TORONTO, ONTARIO M3J 1Z5
(416) 630-9702

PHOENIX FLOOR & WALL PRODUCTS
111 WESTMORE DRIVE
REXDALE, ONTARIO M9V 3Y6
(416) 745-4200

RAMCA TILES LTD.
354 DAVENPORT ROAD
TORONTO, ONTARIO M5R 1K6
(416) 781-5521

RAYETTE FOREST PRODUCTS
60 RAYETTE ROAD
CONCORD, ONTARIO L4K 2G4
(416) 661-0831

RODGERS WALLCOVERINGS LTD.
1809 BRITANNIA ROAD EAST
MISSISSAUGA, ONTARIO L4W 1S6
(416) 673-1600

SCREEN PRINT DISPLAY ADVERTISING LTD.
100 ELGIN STREET
BRANTFORD, ONTARIO N3T 5N3
(519) 756-6185

STEPTOE & WIFE ANTIQUES LTD.
3626 VICTORIA PARK AVENUE
WILLOWDALE, ONTARIO M2H 3B2
(416) 497-2989

STONE FACING LTD.
25 FAULKLAND ROAD
SCARBOROUGH, ONTARIO M1L 3S4
(416) 752-1525

T.M.T. MARBLE SUPPLY LTD.
900 KEELE STREET
TORONTO, ONTARIO M6N 3E7
(416) 653-6111

THAMES VALLEY BRICK & TILE
14 DORCHESTER AVENUE
TORONTO, ONTARIO M8Z 4W3
(416) 252-5811

▶ ATLANTIC CANADA

**ATLANTIC
VENETIAN BLINDS AND DRAPERIES LTD.**
22 WADDELL AVENUE
DARTMOUTH, NOVA SCOTIA B3B 1K3
(902) 463-2263

▶ QUEBEC

**CONNAISSANCE
FABRICS & WALLCOVERINGS LTD.**
1632 SHERBROOKE STREET WEST
MONTREAL, QUEBEC H3H 1C9
(514) 931-2437

DRACO LTD.
605, BOUL. IBERVILLE
REPENITIGNY, QUEBEC J6A 2C2
(514) 581-6600

SALETEX FABRICS LTD.
4716 THIMENS BLVD.
ST. LAURENT, QUEBEC H4R 2B2
(514) 334-7533

TELIO & CIE
5800 ST-DENIS
MONTREAL, QUEBEC H2S 3L5
(514) 842-9116

VAL-ABEL TEXTILES LTD.
55 MT. ROYAL AVENUE WEST
MONTREAL, QUEBEC H2T 2S6
(514) 842-9503

▶ ONTARIO

ACCESSORIES CANADA
P.O. BOX 1273
GUELPH, ONTARIO N1H 6N6
(519) 836-3283

AVEBLA LTD.
442 BRIMLEY ROAD, UNIT 9
SCARBOROUGH, ONTARIO M1J 1A1
(416) 264-4345

BAUMANN FABRICS LTD.
302 KING STREET EAST
TORONTO, ONTARIO M5A 1K6
(416) 869-1221

W.H. BILBROUGH & CO. LTD.
326 DAVENPORT ROAD
TORONTO, ONTARIO M5R 1K6
(416) 960-1611

BRUNSCHWIG & FILS LTD.
320 DAVENPORT ROAD
TORONTO, ONTARIO M5R 1K6

CANADIAN WINDOW COVERINGS
55 JUTLAND ROAD
TORONTO, ONTARIO M8Z 2G6
(416) 252-3751

CURBSUN SYSTEMS INC.
555 HANLAN ROAD
WOODBRIDGE, ONTARIO L4L 4R8
(416) 656-0394

D.C.S. DRAPERY LTD.
334 LAUDER AVENUE
TORONTO, ONTARIO M6E 3H8
(416) 651-5757

**EMHART CAN. LTD.
INTERNATIONAL HARDWARE DIVISION**
P.O. BOX 396, 180 COLEMAN STREET
BELLEVILLE, ONTARIO K8N 5A8
(416) 962-5311

• **HABERT ASSOCIATES LTD.**
321 DAVENPORT ROAD
TORONTO, ONTARIO M5R 1K5
(416) 960-5323 **Pg. 221**

HEESHADE CO. LTD.
132 RAILSIDE ROAD
DON MILLS, ONTARIO M3A 1A3
(416) 449-5580

• **HUNTER DOUGLAS**
7535 BATH ROAD
MISSISSAUGA, ONTARIO L4T 4C1
(416) 678-1133 **Pg. 243**

• **JEFF BROWN FINE FABRICS LTD.**
1785 ARGENTIA ROAD
MISSISSAUGA, ONTARIO L5N 3A2
(416) 821-3666 **Pg. 220**

JOANNE FABRICS CO. LTD.
1090 AEROWOOD DRIVE, UNIT 4
MISSISSAUGA, ONTARIO L4W 1Y5
(416) 624-2744

KOBEFAB INTERNATIONAL INC.
BOX 939, 5380 SOUTH SERVICE ROAD
BURLINGTON, ONTARIO L7R 3Y7
(416) 639-2730

KAREN BULOW LTD.
14 DUNCAN STREET
TORONTO, ONTARIO M5H 3G8
(416) 977-2004

**KIRSCH COOPER INDUSTRIES
CANADA INC.**
100 NORWICH AVENUE
WOODSTOCK, ONTARIO N4S 7Z1
(519) 537-5531

• **LAURII TEXTILES**
354 DAVENPORT ROAD
TORONTO, ONTARIO M5R 1K6
(416) 922-5514 **Pg. 222**

LOUVRE DRAPE CANADA LTD.
6310 VIPOND DRIVE
MISSISSAUGA, ONTARIO L5T 1J9
(416) 673-2869

**MODERN WINDOW SHADES LTD. –
AVENUE CUSTOM SEWING**
267 DAVENPORT ROAD
TORONTO, ONTARIO M5R 1J9
(416) 927-0292

PRIDE OF PARIS FABRICS LTD.
WEST RIVER STREET, BOX 130
PARIS, ONTARIO N3L 3E9
(519) 443-6351

• **PRIMAVERA
INTERIOR ACCESSORIES LTD.**
300 KING STREET EAST
TORONTO, ONTARIO M5A 1K4
(416) 368-3456 **Pg. 223**

RODA WALLCOVERINGS
80 TYCOS DRIVE
TORONTO, ONTARIO M6B 1V9
(416) 782-1167

ROPER
233 SIGNET DRIVE
WESTON, ONTARIO M9L 1V1
(416) 745-8860

• **SAMO INTERNATIONAL**
320 DAVENPORT ROAD
TORONTO, ONTARIO M5R 1K6
(416) 920-3020 **Pg. 224**

A. SANDERSON & SONS LTD.
320 DAVENPORT ROAD
TORONTO, ONTARIO M5R 1K6
(416) 323-1168

SEWING ROOM, THE
209 DAVENPORT ROAD
TORONTO, ONTARIO M4R 1J4
(416) 961-5536

SILENT GLISS
705 PROGRESS AVENUE
SCARBOROUGH, ONTARIO M1H 2T1
(416) 431-3330

SOLARFECTIVE PRODUCTS LTD.
14 DUNCAN STREET
TORONTO, ONTARIO M5H 3G8
(416) 977-7509

STURDI-BILT WOOD PRODUCTS LTD.
275 DON PARK ROAD
MARKHAM, ONTARIO L3R 1C2
(416) 475-1050

TANDEM FABRICS INC.
129 DOLPH STREET WEST
CAMBRIDGE, ONTARIO N3H 2B9
(519) 653-5781

• **WALTER L. BROWN LTD.**
17 VICKERS ROAD
TORONTO, ONTARIO M9B 1C2
(416) 231-4499 **Pg. 226**

COMMUNICATIONS/ AUDIO–VISUALS

BUSINESS ACCESSORIES
45 DUNDAS STREET
CAMBRIDGE, ONTARIO N1R 5Y2
(519) 622-2222

EGAN VISUAL INC.
8201 KEELE STREET
CONCORD, ONTARIO L4K 1B1
(416) 669-9441

ELECTROHOME LTD.
809 WELLINGTON STREET NORTH
KITCHENER, ONTARIO N2G 4J6
(519) 744-7111

GUTMAN, KARL INC.
605 EDUCATION ROAD
CORNWALL, ONTARIO K6H 5V6
(613) 932-0108

INTALITE INC.
9855 MEILEUR STREET
MONTREAL, QUEBEC H3L 3J6
(514) 382-2793

3M CANADA LTD.
P.O. BOX 5757
LONDON, ONTARIO N6A 4T1
(519) 451-2500

PHASE THREE AUDIO & LIGHTING
358 QUEEN STREET EAST
TORONTO, ONTARIO M5A 1T1
(416) 865-1161

PHILIPS ELECTRONICS LTD.
601 MILNER AVENUE
SCARBOROUGH, ONTARIO M1B 1M8
(416) 691-7372

ROBLOK LIMITED
880 WELLINGTON STREET
OTTAWA, ONTARIO K1R 6K7
(613) 237-7236

• **RUTHERFORD
AUDIO VISUALS**
23 PRINCE ANDREW PLACE
DON MILLS, ONTARIO M3C 2H2
(416) 443-9300 **Pg. 265**

TALBOT KELLY ASSOCIATES LIMITED
2 BERKELEY STREET
TORONTO, ONTARIO M5A 2W3
(416) 360-7915

GLENN J. WYLIE & ASSOC. LTD.
114 WEST DEANE PARK DRIVE
ISLINGTON, ONTARIO M9B 2S3
(416) 626-6556

INTERIOR CONTRACTORS

ALDAN CONSTRUCTION LTD.
275 MACPHERSON AVENUE
TORONTO, ONTARIO M4V 1A4
(416) 298-8600

• **BEGG & DAIGLE**
110 MILNER AVENUE
SCARBOROUGH, ONTARIO M1S 3R2
(416) 298-8600 **Pg. 249**

• **CAS INTERIORS INC.**
549 OAKDALE ROAD, UNIT 38
DOWNSVIEW, ONTARIO M3N 1W7
(416) 743-6291 **Pg. 250**

• **CAMERON – McINDOO INTERIORS LTD.**
20 UPJOHN ROAD
DON MILLS, ONTARIO M3B 2V9
(416) 447-3301 **Pg. 252**

• **CENTRE LEASEHOLD IMPROVEMENTS
LIMITED**
STE 3306 ROYAL TRUST TOWER, P.O. BOX 184
TORONTO, ONTARIO M5K 1H6
(416) 363-6131 **Pg. 253**

DESIGN TEAM PLUS LTD.
111 RAILSIDE ROAD
DON MILLS, ONTARIO M3A 1B2
(416) 443-1516

FARMER CONSTRUCTION
2925 DOUGLAS STREET
VANCOUVER, B.C. V8T 4N8
(604) 388-5121

• **FORREC INTERNATIONAL CORPORATION**
33 BRITAIN STREET
TORONTO, ONTARIO M5A 1R7
(416) 362-5782 **Pg. 254**

• **GILLANDERS CONSTRUCTION INC.**
3 CHURCH STREET
TORONTO, ONTARIO M5E 1M2
(416) 363-5121 **Pg. 255**

• **GILLANDERS**
33 ATOMIC AVENUE
ETOBICOKE, ONTARIO M8Z 5K8
(416) 259-5446 **Pg. 255**

HOLMAN DESIGN LTD.
21 KERN ROAD
DON MILLS, ONTARIO M3B 1S9
(416) 441-1877

**INTERIOR CONSTRUCTION
SPECIALISTS INC.**
151 NASHDENE ROAD
SCARBOROUGH, ONTARIO M1V 2T3
(416) 292-4041

• **INTERIOR DIMENSIONS LTD.**
980 YONGE STREET
TORONTO, ONTARIO M4W 2J5
(416) 922-7165 **Pg. 256**

LAURNA MAR INC.
1111 FINCH AVENUE WEST
DOWNSVIEW, ONTARIO M3J 2E5
(416) 665-7505

B.C. MILLWORK PRODUCTS LTD.
150 WEST 1ST AVENUE
VANCOUVER, B.C. V5Y 1A4
(604) 876-2131

• **PANCOR INDUSTRIES LTD.**
910 WESTPORT CRESCENT
MISSISSAUGA, ONTARIO L5T 1G1
(416) 673-2910 **Pg. 257**

• **PATELLA CONSTRUCTION INC.**
124 BERMONDSEY ROAD
TORONTO, ONTARIO M4A 1X5
(416) 752-7750 **Pg. 260**

**PROFESSIONAL CONSTRUCTION
CO-ORDINATORS LTD.**
575 EGLINTON AVENUE WEST
TORONTO, ONTARIO M5N 1B5
(416) 486-9772

• **QUALITY GENERAL CONTRACTING CO.**
140 BENTLEY
MARKHAM, ONTARIO L3R 3L2
(416) 475-1315 **Pg. 258**

RETAIL ENVIRONMENTS LTD.
2382 DUNDAS STREET WEST
TORONTO, ONTARIO M6P 1W9
(416) 536-2204

• **ROBINSON GROUP LTD., THE**
263 DAVENPORT ROAD
TORONTO, ONTARIO M5R 1J9
(416) 960-2444 **Pg. 141**

• **WOODRITES CUSTOM BUILDERS AND
RENOVATORS LTD.**
940 QUEEN STREET WEST
TORONTO, ONTARIO M6J 1G8
(416) 532-9621 **Pg. 261**

LIGHTING/ ENGINEERING CONSULTANTS

AC/DC DESIGN LTD.
2667 WEST 14TH AVENUE
VANCOUVER, B.C. V6K 2W8
(604) 732-1919

• **H.H. ANGUS & ASSOCIATES LTD.**
1127 LESLIE STREET
DON MILLS, ONTARIO M3C 2J6
(416) 443-8200 **Pg. 263**

• **CROSSEY ENGINEERING**
4141 YONGE STREET
TORONTO, ONTARIO M2P 2A8
(416) 221-3111 **Pg. 264**

JACK A. FROST LTD.
3245 WHARTON WAY
MISSISSAUGA, ONTARIO L4X 2R9
(416) 624-5344

GIFFELS ASSOCIATES LTD.
30 INTERNATIONAL BLVD.
REXDALE, ONTARIO M9W 5P3
(416) 675-5950

INTERIOR LANDSCAPING

ARSENAULT, MAURICE –
CONSULTANT HORTICULTURE
C.P. 72, SUCC. CHOMEDEY
LAVAL, QUEBEC H7W 3S8
(514) 337-1222

BEACH McLEOD NORTHERN
116A VICEROY ROAD
CONCORD, ONTARIO L4K 2M1
(416) 669-5777

BRUCE JENSEN NURSERIES INC.
RR NO. 2
NEWCASTLE, ONTARIO L0A 1H0
(416) 686-0783

HYDRO-GRO INTERIOR LANDSCAPE
25 WALNUT CRESCENT
TORONTO, ONTARIO M8W 2Z9
(416) 251-3228

• **INTERIOR LANDSCAPE GROUP INC., THE**
80 OAKDALE ROAD
DOWNSVIEW, ONTARIO M3N 1V9
(416) 746-3765 **Pg. 269**

• **THE FINAL TOUCH DECOR GROUP INC.**
16 LESMILL ROAD
TORONTO, ONTARIO M3B 2T5
(416) 449-1974 **Pg. 271**

• **JENSEN INTERNATIONAL INC.**
140 MILNER AVENUE
SCARBOROUGH, ONTARIO M1S 3R3
(416) 299-6466 **Pg. 270**

MOORHEAD FLEMING
CORBAN McCARTHY
33 BRITAIN STREET
TORONTO, ONTARIO M5A 1R7
(416) 366-9238

PLANTASTIC
43 TOWNS ROAD
TORONTO, ONTARIO M8Z 1A2
(416) 252-5061

PLANTATION
3863, BOUL. ST-LAURENT
MONTREAL, QUEBEC
(514) 842-8549

PLANTES TROPICALES G.L. INC., LES
4044 ROUEN
MONTREAL, QUEBEC H1W 1N5
(514) 252-8510

R.V. WOOD AND ASSOCIATES
825 DENISON STREET
MARKHAM, ONTARIO L4R 1C8
(416) 475-8388

SILK-SCAPING LTD.
110 RIVIERA DRIVE
MARKHAM, ONTARIO L3R 5M1
(416) 477-8733

PAINT

• **BENJAMIN MOORE & CO. LTD.**
15 LLOYD AVENUE
TORONTO, ONTARIO M6N 1G9
(416) 766-1173 **Pg. 245**

CROWN PAINT & WALLPAPER
88 RONSON DRIVE
REXDALE, ONTARIO M9W 1B9
(416) 245-2900

PAINT COLORS UNLIMITED
502 ADELAIDE STREET WEST
TORONTO, ONTARIO M5V 1T2
(416) 366-2941

PARA PAINTS CANADA INC.
25 RACINE ROAD
REXDALE, ONTARIO M9W 2Z4
(416) 743-7860

PLASTIC LAMINATES

CONTOUR DISTRIBUTORS
104 GLENVIEW AVENUE
TORONTO, ONTARIO M4R 1P8
(416) 488-0245

• **FORMICA CANADA INC.**
2255 SHEPPARD AVENUE EAST
WILLOWDALE, ONTARIO M2J 4Y5
(416) 498-9405 **Pg. 236**

• **OCTOPUS PRODUCTS LTD.**
200 GEARY AVENUE
TORONTO, ONTARIO M6H 2B9
(416) 531-5051 **Pg. 237**

• **WILSONART**
1500 SUPERIOR PARKWAY
WESTLAND, MICHIGAN 48185
(313) 721-3600 **Pg. 238**

GLENN J. WYLIE & ASSOCIATES LTD
81 KELFIELD STREET
REXDALE, ONTARIO M9W 5A3
(416) 243-7770

ART & ANTIQUES

▶ ATLANTIC CANADA

THE GALLERY
282 DUCKWORTH STREET
ST. JOHN'S, NEWFOUNDLAND A1C 1H3
(709) 753-1511

MORRIS ART GALLERY LTD.
221 UNION STREET
SAINT JOHN, NEW BRUNSWICK E2L 1B2
(506) 657-6860

▶ QUEBEC

CANADIAN GUILD OF CRAFTS (QUE.)
2025 PEEL STREET
MONTREAL, QUEBEC H3A 1T6
(514) 849-6091

GALERIE ELCA LONDON
1616 SHERBROOKE STREET WEST
MONTREAL, QUEBEC H3H 1C9
(514) 931-3646

GALERIE GRAFF
963, RUE RACHEL EST
MONTREAL, QUEBEC H2J 2J4
(514) 526-2616

GALERIE VERRE D'ART
1518, RUE SHERBROOKE OUEST
MONTREAL, QUEBEC H3G 1L3
(514) 932-3896

GALERIE WADDINGTON & GORCE INC.
1504, RUE SHERBROOKE OUEST
MONTREAL, QUEBEC H3G 1L3
(514) 933-3653

ARBOUR, MADELEINE ET ASSOCIES
266, RUE ST-PAUL EST
MONTREAL, QUEBEC H2Y 1G9
(514) 878-3846

SHAYNE GALLERY, THE
5471 ROYALMOUNT AVENUE
MONTREAL, QUEBEC H4P 1J3
(514) 739-1701

▶ ONTARIO

ARTS AND COMMUNICATIONS
55 BLOOR STREET WEST
TORONTO, ONTARIO M4W 1A5
(416) 966-3421

**ANSELMO ART STUDIO
& ASSOCIATES INC.**
280 AVENUE ROAD
TORONTO, ONTARIO M4V 2G7
(416) 966-3856

**ART COLLECTION CANADA OF
TORONTO LTD.**
315 QUEEN STREET WEST
TORONTO, ONTARIO M5V 2X2
(416) 977-4456

ASHTON'S
267 QUEEN STREET EAST
TORONTO, ONTARIO M5A 1S6
(416) 366-6846

BAAS STUDIO GALLERY
322 KING STREET WEST
TORONTO, ONTARIO M5V 1J2
(416) 979-2705

BENITZ, JEAN
355 BERKELEY STREET
TORONTO, ONTARIO M5A 2X6
(416) 926-1632

BRASS ROOTS
220 BAYVIEW DRIVE
BARRIE, ONTARIO L4N 4Y8
(416) 698-1353

CANADIAN ART PRINTS
77 MOWAT AVENUE, SUITE 102
TORONTO, ONTARIO M6K 3E3
(416) 533-2444

CHRISTIE'S AUCTIONEERS
94 CUMBERLAND STREET
TORONTO, ONTARIO M5R 1A3
(416) 960-2063

• **CONTEMPORARY FINE ART SERVICES**
411 RICHMOND STREET EAST
TORONTO, ONTARIO M5A 3S5
(416) 366-9770 **Pg. 273**

DESGAGNES, GENEVIEVE
783 BATHURST STREET, 4TH FLR.
TORONTO, ONTARIO M5S 1Z4
(416) 364-3700

DE FOREST STUDIOS
BOX 387
SCHOMBERG, ONTARIO L0G 1T0
(416) 939-7216

• **DESIGN COLLECTIONS/GALLERY 400**
400 SUMMERHILL AVENUE
TORONTO, ONTARIO M2W 2E4
(416) 920-1921 **Pg. 274**

DIRSTEIN ROBERTSON LIMITED
77 YORKVILLE AVENUE
TORONTO, ONTARIO M5R 1C1
(416) 961-6211

ESTEE GALLERY
198½ DAVENPORT ROAD
TORONTO, ONTARIO M5R 1J2
(416) 964-7613

EVELYN AMIS FINE ART
14 HAZELTON AVENUE
TORONTO, ONTARIO M5R 2E2
(416) 961-0878

• **FIVE SIGNATURES**
111 QUEEN STREET EAST
TORONTO, ONTARIO M5C 1S2
(416) 865-1803 **Pg. 275**

GALLERY DRESDNERE
12 HAZELTON AVENUE
TORONTO, ONTARIO M5R 2E2
(416) 923-4662

GALLERY MOOS LTD.
136 YORKVILLE AVENUE
TORONTO, ONTARIO M5R 1C2
(416) 922-0627

GALLERY QUAN
112 SCOLLARD STREET
TORONTO, ONTARIO M5R 1G2
(416) 968-7822

GALLERY ONE
121 SCOLLARD STREET
TORONTO, ONTARIO M5R 1G4
(416) 929-3103

GERALDINE DAVIS GALLERY
225 RICHMOND STREET WEST
TORONTO, ONTARIO M5V 2C7
(416) 595-5225

ISAACS GALLERY, THE
832 YONGE STREET
TORONTO, ONTARIO M4W 2H1
(416) 923-7301

MARIANNE FRIENDLAND GALLERY
122 SCOLLARD STREET
TORONTO, ONTARIO M5R 1G2
(416) 961-4900

• **MARCUS, H.D. ENTERPRISES INC.**
294 BERKELEY STREET
TORONTO, ONTARIO M5A 2X5
(416) 967-7617 **Pg. 276**

MICHAEL REEVES ANTIQUES
171 QUEEN STREET EAST
TORONTO, ONTARIO M5C 1S2
(416) 368-0257

MIRRA GODDARD
22 HAZELTON AVENUE
TORONTO, ONTARIO M5R 2E2
(416) 964-8197

PAISLEY SHOP LIMITED
889 YONGE STREET
TORONTO, ONTARIO M4W 2H2
(416) 923-5830

SOTHEBY'S
9 HAZELTON AVENUE
TORONTO, ONTARIO M5R 2E1
(416) 926-1774

WADDINGTON'S AUCTIONEERS
189 QUEEN STREET EAST
TORONTO, ONTARIO M5A 1S2
(416) 362-1678

WADDINGTON & SHIELL GALLERIES
33 HAZELTON AVENUE
TORONTO, ONTARIO M5R 2E3
(416) 925-2461

▶ WESTERN CANADA

**EAU CLAIRE FINE ARTS LTD. –
WESTIN HOTEL**
340 4TH AVENUE SW
CALGARY, ALBERTA T2P 2S6
(403) 262-5133

▶ BRITISH COLUMBIA

CANADIAN ART PRINTS
736 RICHARD STREET
VANCOUVER, B.C. V6B 3A4
(604) 681-3485

**CRAFTS ASSOCIATION OF
BRITISH COLUMBIA**
1411 CARTWRIGHT STREET
VANCOUVER, B.C. V6H 3R7
(604) 687-6511

DIANE FARRIS GALLERIES
165 WATER STREET
VANCOUVER, B.C. V6B 1A7
(604) 687-2629

RENDERERS

▶ QUEBEC

**SCHNEIDER, FRANK
ARCHITECTURAL RENDERER**
2024 PEEL STREET
MONTREAL, QUEBEC H3A 1W5
(514) 843-6462

▶ ONTARIO

ARCHITECTURAL RENDERINGS
2025 SHEPPARD AVENUE EAST
WILLOWDALE, ONTARIO M2J 1V7
(416) 496-0635

AU-YEUNG DESIGNS
27 GREENBRIAR ROAD, NO. 1
WILLOWDALE, ONTARIO M2K 1H7
(416) 229-2545

• **G.A. DESIGN**
31 SILVERTON AVENUE
DOWNSVIEW, ONTARIO M3H 3E7
(416) 638-4933 **Pg. 281**

GRICE GORDON ARCHITECT ILLUSTRATOR
878 QUEEN STREET WEST
TORONTO, ONTARIO M6J 1G3
(416) 536-9191

HEART RENDER INC.
236 AVENUE ROAD
TORONTO, ONTARIO M5R 2J4
(416) 964-1545

• **KEOGH RENDERING**
10 GRENOBLE DRIVE, NO. 1419
DON MILLS, ONTARIO M3C 1C7
(416) 423-2412 **Pg. 282**

McCANN, MICHAEL ASSOCIATES LTD.
2 GIBSON AVENUE
TORONTO, ONTARIO
(416) 964-7532

McCARTY, BERNARD – ILLUSTRATION
1010 VISTULA DRIVE
PICKERING, ONTARIO M1W 2L9
(416) 496-0635

MILHOUSE, CAM
P.O. BOX 157, STN. C
TORONTO, ONTARIO M6J 3M9
(416) 534-3632

• **MORELLO DESIGN & CO.**
61 MARLBOROUGH AVENUE
TORONTO, ONTARIO M5R 1X5
(416) 963-4315 **Pg. 283**

SULLIVAN STUDIOS
51 BULWER
TORONTO, ONTARIO M5T 1A1
(416) 593-0543

TURNER, G.B. GRAPHIC DESIGN INC.
5 POLSON STREET
TORONTO, ONTARIO M5A 1A4
(416) 466-0812

VERSTEEG DESIGNS LTD.
600 MARKHAM ROAD
TORONTO, ONTARIO
(416) 537-9641

YUJI YOSHIZAWA – ILLUSTRATION
60 PAVANE LINKWAY, NO. 1105
DON MILLS, ONTARIO M3C 1A2
(416) 429-0529

▶ ALBERTA

CREATIVE GROUP DESIGN LTD.
300 B 17TH AVENUE SW
CALGARY, ALBERTA
(403) 263-8100

ODIN CREATIVE DIMENSIONS LTD.
6216 TOUCHWOOD DRIVE NW
CALGARY, ALBERTA
(403) 274-4886

PHOTOGRAPHERS

▶ QUEBEC

ALLARD, PHOTOGRAPHERS INC.
1394 MONT ROYAL EST
MONTREAL, QUEBEC
(514) 526-1691

**DRUMMOND, MICHAEL
DESIGN & PHOTOGRAPHY LTD.**
1235A, AVENUE GREENE
MONTREAL, QUEBEC H3Z 2A4
(514) 933-5205

LECLAIR, BERNARD PHOTOGRAPHE
5919, HENRI BOURASSA OUEST
MONTREAL, QUEBEC
(514) 335-1785

• **PRODUCTIONS MILNOX, LES**
1573, RUE DUCHARME
MONTREAL, QUEBEC H2V 1G4
(514) 279-1352 **Pg. 288**

STUDIO ALAIN ENR.
7562, ST-DENIS
MONTREAL, QUEBEC
(514) 279-9225

VACHON, JEAN
95, RUE PRINCE
MONTREAL, QUEBEC H3C 2M7
(514) 395-2227

▶ ONTARIO

ALKIN CROMWELL & ASSOCIATES
101 NIAGARA STREET, NO. 205
TORONTO, ONTARIO M5V 1C3
(416) 362-6913

AMESTOY, JUAN PHOTOGRAPHY
67 MOWAT AVENUE, SUITE 148
TORONTO, ONTARIO M6K 3E3
(416) 534-7729

BRODIE, RALPH PHOTOGRAPHICS
1499 QUEEN STREET WEST
TORONTO, ONTARIO M6R 1A3
(416) 536-9463

DAVIDSON BENARD GROUP
390 DUPONT STREET
TORONTO, ONTARIO M5R 1V9
(416) 922-5212

• **DAY, FRASER PHOTOGRAPHY**
34 BARBARA CRESCENT
TORONTO, ONTARIO M4C 3B2
(416) 463-9052 **Pg. 285**

EVANS, STEVEN PHOTOGRAPHY INC.
27 DAVIES AVENUE
TORONTO, ONTARIO M4M 2A9
(416) 463-4493

• **HANRAHAN, TIM PHOTOGRAPHER INC.**
3717 CHESSWOOD DRIVE
DOWNSVIEW, ONTARIO M3J 2P6
(416) 636-7263 **Pg. 286**

HOZ, GADI PHOTOGRAPHICS
105 DOLOMITE DRIVE
DOWNSVIEW, ONTARIO M3J 2N1
(416) 665-2233

INTERIOR IMAGES
312 ADELAIDE STREET WEST, NO. 704
TORONTO, ONTARIO
(416) 598-0272

• **LEITH, IAN & ASSOCIATES
PHOTOGRAPHY**
1515 MATHESON BLVD. C 11
MISSISSAUGA, ONTARIO L4W 2P5
(416) 625-2410 **Pg. 287**

LENSCAPE INC.
645 KING STREET EAST
TORONTO, ONTARIO M5A 4L7
(416) 368-9567

MELAINE PHOTOGRAPHY
11 GOREVALE AVENUE, SUITE 46
TORONTO, ONTARIO M6J 2R5
(416) 947-1449

NEW IMAGES
955 BAY STREET (SUTTON PLACE) N°. 206
TORONTO, ONTARIO M5S 2A2
(416) 922-3636

PANDA ASSOCIATES PHOTOGRAPHERS
524 WELLINGTON STREET WEST
TORONTO, ONTARIO
(416) 593-9266

RAHMER, LUCY PHOTOGRAPHY
20 AVOCA AVENUE, SUITE 606
TORONTO, ONTARIO M4T 2B8
(416) 925-2029

SAMSON PRODUCTIONS
100 WHITEHORN CRESCENT
TORONTO, ONTARIO M2J 3B2
(416) 493-1131

SPALDING-SMITH, FIONA
70 HOGARTH AVENUE
TORONTO, ONTARIO
(416) 463-5073

ELLEN B. TAUB PHOTOGRAPHY
44 CHARLES STREET WEST, NO. 2911
TORONTO, ONTARIO M4Y 1R7
(416) 968-7175

SUGINO, SHIN
46 McGEE STREET
TORONTO, ONTARIO M4M 2K9
(416) 469-4588

WEBSTER, CLIVE PHOTOGRAPHY INC.
56 THE ESPLANADE
TORONTO, ONTARIO
(416) 363-2081

▶ W E S T E R N   C A N A D A

• **BILODEAU/PRESTON LTD.**
162 HESTON STREET NW
CALGARY, ALBERTA T2K 2C4
(403) 284-4400 **Pg. 284**

KOPELOW, GERRY PHOTOGRAPHICS
18 EINARSON
WINNIPEG, MANITOBA
(204) 775-5113

▶ B R I T I S H   C O L U M B I A

FULKER, JOHN
1755 – 29TH STREET
W. VANCOUVER, B.C.
(604) 922-6857

OTTE, GARY PHOTOGRAPHERS LTD.
21, 1551 JOHNSTON STREET
VANCOUVER, B.C.
(604) 681-8421

PULLAN, SELWYN
233 WOODALE
N. VANCOUVER, B.C.
(604) 988-8155

SCOTT, SIMON ASSOCIATES LTD.
1627 W 2ND
VANCOUVER, B.C.
(604) 733-9797

SHERLOCK, JOHN
225 SMITHE STREET
VANCOUVER, B.C.
(604) 683-2614

M O D E L   M A K E R S

▶ Q U E B E C

LUCRAFT ENR.
1600, RUE NOTRE DAME OUEST
MONTREAL, QUEBEC
(514) 931-7737

MAQUETTES FRANCOIS PELLETIER ENR.
6512, GUILLAUME COUTURE AVENUE
MONTREAL, QUEBEC
(514) 254-8250

MAQUETTES 2 D INC.
2383, RUE JEANNE D'ARC
MONTREAL, QUEBEC
(514) 254-1011

MIGNAPRO INC.
2870, RUE ROUEN
MONTREAL, QUEBEC
(514) 524-5145

MODELTECH INC.
3618, RUE LOUIS VEUILLOT
MONTREAL, QUEBEC
(514) 255-4455

▶ O N T A R I O

ANDOFF MICHAEL WORKSHOP
32 SCOLLARD
TORONTO, ONTARIO
(416) 921-0836

ARCHITECTURAL DIMENSIONS
2600 JOHN
MARKHAM, ONTARIO
(416) 475-1602

ARTICULATIONS
77 MOWAT AVENUE
TORONTO, ONTARIO
(416) 532-7855

BRAUND MODELS
1177-A KING STREET WEST
TORONTO, ONTARIO
(416) 535-4423

DAVAN SCALE MODELS
666 KING STREET WEST
TORONTO, ONTARIO
(416) 862-1447

McCANN, PETER
ARCHITECTURAL SCALE MODELS
666 KING STREET WEST
TORONTO, ONTARIO
(416) 366-0326

MINIKIN SCALE MODELS
168 DEAN PARK
SCARBOROUGH, ONTARIO
(416) 281-2978

MODEL DESIGN INTERNATIONAL
72 FRASER AVENUE
TORONTO, ONTARIO M6K 3K2
(416) 533-4642

MODELS UNLIMITED
666 KING STREET WEST
TORONTO, ONTARIO
(416) 366-6785

SCALE MODELS
180 SPRING GARDEN AVENUE
WILLOWDALE, ONTARIO
(416) 225-0403

THREE-D IMAGERY
222 QUEEN'S QUAY WEST
TORONTO, ONTARIO
(416) 368-6878

ULTRA SCALE LTD.
51 WOLSELEY
TORONTO, ONTARIO
(416) 368-6839

UPLIS LTD.
237 CLINTON
TORONTO, ONTARIO
(416) 563-8600

▶ W E S T E R N   C A N D A

MARK DESIGN STUDIO
5032 16TH AVENUE NW
CALGARY, ALBERTA
(403) 247-2703

MITCHELL, MARK & ASSOCIATES INC.
245 BELL
WINNIPEG, MANITOBA
(204) 477-0481

PROFESSIONAL SCALE MODEL BUILDING
WESTWIND INDUSTRIAL PK
EDMONTON, ALBERTA
(403) 470-3023

SUNDERLAND MODELS LTD.
6814 N 6TH STREET EAST
CALGARY, ALBERTA
(403) 252-2623

▶ B R I T I S H   C O L U M B I A

B & B SCALE MODELS
1459 ANDERSON
VANCOUVER, B.C.
(604) 681-1536

BRINKWORTH MODEL &
DESIGN CONSULTANTS LTD.
4151 NO. 4 ROAD
RICHMOND, B.C.
(604) 278-2942

DIMENSIONS 3 PLASTICS LTD.
7532 CONWAY
BURNABY, B.C.
(604) 437-5210

LINDSAY MODELS & DESIGN CONSULTANTS
1107 W 14TH
NORTH VANCOUVER, B.C.
(604) 988-5751

▶ QUEBEC

**DAWSON COLLEGE
DELORIMIER CAMPUS**
2120 SHERBROOKE STREAT EAST
MONTREAL, QUEBEC H2K 1C1
(514) 931-8731

CEQEP F.X. GARNEAU
1660 BOULEVARD DE L'ENTENTE, C.P. 6300
SILLERY, QUEBEC G1T 2S5
(418) 688-8310

▶ ONTARIO

**ALGONQUIN COLLEGE OF APPLIED
ARTS AND TECHNOLOGY**
COLONEL BY CAMPUS, 281 ECHO DRIVE
OTTAWA, ONTARIO K1S 1N3
(613) 237-5343

**CONFEDERATION COLLEGE OF APPLIED
ARTS AND TECHNOLOGY**
P.O. BOX 398
THUNDER BAY, ONTARIO P7C 4K1
(807) 475-6110

**DURHAM COLLEGE OF APPLIED ARTS
AND TECHNOLOGY**
SIMCOE ST. N. CAMPUS, P.O. BOX 385
OSHAWA, ONTARIO L1H 7L7
(416) 576-0210

**FANSHAWE COLLEGE OF APPLIED ARTS
AND TECHNOLOGY**
520 FIRST STREET, UNIT 6
LONDON, ONTARIO N5Y 3C6
(519) 452-4225

**GEORGIAN COLLEGE OF APPLIED ARTS
AND TECHNOLOGY**
1 GEORGIAN DRIVE
BARRIE, ONTARIO L4M 3X9
(705) 728-1951

**HUMBER COLLEGE OF APPLIED ARTS
AND TECHNOLOGY**
P.O. BOX 1900
REXDALE, ONTARIO M9W 5L7
(416) 675-3111

• **INTERNATIONAL ACADEMY OF
MERCHANDISING & DESIGN LTD.**
31 WELLESLEY STREET EAST
TORONTO, ONTARIO M4Y 1G7
(416) 922-3666 **Pg. 290**

**NIAGARA COLLEGE OF APPLIED ARTS
AND TECHNOLOGY**
WELLAND CAMPUS, P.O. BOX 1005
WOODLAWN ROAD
WELLAND, ONTARIO L3B 5S2
(416) 735-2211

ONTARIO COLLEGE OF ART
100 McCAUL STREET
TORONTO, ONTARIO M5T 1W1
(416) 977-5311

RYERSON POLITECHNICAL INSTITUTE
350 VICTORIA STREET
TORONTO, ONTARIO M5B 2K3
(416) 979-5188

**SENECA COLLEGE OF APPLIED ARTS
AND TECHNOLOGY**
YORKDALE CAMPUS, 2999 DUFFERIN ST.
TORONTO, ONTARIO M6B 3T4
(416) 491-5050

**SHERIDAN SCHOOL OF
CRAFT AND DESIGN**
1460 SOUTH SHERIDAN WAY
MISSISSAUGA, ONTARIO L5H 1Z7
(416) 274-3685

**ST. CLAIR COLLEGE OF APPLIED ARTS
AND TECHNOLOGY**
2000 TALBOT ROAD WEST
WINDSOR, ONTARIO N3A 6S4
(416) 979-5188

▶ MANITOBA

UNIVERSITY OF MANITOBA
DEPARTMENT OF INTERIOR DESIGN
FACULTY OF ARCHITECTURE
WINNIPEG, MANITOBA R3T 2N2
(204) 474-9386

▶ SASKATCHEWAN

COLLEGE OF HOME ECONOMICS
SASKATOON, SASKATCHEWAN S7N 0W0
(306) 966-5823

▶ ALBERTA

LAKELAND COLLEGE
VERMILION CAMPUS
VERMILION, ALBERTA T0B 4M0
(403) 853-2971

MOUNT ROYAL COLLEGE
4825 RICHARD ROAD SW
CALGARY, ALBERTA T3E 6K6
(403) 240-6100

▶ BRITISH COLUMBIA

KWANTIEN COLLEGE
5840 CEDARBRIDGE WAY
RICHMOND, B.C. V6X 2A7
(604) 273-5461

▶ NATIONAL

A.C.I.D
ASSOCIATION OF
CANADIAN INDUSTRIAL DESIGNERS
181 UNIVERSITY AVENUE
TORONTO, ONTARIO M5H 3M7
(416) 862-1799

C.A.P.I.C.
THE CANADIAN ASSOCIATION OF
PHOTOGRAPHERS AND ILLUSTRATORS
IN COMMUNICATION
69 SHERBOURNE STREET, SUITE 315
TORONTO, ONTARIO M5A 3X7
(416) 364-1223/4

C.B.E.M.A.
CANADIAN BUSINESS EQUIPMENT
MANUFACTURERS ASSOCIATION
1 YORKDALE ROAD, SUITE 212
TORONTO, ONTARIO M6A 3A1
(416) 789-0508

E.D.A.C.
EXHIBIT AND DISPLAY ASSOCIATION
OF CANADA
25 ADELAIDE STREET EAST
TORONTO, ONTARIO M5H 1N3
(416) 368-0973

F.I.D.E.R.
THE FOUNDATION FOR INTERIOR DESIGN
EDUCATION RESEARCH
322 8TH AVENUE
NEW YORK, N.Y., 10001 U.S.A.
(212) 929-8366

I.D.C.
INTERIOR DESIGNERS OF CANADA
168 BEDFORD ROAD
TORONTO, ONTARIO M5R 2K9
(416) 961-8577

I.F.M.A.
INTERNATIONAL FACILITY
MANAGEMENT ASSOCIATION–
TORONTO CHAPTER
P.O. BOX 29, T.D. CENTRE
TORONTO, ONTARIO M5K 1B9

N.D.C.
NATIONAL DESIGN COUNCIL
110 CONNOR STREET, 5TH FLOOR
OTTAWA, ONTARIO K1A 0H5
(613) 992-5004

▶ NEW BRUNSWICK

I.D.N.B
INTERIOR DESIGNERS OF
NEW BRUNSWICK
P.O. BOX 1541
FREDERICTON, NEW BRUNSWICK E3B 5G2
(506) 472-1003

▶ NOVA SCOTIA

A.I.D.N.S
ASSOCIATION OF INTERIOR DESIGNERS
OF NOVA SCOTIA
6270 LAWRENCE STREET
HALIFAX, NOVA SCOTIA B3L 1J2
(902) 469-8190

▶ QUEBEC

S.D.E.Q.
LA SOCIETE DES DECORATEURS–
ENSEMBLIERS DU QUEBEC
451, RUE ST-SULPICE
MONTREAL, QUEBEC H2Y 2V9
(514) 288-9046

▶ ONTARIO

ARIDO
ASSOCIATION OF REGISTERED
INTERIOR DESIGNERS OF ONTARIO
168 BEDFORD ROAD
TORONTO, ONTARIO M5R 2K9
(416) 921-2127

▶ MANITOBA

M.D.I.
MANITOBA DESIGN INSTITUTE
800–155 CARLTON STREET
WINNIPEG, MANITOBA R3C 3H8
(204) 944-2468

P.I.D.I.M.
PROFESSIONAL INTERIOR DESIGNERS
INSTITUTE OF MANITOBA
100 OSBORNE SOUTH
WINNIPEG, MANITOBA R3L 1Y5
(204) 453-6718

▶ SASKATCHEWAN

I.D.S
INTERIOR DESIGNERS OF SASKATCHEWAN
204 ANGUS CRESCENT
REGINA, SASKATCHEWAN S4T 6Z4
(306) 525-5600

▶ ALBERTA

R.I.D.I.A
REGISTERED INTERIOR DESIGNERS
INSTITUTE OF ALBERTA
205-1235 17TH AVENUE SW
CALGARY, ALBERTA T2T 0C2
(403) 244-4487

▶ BRITISH COLUMBIA

I.D.I.
INTERIOR DESIGNERS INSTITUTE OF
BRITISH COLUMBIA
205 – 1836 WEST 5TH AVENUE
VANCOUVER, B.C. V6J 1P3
(604) 734-7631

B.C.D.R.A.
BRITISH COLUMBIA DESIGN RESOURCE
ASSOCIATION
1237 HOWE STREET
VANCOUVER, B.C. V6Z 1R3
(604) 683-0521